SAMOAN ART AND ARTISTS
O MEASINA A SAMOA

SAMOAN ART AND ARTISTS
O MEASINA A SAMOA

SEAN MALLON

University of Hawai'i Press
Honolulu

First published in 2002 by
Craig Potton Publishing
98 Vickerman Street
PO Box 555
Nelson, New Zealand
www.craigpotton.co.nz

This edition published in 2002 by
University of Hawai'i Press

© Text: Sean Mallon
© Individual photographers
© University of Hawai'i Press

Filmwork by i2i imaging, Auckland, New Zealand
Printed by Everbest Printing, China

Library of Congress Cataloging-in-Publication Data

Mallon, Sean.
    Samoan art and artists / Sean Mallon.
        p. cm.
    "A latitude 20 book."
    Includes bibliographical references and index.
    ISBN 0-8248-2675-2
    1. Arts, Samoan–Samoan Islands. 2. Arts, Samoan–New Zealand.
I. Title.

    NX596.S26 M35 2002
    745'.09961'3--dc21

                            2002026628

CONTENTS

ACKNOWLEDGEMENTS

A project like this is not possible without the assistance of many people. My sincere thanks to all the artists featured in this book for their hospitality and generosity. I am grateful to Janet Davidson, Fuli and Jeff Evans and Roger Neich who read early chapter drafts and were a great source of information and encouragement. Alessandro Duranti, Muagututia Harry Paul, Malama Meleisea, Richard Moyle, Penelope Schoeffel, Peggy Fairburn-Dunlop and Damon Salesa also read parts of the book and offered helpful comments. However any errors are entirely my own. My mother Iutita and relatives Tongia'i Kaietano Smith and So'oamali'i Lefaoseu supplied many useful contacts, insights and anecdotes. As deadlines approached my sisters Theresa and Kathleen transcribed the last of the interviews.

In Samoa Sanele and Telesia Afoa, Afitu Smith of Safotu, and Mosie Sua and his family provided great hospitality and company. Muagututia Harry Paul and his wife Heidi shared their knowledge and many contacts. Sanele and Des Mallon, Mick Pendergrast, Craig Potton, Dave Armstrong and members of the extended aiga were great travelling companions and drinking partners.

I am grateful to Janet Davidson, Ngahuia Te Awekotuku, Albert Wendt, Vishvajit Pandya, Niko Besnier and James Urry for encouraging my interest in art and culture, and Craig Potton, Robbie Burton, and James Brown for their commitment and enthusiasm for the project. Kate Corbett helped me get going but I must thank Teresia Teaiwa and Gerry Mallon for always remembering to ask that motivating question...'have you finished your book yet?'.

My thanks to the following individuals and institutions who contributed directly or indirectly to this book. Research for this book was supported by a grant from the Pacific Islands Arts Committee of Creative NZ (1998).

SAMOA: Joe Annandale; Tyrone Laurenson; Keith and Lanu Martin; Togi Tonupopo; Tanu Beach Fales; Adi Tafuna'i and Theresa Fepulua'i – Women in Business Foundation, Apia; Samoa Museum; Samoa Visitors Bureau, Apia.

NEW ZEALAND: Caroline Armstrong; Mark Adams; Ron Brownson – Auckland Art Gallery; Anton Carter; City Gallery – Wellington; Eteuati Ete; Igelese Ete and Jakkie Leota Ete; Arno Gasteiger; Jeremy Glyde; Micheal Hall; Norman Heke; Te Aka Matua – Te Papa Library, Galumalemana Alfred Hunkin – Samoan Studies Victoria University; Alice Hunt, Sarah Hunter; Suzanne Knight; Lane Gallery – Auckland; David Lupton; Alastair Mc Lean; Remi Mata; Fiona McKergow; Richard Moyle – University of Auckland; Oedipus Rex Gallery – Auckland; Giles Peterson; Krzysztof Pfeiffer; Lemi Ponifasio; Samson Samasoni; Justine Semei Barton; Joseph Smith; Sean Shadbolt; John Sullivan – Alexander Turnbull Library; Lisa Taouma, Makerita Urale.

Coconut leaf hats. (Craig Potton)

AMERICAN SAMOA: John Enright; Sven Ordquist; Marilyn Walker.
GERMANY: Dr Berkhard Fenner; Dr Ingrid Heerman; Dr Gerda Kroeber Wolfe and family, Dr Marion Melk Koch ; Peter Messenholler; Dietrich Schleip.
UNITED STATES: Christina Hellmich Scarangello – Peabody Essex Museum Salem; April Henderson; Cristina Veran; Mark Westenra.
HAWAI'I: Herb Kawainui Kane; Victoria Kneubuhl.
GREAT BRITAIN: Ro and Dick Brown; Stephen Ruscoe, Jill Hasell and Dorota Starzecka – British Museum of Mankind; Anne Masoe.

INTRODUCTION

THE ARTISTIC HERITAGE OF SAMOA

Samoa is one of the most written about and widely discussed island groups in Polynesia. Its history, society and culture have for many years attracted the attention of travellers, scientists, anthropologists and writers. Some of the most interesting and informative accounts of the history and culture of Samoa are found in unpublished sources, such as diaries, logbooks and journals. Academic publications and specialist reports are also rich in information. The difficulty is that many of these important and valuable sources are written for and by specialists. Some are out of print or too fragile or rare to be easily accessed and therefore housed in specialist or university libraries, or in private or institutional collections.

Because of this the opportunities for the general reader to read and learn about Samoa's artistic heritage are limited. There has been no broad survey of the Samoan arts since Te Rangi Hiroa's (Peter Buck) *Samoan Material Culture* published in 1930. Prior to this there was Augustin Kramer's monograph *The Samoan Islands* which covered art and material culture. However, this was only translated into English and widely distributed in 1995. There have been several other 20th century studies, but with the exception of Roger Neich's *Material Culture of Western Samoa* (1985) they have tended to specialise and focus on a particular art form or particular period. Te Rangi Hiroa's *Samoan Material Culture* thus provides the baseline upon which this book is built. Other sources and accounts from both 19th century and 20th century have been consulted, but always using Te Rangi Hiroa's study as a reference point.

This book is intended as an introduction to the Samoan arts and sets out to bring aspects of the artistic heritage of Samoa to the general reader. It is partly a history but also quite simply a catalogue of images documenting the creativity of Samoan artists over the last 200 years. The book is mainly concerned with Samoan artists in Samoa and New Zealand but also features artists from other places where Samoan communities are well established. The aim is to provide a starting point and introduction that will direct the reader towards further research and more detailed sources. My own contribution to the survey of work by so many others has been to provide an overview supplemented with recent observations and notes on contemporary developments. In some chapters excerpts from interviews with artists have been included in an effort to bring 'living voices' to the text. New images and objects have also been included, some of them published here for the first time. It is my hope that

Opposite: Tuataga Levao of Siumu.
(Craig Potton)

Siapo manamu (freehand painted tapa). Donated by the late Thomas Trood Esquire, Acting British Vice Consul, Apia, Samoa. Forwarded to the museum by direction of the administration of Samoa in 1917. (Museum of New Zealand, Te Papa Tongarewa, Ref. No: FE001423)

they will help to challenge our ideas about what the arts of Samoa were and how they are manifest today.

A quick survey of books on Oceanic and Pacific art largely gives the false impression that art of Pacific island cultures was something that stopped developing in the late 19th or early 20th century. It is only in the last five years or so that contemporary or late 20th century work has rated a mention in any meaningful way. Authentic Pacific art was widely seen as something of the past and the prevailing attitude was that indigenous forms of creativity and thinking disappeared with the arrival of the first Europeans. However, this was just the next chapter in a long history of changes and transformations that have occurred in the Pacific islands since first settlement. The arts and their unique characteristics changed, but they continued to thrive.

One of the things I have come to recognise while writing this book is that it is not always appropriate to attempt to put the development of the arts in a chronological or evolutionary order. Some art forms, such as dance, do not have a linear development; '...aspects are revived after being discarded or they are continued and transformed by new materials. What appears to be boldly innovative may, in a longer term view, be a return to an earlier manifestation or simply a briefly adopted form'.[1] Likewise the development of the arts is not always about moving from a less sophisticated state to another more sophisticated one, but more about making use of new opportunities as they arrive. As Samoan author Albert Wendt recalls:

It's like what Tom Davis[2] said to me when I went to the Cook Islands a few years ago. He was just in the process of finishing building his sailing craft and I think he was using marine plywood or fibreglass. I said to him 'Why are you using it? You know your people in the old days never used it.' He said 'But if they had had it in those days they would have used it.'[3]

Samoans' creativity has been shaped by the mixture of influences and conditions specific to them at different times. While it is important to see the broader historical context for an art form or work, the arts of one so-called homogeneous group can also develop differently at different locations at the same time. Some areas in Samoa for example specialised in making wooden bowls, others in siapo (tapa) production, or in va'a (canoe) building.

As Samoans have migrated overseas their art and creative motivations have gone with them and changed according to the circumstances of their new locations. So in an attempt to keep up with what Samoan artists were creating in the 1990s and are creating in the 21st century, especially in Samoan communities overseas, this book includes work in a range of media from Samoan artists living abroad. The artists and arts in this book are testimony to the many different ways fa'asamoa (Samoan custom) can be interpreted and understood. We need go no further than the oratorical arts of the tulafale or orators of Samoa to find a wellspring of interpretation and reinterpretation of the history and culture of Samoa. Samoan artists are writers, filmmakers, photographers, actors, painters, weavers, sculptors and orators. What connects them is their heritage and their exploration and interpretation of Samoan culture and life experiences. These processes are important, for it is through them and the interplay of representations, knowledge and the influences outside, that a sense of Samoan identity is constructed. In this way the arts provide one of the most accessible means for people to connect with their heritage and explore who they are.

As a general survey book I hope there is still something here for the specialist, anthropologist, historian and art historian. As with any survey, you are dealing with small pieces of what is often a very large and complex picture. Here we are dealing with a representation of Samoa's artistic heritage, not a presentation. A broad cross-cultural understanding of art is needed to unravel the intricacies and aesthetics unique to the Samoan culture and experience. The way Samoans think of art and how their ideas interplay and interact within a world system and global community are fertile territory for further study and research. Some people have already made some investigations and work is in progress. There are so many more questions to ask and avenues to explore. I hope this book and the stories and the work of the artists within it inspire others to create new things and ask new questions.

INTRODUCTION
1. Allan Thomas, 'Dance Costume in the Central Pacific Islands', *Studia Choreologica*, Vol. 1 (Instytut Dhoreologii w Poznaniu: 1999), pp. 39-56
2. A former Cook Island Prime Minister, scientist and sailor/navigator.
3. Albert Wendt, interview with author, (April 2000)

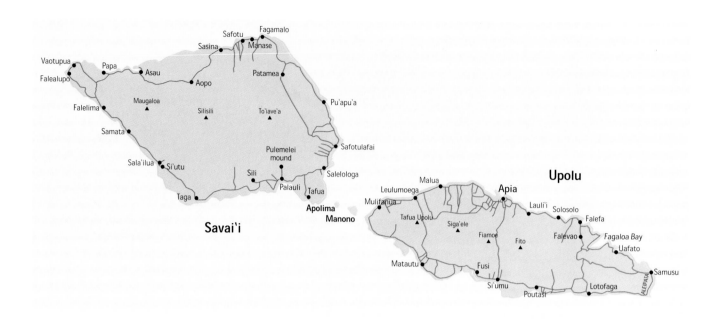

Savai'i

Vaotupua
Falealupo
Papa
Asau
Aopo
Falelima
Maugaloa ▲
Samata
Sala'ilua
Si'utu
Taga
Safotu
Sasina
Fagamalo
Manase
Patamea
Pu'apu'a
Silisili ▲
To'iave'a ▲
Safotulafai
Pulemelei mound
Saleloga
Sili
Palauli
Tafua
Apolima
Manono

Upolu

Leulumoega
Malua
Mulifanua
Apia
Tafua Upolu ▲
Lauli'i
Solosolo
Falefa
Siga'ele ▲
Falevao
Fagaloa Bay
Matautu
Fiamoe ▲
Fito ▲
Uafato
Fusi
Samusu
Si'umu
Poutasi
Lotofaga
ALEIPATA

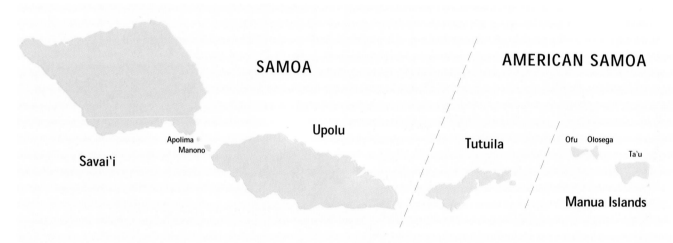

SAMOA

AMERICAN SAMOA

Savai'i
Apolima
Manono
Upolu

Tutuila

Ofu   Olosega
Ta'u

Manua Islands

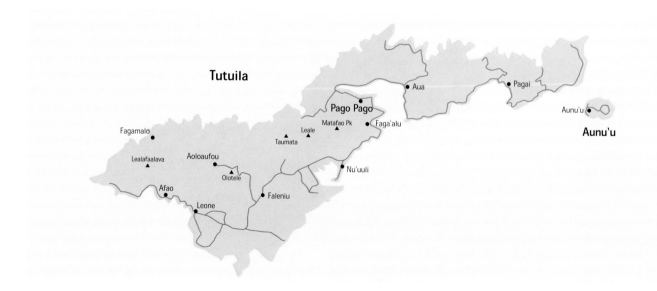

Tutuila

Fagamalo
Lealafaalava ▲
Aoloaufou
Afao
Olotele ▲
Leone
Faleniu
Taumata ▲
Leale ▲
Matafao Pk ▲
Pago Pago
Faga'alu
Nu'uuli
Aua
Pagai
Aunu'u

Aunu'u

CHAPTER 1

THE SAMOAN ARTS

Part of the distinctive character and identity of Samoa and Samoans around the world derives from the arts. The arts are a popular and diverse vehicle for communication, exchange and expressions of creativity and identity. From first settlement of the Samoan islands to the recent emigration of Samoans to New Zealand, Australia, Hawai'i and the United States, Samoan art has been part of many journeys, crossings and meetings of both people and ideas. These processes and interactions have transformed the arts as they have the life and culture of Samoa. In 1984 Sefulu Ioane in his article *Western Influences on Samoan Poetry* said that 'No man or country is an "island" anymore'.[1] One would have to argue that this has always been the case. The stories, languages, genealogy and material culture of the Pacific demonstrate that there were many shared histories, interconnections, routes of trade and communication among the Pacific islands long before the arrival of European ships. Samoa was not an island, so to speak, but part of a chain of distinct communities along which ideas, objects and people flowed. At times the connections were broken and former relationships were forgotten, but new relationships were made and new societies, identities and cultures developed. Through this interplay and the continual shifting of boundaries and people, Pacific and Samoan art in the 20th century has been part of a transforming and dynamic process. As new technologies and ideas have changed the cultures of the Pacific, so too have they changed the arts and the way Pacific peoples see, think, talk about and express themselves.

However, these processes of change are not widely understood when we talk about Samoan art today. Working in the museum environment for the last ten years, I have been interested to note some of the general perceptions of Samoan history, art and culture, from both Samoan and non-Samoans. A common impression, particularly among younger people is that with the arrival of Europeans, and in particular the missionaries, the arts and culture of Samoa were destroyed beyond recovery, and that the arts and culture since that time and including today are less authentic, less Samoan. However, for more than a generation, historians have been thinking more critically about these issues of encounter, agency and change in the Pacific.

This first chapter provides a brief background to Samoan society. It highlights some of the ways in which internal and external influences have shaped not only the course of Samoa's history but also its arts. It aims to remind us that Samoan art did

Fig. 1.1 Map of Samoa.

not disappear with the arrival of Europeans. Samoans were often creative and active agents of change, not merely passive victims, and as has always been the case, culture and art were not merely replicated but reproduced in new and innovative ways. As anthropologist Marshall Sahlins and others have pointed out:

In too many narratives of Western domination, the indigenous peoples appear merely as victims - neo-historyless peoples whose own agency disappeared more or less with their culture, the moment Europeans erupted on the scene. It is as if they had no historical relations with other societies, were never forced to adapt their existence.[2]

Samoa has an artistic heritage spanning almost 3000 years. In that time Samoans have adapted, appropriated, borrowed and exchanged as a result of interactions and influences within and outside their island group. The transformations made since the arrival of Europeans continues a process that began well before, and is central to the way that culture is understood to work. This chapter and those that follow focus largely on the last 200 years of Samoa's artistic heritage and argue that the arts of Samoans today are an outcome of the ongoing dynamic processes of cultural change and are just as authentic, living and vibrant as those of the past.

SAMOA AND ITS PEOPLE

Samoa is a chain of islands in the central Pacific Ocean which runs between latitude 13° and 15°S and longitude 171° and 176°W. The islands are high and volcanic in origin with the exception of Rose Atoll which lies at the chain's eastern end. The

Fig. 1.2 Samoan dancer performing the fa'ataupati (slap dance), 1999. (Craig Potton)

highest peak is Mount Silisili on Savai'i which rises to a height of over 1850 metres. The larger islands are rich in lush tropical vegetation but have few native animals. Most settlement is in the coastal lowlands where plantations have been established and the lagoons and ocean can be easily fished.

Archaeological investigations suggest that the earliest human inhabitants settled in Samoa almost 3000 years ago. The first settlers were a seafaring people whose ancestors originated in South East Asia, and over time populated most of island Melanesia and eventually Fiji, Samoa and Tonga. They brought with them crops, animals and a distinctive type of pottery known as Lapita ware, named after an archaeological site in New Caledonia where it was first rediscovered. They were people initially connected by a shared culture who developed unique and distinct societies over time in the different archipelagos and islands they settled. Three of these societies are those we now know as Samoa, Tonga and Fiji. They form what is sometimes described as the 'Cradle of Polynesia': the place where aspects of culture distinctly Polynesian developed and dispersed from and were transformed into many of the other cultures and societies of the Pacific that we know today.

The first written descriptions of Samoa were made in the 18th century. What we know of the history of Samoa before then relies upon oral historical accounts that take the form of genealogies, songs, legends and stories. These have been passed on from generation to generation and differ in the telling and the details depending on who you are and what part of Samoa you are from. Many of these accounts relate to events such as wars, journeys, the origins of titles and the beginnings of certain customs or things. They are evidence of a long and rich history and give us important glimpses of Samoa's past and the foundations of its customs and culture.

Before the arrival of the Christian missionaries in the 1830s Samoa's own religious and political leadership system was very different from the system today. According to historian Malama Meleisea, government and community authority in 18th century pre-Christian Samoa were the domain of two kinds of matai (chief) known as ali'i and tulafale. Ali'i titles were those which traced sacred origins through genealogies that began with Tagaloa-a-lagi, the creator, and were linked to major aristocratic lineages. Tulafale had more utilitarian associations, in accordance with their role of rendering service to and oratory on behalf of the ali'i.[3] This is not to say that tulafale were not powerful and influential in their own right. They had different responsibilities and influences that were to change over time. In some cases and circumstances tulafale titles could outrank ali'i titles, the rank of each being understood most clearly in 'the context of the nu'u, district and genealogical origins'.[4]

In 18th century Samoa the matai had responsibility for and leadership roles within the nu'u (village) and 'aiga (the smallest community or political entity made up of a number of families). Several nu'u were combined to create a sub-district, which in turn combined with other sub-districts to create a greater entity or district known as an itu malo.[5] At each level of society different matai or groups of matai would provide leadership.[6] The government of the nu'u was the fono or council of matai. The fono would make decisions on behalf of the village and supervise and administer food production, labour and group affairs.

The matai system in present day Samoa retains some of the character of former times but has changed a great deal since the 18th century. Meleisea argues that the current system is '... a modern political order which developed after 1830, the year in which the Christian gospel was first formally proclaimed in Samoa'. He describes Christianity as changing the whole nature of relationships within Samoan society,

Fig. 1.3 The pe'a, Samoan male tattoo, Independence Day Celebrations, Apia, Upolu, 1999. (Craig Potton)

replacing the indigenous religious system and aspects of its customs and beliefs. As part of this process he notes that the status and role of matai changed and 'The Pre-Christian role and status of titles were redefined to accommodate Christian ideology and the day-to-day business of family and village government'.[7] Today the term fa'amatai is used to refer to the leadership of families and villages by groups of ali'i and tulafale. But Meleisea observes that 'there are resonances of the old order in the rituals of kava ceremonies and on other ceremonial occasions, when ali'i and tulafale assume distinctly different roles'.[8]

Under the leadership of the matai, the 'aiga have historically supported themselves through subsistence agricultural activities as well as hunting and fishing. Different tasks relating to the everyday necessities of life were generally assigned according to age and gender. Within certain activities, such as hunting and fishing, tattooing, house and canoe building, there were highly skilled individuals who specialised in, oversaw and controlled aspects of the work. They were known as tufuga and their skills and expertise in these fields were recognised and respected. In some cases aspects of their work was marked with special ceremony and ritual. Presentations made to tufuga as payment for their work could include valuables such as 'ie toga (fine mats) and food, and could amount to a massive commitment of resources from the commissioning party. Despite this some tufuga were well known throughout Samoa and there was much competition to obtain their skills and services.[9] Historically there were also many other experts and specialists in the community skilled in such arts as the manufacture of mats, clothing, wooden articles and medicine.

The tufuga have continued to hold a respected place in Samoan society with some specialist roles carrying titles or being associated with particular 'aiga. In the village of Malie in the 1960s there were 36 kinds of specialist occupation known, all of which carried a matai title.[10] In the past some areas of specialisation had an apprentice and guild system where individuals with an aptitude and talent for a particular activity would connect themselves to an 'aiga associated with that specialist craft. The apprentice was then trained and nurtured in the necessary skills under expert tutelage. House and canoe building in particular have a long history in which a number of groups or guilds had their own trademarks, conventions and standards, and a hierarchy consisting of master craftsmen and their apprentices.[11] In some instances the apprentice/master relationship continues today, although it is much less formalised.

Today Samoa's economy is largely based on its subsistence and cash crop agriculture and its fishery. Tourism and light industry are slowly gaining a foothold, but there is a strong reliance on foreign aid and remittances from overseas. Within the difficult economic environment there are still many individuals working as specialists and their goods and services retain an important role in the village economy. In some cases there has been a decline in demand for certain goods and skills as imported items and methods replace local ones. Some arts, like the building of plank canoes such as the 'alia and va'aalo, have disappeared from living memory and only recently have there been attempts to recover these skills. But apart from the tufuga who were expert in these arts there still remain other specialists expert in the arts of medicine and healing, siapo making, basket and mat weaving, faleaitu (comic theatre), fagogo (story telling), music and dance.

Many internal and external forces and influences have shaped the course of Samoa's history. Not only have they changed Samoa's environment, but also the politics, customs and arts of its people. Long before the arrival of Europeans, the arts and customs of Samoa were influenced by contact with places such as Fiji and Tonga and islands further abroad. Technologies were shared between these societies and items such as adzes, whalebone, fine mats, feathers and women were traded across great distances.

In the same way that this trade took place between different island groups, Samoan art was also shaped by the local environment and the relationships between the different villages and districts. Certain areas specialised in different crafts or services depending upon the available local resources, but probably also because specialisation was a useful means of promoting inter-village and in some cases inter-island trade. Certain regions of Samoa were noted for their wooden bowls, carving and timber resources, others for their access to stone quarries for adzes or red earth for dye making. At different times in the last 200 years different regions or villages specialised in making the various products. For example, Falealupo and Asau made 'ava (kava) bowls, Safotu supplied 'ava, Manono made cuttlefish hooks, Malua was known for its fine mats, Vaiulu'utai for stone adzes and North-East Savai'i for its dyes.[12]

EUROPEAN ENCOUNTERS

With the arrival of Europeans in the Pacific came the first written descriptions of Samoa as well as the first exchanges in European material goods. The first European to visit and describe Samoa was Dutchman Jacob Roggeveen, who sailed into the waters off Manu'a in 1722 and engaged in some trade, exchanging mirrors and beads for food, but didn't actually make a landing. Nearly 50 years later, in 1768, Frenchman Louis Antoine de Bougainville sighted Samoa. He decided to name the archipelago the Navigator Islands, 'warranted on account of a dozen canoes with large sails'[13] and assuming that the Samoans must be skilled navigators. He was followed nearly 20 years later by another Frenchman, explorer Jean-Francois de Galaup de la Perouse. In 1787 he and his crew encountered violence on Tutuila after a series of misunderstandings with the locals. These were the beginnings of an era of cultural contact with Europeans that would bring sickness and disease, new knowledge and ideologies, new relationships and a range of new material items and technologies.

As different parts of the Pacific were explored and mapped by European vessels, the region quickly opened up for trade and other commercial opportunities. By the early 1800s whalers and merchants had made their way into the Pacific and established ports and settlements. Consequently new religious ideas and ideology came with the arrival of the first missionaries in the 1830s. They introduced a number of changes that affected not only the ideological world but the artistic, cultural and physical landscape. These included new forms of dress and ideas of modesty and extended to prohibitions by some denominations on arts such as tattooing and certain forms of dance. What remained of Samoa's indigenous religion was transformed in a manner similar to that experienced in other parts of the Pacific, with the first missionary teachers requiring that Samoans desecrate their aitu objects in evidence of their new convictions.[14] Despite these prohibitions and the adoption of Christianity, arts like dance and tattooing and some beliefs such as those concerning aitu, are still strong in contemporary Samoan communities.[15] The missionaries also introduced new forms of song and music that were embraced and modified by the Samoan congregations to suit their taste and aesthetic. In fact, at one point missionary attempts to teach Samoans Christian hymns were abandoned for a short time. No sooner had the missionary teachers taught them the words, than the Samoan women took them for use in their erotic night dances, much to their teachers' disapproval.[16]

Literacy and the written word also had a transforming influence. Spurred on by the initiatives of the church the Samoan translations of the new testament and bible introduced new imagery, cultures and histories, that would transform the Samoan perceptions of the world forever. The paperwork that came with western trade and government offered new ways to record and document, improving communication, and enabling Samoans to read and be more informed about local and international events.

Later in middle to late 19th century Samoa, church building became an important focus and became particularly competitive between different villages and denominations. (This spirit of competition continues to this day.) Some of the stone and coral churches built at this time incorporated European styles of architecture and were elaborate in both design and scale. It was not long before they surpassed the great fale tele (round house) as the most dominant feature of the village landscape. The building of churches can be seen as symbolic of the way Samoans accommodated the new ideas of the time and Christianity in general. As historian R.P. Gilson states, Samoans were:

...able to adopt Christianity, and adapt it, with greater resilience, experiencing scarcely any disintegration of their traditional social structure and way of life. There are historical as well as social reasons for this, but in general, the village church, however out of keeping with the island landscape, may be seen as a monument to the selectivity of the Samoan reaction to European contact.[17]

LATE 19TH AND EARLY 20TH CENTURY

From the 1850s through to the turn of the century, overseas colonial interests began to get a foothold in the port towns and surrounding lands of Apia and Pago Pago. Businesses and commercial enterprises had become well established and there were increasing numbers of foreign traders and speculators. Late in the century the beginnings of Samoan tourism started with companies such as the Union Steamship Company offering passage to Samoa. With the increase in western visitors, items such as weapons, baskets, bowls and model canoes were made as a market for tourist souvenirs grew. However, as overseas interest in the Samoan Islands intensified, the region became plagued with power struggles and conflicts between rival Samoan political factions and the imperial powers of the United States, Germany and Great Britain. After much bloodshed among the Samoan population and a near war between

Fig. 1.4 Making cord ('afa) from coconut fibre, Palauli, Savai'i, 1999. (Craig Potton)

the three imperial powers Samoa was annexed in 1899. Western Samoa (Savai'i and Upolu) was taken by the Germans and eastern Samoa (Tutuila and Manu'a) by the United States. Great Britain renounced all claims.

The colonial administration of the late 19th and early 20th centuries had both positive and negative consequences for the arts and customs of Samoa. Happily for some Samoans at least, the Europeans continued to introduce the latest styles of dress and fashion. Blazers and hats became popular and were highly sought after by locals despite their unsuitability to the climate. New entertainment such as brass bands and European songs and music became popular.

Other significant influences on the local culture include labourers brought to Samoa from overseas. In the 1870s German estate owners introduced Melanesian labour to Samoa to assist with commercial planting. By 1903 the plantation economy in Samoa was well developed, and so 279 labourers from Hong Kong were introduced to assist. By the outbreak of the war there were 2184 Chinese and 877 Melanesian indentured labourers in Samoa.[18] Later, in the 1920s, a small number of Niueans were also recruited for a year's service as labourers and began a small settlement near Apia.[19] There was also the sustained presence of workers and communities from nearby Tokelau and the Cook Islands. These communities made their mark in Samoan community life through the businesses and trades they established, through intermarriage, and through the variations and ideas they introduced to the local customs and material culture. The Chinese, for example, introduced new cuisine such as chop suey and the Niueans are likely to have been responsible for the introduction of the va'a niue (a Niuean-styled dugout canoe).

The colonial administration of Western Samoa changed hands on August 30, 1914 in an early action of the First World War when New Zealand troops occupied

Western Samoa. There was no resistance from the resident Germans, but local Samoan resistance to the New Zealand governorship was soon to reveal itself.

The Mau a Pule was a Samoan resistance movement started during the German administration by orator chief Lauaki Namulau'ulu Mamoe. Because of his resistance to the German authorities meddling in Samoan affairs and customs, Lauaki was exiled to Saipan in 1909. Organised resistance dwindled, but in 1926 a new movement simply called Mau was established; it had the same resistance objectives, but this time they were directed at the New Zealand administration.

Fig. 1.5 Patterns in pandanus weaving. (Craig Potton)

Since 1914 New Zealand's track record in Samoan affairs had not been impressive. A major incident was an influenza epidemic in 1918. The sickness was brought to the country when the New Zealand authorities failed to quarantine the infected ship *Talune*. This oversight had a terrible impact resulting in 7000 to 8000 deaths out of a population of approximately 38,302.[20] In terms of the arts, the skills, knowledge and memory lost at this time must have been immense.

Resentment toward the New Zealand administration grew throughout the 1920s with the passing of laws and regulations that interfered with the authority of the matai and the rights over titles.[21] This extended to other areas of cultural life and customs. For example in 1926 the administration tried to regulate the exchange of 'ie toga and the associated malaga or travelling parties. Anthropologist F.M. Keesing quotes an orator at the time as saying:

The white people condemn many Samoan customs as being wasteful. Their idea is that customs that interfere with working and making money are bad. But such customs give pleasure to the Samoans and are almost their only form of amusement. To travel and to entertain those who travel makes life interesting. A life filled with nothing but work would not be worth living. [22]

Fuelled by the impositions and interference with local institutions the Mau independence movement gained momentum and support. This was further strengthened in 1929 when during a peaceful demonstration in Apia nine members of the Mau were killed by New Zealand troops. The following year the Mau was declared a seditious organisation. However, a change of government in New Zealand in 1935 saw this declaration revoked. This change in circumstances for the Samoan people sowed the seeds for Western Samoa's eventual political independence in 1962.

World War II was a transformative period that saw a huge influx of foreigners into Samoa as the threat of Japanese attack became a concern. By 1942 there were hundreds of United States marines stationed in Samoa. One estimate cites one marine for every six Samoans. Their presence introduced new infrastructures, improved roads and communications. This temporary influx of people, money and machines also created new business opportunities and wealth. War and its associated activities were significant not only for the new technology and entertainments they introduced, but also the exposure to new ideas, markets and products.

America's association with the Samoas had been fairly formal from at least 1878 when they set up a naval station in Pago Pago harbour. Tutuila in the east of the Samoan archipelago had come under U.S. Navy governance from 1905 and from 1911 was to become known as American Samoa. However, Congress did not accept the deeds of cession until 1929. After control was transferred to the U.S. Department of the Interior in 1951 the development of the islands' infrastructure and services greatly increased. There was also growth in tourism and ongoing exposure to American products and markets. Increased emigration to the US mainland saw new communities established in places such as California and Hawai'i. Between these locations new routes and forms of communication and exchange developed, and culture, art and ideas travelled, as they had and continued to do so to other parts of the Pacific.

Western Samoa opened up even more to foreign visitors and investment throughout the 1960s and 70s, and this growth continues today. There has been corresponding growth in the number of arts and culture visitor experiences geared toward the tourist industry. This commercialisation of many of Samoa's arts is not necessarily all negative. The tourist arts have nurtured and encouraged aspects of Samoan arts and culture, although there is always the potential for the tourist market to overly distort or destroy them. For instance, the art of fale (house) building has recently benefited from tourism, with several fales being built as part of a new resort. But when imported baskets and carvings are sold as being authentically Samoan, local creativity is losing out to the desire for easy profits.

THE MID TO LATE 20TH CENTURY

The mid to late 20th century has seen Samoans migrating in great numbers to different parts of the world. Large Samoan communities can be found in Hawai'i, the United States mainland, Australia and New Zealand. Despite geographical distance, many Samoan migrants and their families maintain strong social, spiritual and family ties with their homeland.

One of the largest Samoan communities overseas is in New Zealand, a close and popular destination for many Pacific island people since the 1950s and 60s. They were encouraged to emigrate to New Zealand at this time by a government seeking a cheap industrial labour force. But many migrated for other reasons: to seek better educational opportunities, to connect with friends and relatives, to find employment and support family left behind in Samoa, and in some cases just for the adventure or novelty of travelling to another country.[23] These first waves of immigrants took aspects of their material and social culture such as 'ie toga, tatau (tattoo), siapo (tapa) and fa'asamoa customs and values to their new homeland. Some of these have been maintained or

Fig. 1.6 Supporting post in fale, Sinalei
Reef Resort, Upolu. (Craig Potton)

transformed to suit the conditions and circumstances of living in a new country.
Others have been discarded.

The families raised by these immigrants have likewise made choices about the
relevance and place of their culture in their lives. This has created a diverse range of
responses and attitudes toward aspects of fa'asamoa, especially in the last two to three
generations.[24] These processes are not confined to migrant Samoans, however. Samoans in Samoa are also part of the global community and are therefore subject to some
of the same choices, decisions and opportunities. The many ways in which artists
respond to their heritage, origins and the environment in which they find themselves,
are as varied as the ways they see and perceive the values and place of fa'asamoa.

SAMOAN ARTS TODAY

In Samoan communities, there are artists in many fields and media who work primarily for and in the market of museum, art dealer and gallery. Others work as commercial photographers and filmmakers and some are involved in education or the media.
To date the majority of gallery-based artists migrated, were born, or raised outside
Samoa and are either self taught or trained in western educational institutions.
Increasingly, a growing number of artists are being trained in a similar system and are
working for similar markets within Samoa itself. Art in the broadest sense is gradually
becoming recognised as an acceptable and valid occupation as well as a form of
individual expression outside the customary environments. Samoan artists are discov-

ering what the possibilities are in their chosen media and the many ways they can express their ideas.

As social and geographical circumstances have changed, so too has the fa'asamoa in which many of the arts of Samoa are embedded. In Samoan communities there is a great range of attitudes to and experiences of Samoan culture[25] and this is reflected in the many ways that customary values and practices are now manifest. Fa'asamoa as practised in New Zealand has characteristics distinct to the conditions of living there and reflecting the individual criteria set by those who practise it. The way a wedding is organised, how 'ie toga are collected and distributed, the materials used in costume-making, the style in which a song is played or composed, the tools used in tatau, the furnishing and design elements in churches: all are marked by variations in practice but all retain some continuity in social significance. The tanoa fai'ava (kava bowl) still mediates relationships and discussion in the fono whether it is decorated or plain. The matai retain special seating arrangements in the fale fono, whether the roof is coconut leaf or corrugated iron. And the taupou (village maiden) will wear the tuiga (ceremonial headdress) whether it is decorated with nautilus shell or plastic beads.

Likewise, the role of the tufuga raises similar issues, not only in terms of practice, but also perception. In Samoa the work of tufuga has always been appreciated not only for its artistic merit, but also for its economic, social and functional attributes. Some tufuga continue to have a role within the confines of their immediate community, contributing to its economic livelihood and supporting themselves and their family. Others move between different locations both locally and overseas, producing their work in different environments and for different purposes. To some extent this has long been the case, as historically tufuga have travelled far and wide with their expert knowledge - for example, tattooing royalty in the Tongan courts[26] or building canoes among communities in Fiji.[27] Today the arts of tufuga and other specialists find new inspiration and reinterpretation in Samoan communities overseas. In an intertwining of old and new aesthetic values and practice, contemporary artists are reproducing the arts of the tufuga as well as working in their own unique directions.

BEYOND THE STEREOTYPES

To appreciate and value the Samoan arts in the present, it is necessary to be aware of some of the stereotypes that shape our perceptions. In discussions of Samoan art and Pacific art in general, notions of what is 'traditional' and what is 'contemporary', or what is 'tradition' and what is 'change', play a significant role in what we describe and categorise as 'authentic' art. I have found with many Pacific artists and Pacific island peoples that the 'traditional' in art and culture is seen as something to strive for, an ideal model, something to perfect. For others tradition has been an idea to look to for inspiration, an 'authentic' and true foundation to develop their own ideas upon. As anthropologist Nicholas Thomas has suggested, this has been one of the most regrettable stereotypes in the Pacific arts that indigenous knowledge is dominated by the reproduction and perpetuation of tradition. 'This would deny the interpretation and innovation always present in Pacific cultures.'[28]

The term 'tradition' has long been used by anthropologists and others as a convenient way of talking about a 'non time' specific way of life. At one time it was a way for anthropologists to describe the cultures they studied, as if they were somehow pure and untouched by the outside world. One writer has described the term 'traditional' as betraying the anthropologists' desire to fix societies under study in amber so that they could be studied and preserved in their most untouched form. This was important at the time as many peoples of the Pacific were considered 'as something beautiful perhaps or strangely 'other' but nonetheless inescapably doomed to wither and perish with the arrival of the first high tech western prow'.[29]

We have already seen how Samoan culture did not end or begin with the arrival of the first prows of these European ships. However in many societies, including those in the Pacific, 'tradition' seems to be situated at this 'moment of contact' with Europeans. All that was before was 'traditional' and all that has followed has been degeneration and deviation from a more constant and coherent way of life. It is often assumed that ideas and practices possess a considerable continuity which, free of outside influences, are constantly replicated in their entirety. Today many people still consider 'tradition' as something that needs to be recaptured in order to fulfil the real ethos of life and an idealised and legitimate cultural existence. But in reality the 'moment of contact' with the outside world extended over a long and complex period of social and cultural exchange, not only with Europeans, but as already noted, with other Pacific island peoples as well. Despite all this it is important to note that the notion of tradition often becomes a reality when people choose to act upon it. While this reality may be connected to actual past ideas or practices, it connects to them only in a highly selective way.

Some have resented the supposed imposition of new ideas and foreign influences, perceiving that they dilute what is intrinsically Samoan in the arts, that which is 'traditional'. While it is true that the indigenous social and religious contexts for some of the arts transformed with the arrival of the missionaries, over the last 200 years Samoans have been active agents in how these changes and transformations have been managed. To understand processes of change in art and culture we have to remember that the meaning or significance of things is not necessarily imposed on people, but created by people themselves. New ideas, products and materials were introduced or made available in Samoa throughout its history, but Samoan communities modified or rejected them to suit their own situations and purposes.

A Samoan notion of authenticity and 'tradition' is probably best encapsulated by the concept of fa'asamoa. But as a set of cultural practices and values, fa'asamoa is regularly contested and reformulated to suit the needs and criteria of those who practise it. For example, the tulafale (orator) are widely seen as the guardians of fa'asamoa – advocates of a seemingly static unchanging set of ideas and practices of Samoan culture. But in reality they are among the most active agents for its reinterpretation and application. They have to be, in order to deal with the various political and social issues that their role in society entails.

Within other arts and cultural institutions there was a similar creativity in the way things were reinterpreted, revised and made Samoan. Throughout this book you will see many examples. Already I have noted the use of Christian hymns in the erotic Samoan night dances; other appropriations include the use of the whale blubber knife as a weapon of war and later as a dance accessory of the taupou. The English Union Jack, the standard of an empire, was for a short time highly sought after and used as a garment. In the absence of straw bonnets supplied by the missionaries, Samoan women in one instance made their own from turtle shell, and in body adornments the ongoing use of mirrors, plastics and other introduced materials illustrates the way that Samoans have made the most of new opportunities and materials. In contemporary faleaitu (clowning) and dance we see the integration of foreign elements and styles but built upon a foundation of some key Samoan aesthetic values and forms.

As an example of persistence in the arts, tatau is a long established art form that withstood missionary censure by some denominations to exist today as a strong symbol of Samoan identity and culture. However it too is constantly being revised and re-invented by those who create it, as well as those who receive it. Finally, Meleisea describes an example of these processes that shows how even simple things such as tea and tea cups have been imbued with a Samoan sense of significance and meaning.

When all [sic] ali'i or pastor is served tea he receives a china cup and saucer. A tulafale receives his tea in a cup without a saucer, or in a mug. New goods came to be used in old ways to indicate distinctions of rank and status. In this way, in the past one hundred and fifty years of Christian Samoan history, Christian and papalagi customs and institutions have been made distinctively Samoan.[30]

FURTHER QUESTIONS IN SAMOAN ART

While this book looks at the arts largely in terms of categories familiar to the outsider, another question remains: what are the categories of art that have meaning for Samoan people? Can they be separated and distinguished in a world where different systems of knowledge, aesthetics and meaning are so closely intertwined? These questions are difficult to answer; amidst all the introductions and a long history of crossings and the coming together of peoples, is there a thick vein of distinctiveness that enables the Samoan arts to retain a unique character? If there is it probably lies within the way things are done, the structuring principles underlying the surface manifestations that we are conditioned to see as constituting art. In Samoa some of these structures are found in the abstract conceptualisation of space, the way a village is laid out, the way food is presented, the positioning of matai in the fale and the ways arts such as dance and oratory are performed.

Neich touched on these principles in *Material Culture of Western Samoa* as did Shore in his discussions on Samoan dance in *Sala'ilua - A Samoan Mystery*.[31] Neich suggests that 'the focus of most aesthetic effort in Samoa is not on the objects themselves but on the way they are used, worn and exchanged in activities concentrated on the more valued Samoan arts of oratory, ceremonial, music and dance.'[32] Shore remarks on these same complexities in the way aspects of Samoan dance reinforce important social orders and relationships within the community. So despite many material changes in the manufacture of items such as mats and fale, these things retain and embody important structuring principles, classification hierarchies and uses that are central to a Samoan way of understanding and relating to things.

As mentioned in the introduction there is still much more to look at in terms of the Samoan arts. In her essay *Art and Aesthetics*, Adrienne Kaeppler has called for further study into the way in which the arts of the Pacific are often part of society and the structure of social reality: 'How they provide a basis for understanding the nature of society; how artistic and aesthetic structures are social structures; how art and aesthetics communicate meanings on different planes; how symbolic action is social action'.[33] Work in this area can only enrich our understanding of how different cultures and societies perceive and make sense of the world. Another avenue of enquiry that presents a challenge is how to capture the transnational nature of contemporary Samoan society. How do we map the connections and processes of belonging that link Samoan communities across the globe in their culture and their arts.

In the area of Samoan music April Henderson has made a recent investigation into the imagery of Samoan hip hop.[34] In her thesis, *Gifted Flows: Netting the imagery of hip hop across the Samoan diaspora*, she talks of the flow of ideas relating to hip hop music between people from one place who have established communities in many places. This is another example of Samoans taking an art form from one location and set of circumstances, and making something unique by re-applying it to their own set of circumstances, whether in Los Angeles, USA or Auckland, New Zealand. A full investigation of these questions is beyond the scope of this book, but this type of multi-sited research and the transnational study of culture offers new and interesting opportunities. In looking at the work of Samoan artists mainly from Samoa and New Zealand we take a small step in this direction. I hope that through their art and stories we can gain a better appreciation of the great diversity and possibilities that Samoan art can encompass.

Fig. 1.7 Siapo pattern, window frame, MADD Gallery, Apia, Upolu, 1999. (Craig Potton)

CHAPTER 1

1. Sefulu Ioane, *Western Influences on Samoan Poetry* (SPAN: 1984)
2. M. Sahlins, 'On the anthropology of modernity, or some triumphs of culture over despondency theory'; in Hooper, T (ed), *Culture and Sustainable Development in the Pacific* (Canberra: Asia Pacific Press, 2000), pp. 44-45; See also Howe, K.R. The Fate of the 'Savage', in 'Pacific Historiography', *Journal of New Zealand History* vol. 11, No. 2 (1977), pp. 137-154
3. M. Meleisea, *The Making of Modern Samoa* (Suva: Institute for Pacific Studies of the University of the South Pacific, 1987b), p. 8
4. Meleisea, *The Making of Modern Samoa*, p. 8
5. M. Meleisea, 'To whom gods and men crowded: chieftainship and hierarchy in ancient Samoa'; in Huntsman, Judith (ed), *Tonga and Samoa Images of Gender and Polity* (Christchurch, New Zealand: Macmillan Brown Centre for Pacific Studies, University of Canterbury, 1995), p. 23
6. Meleisea, 'To whom gods and men crowded', p. 23
7. Meleisea, 'To whom gods and men crowded', p. 33
8. Meleisea, 'To whom gods and men crowded', p. 35
9. M. Meleisea, *Lagaga: A Short History of Samoa* (Suva: University of the South Pacific, 1987), p. 35
10. D. Pitt, *Tradition and Economic Progress in Samoa* (Oxford: Clarendon Press, 1970), p. 231
11. I. Goldman, *Ancient Polynesian Society* (Chicago & London: University of Chicago Press, 1970), p. 255
12. Pitt, *Tradition and Economic Progress in Samoa*, p. 234
13. J. Dunmore (ed), *The Journal of Jean-Francois de Galaup de la Perouse: 1785-1788* (London: Hakluyt Society, 1995), footnote, p. 386
14. R.P. Gilson, *Samoa 1830-1900 - The Politics of a Multi-cultural Community* (Melbourne: Oxford University Press, 1970), p. 73
15. Spirits in Samoa internet discussion, [online] http://www.samoa.co.uk/qanda/5513.html; See also Neich, L.L. and Neich, R. 'Some modern Samoan beliefs concerning pregnancy, birth and infancy', *The Journal of the Polynesian Society*, vol. 83, No. 4, (1984)
16. John Williams, in Moyle, R.M. (ed), *The Samoan Journals of John Williams 1830 and 1832* (Canberra: Australian National Library Press, 1984), p. 117
17. Gilson, *Samoa 1830-1900*, pp. 14-15
18. F.M. Keesing, *Modern Samoa, Its Government and Changing Life* (London: George Allen & Unwin Ltd, 1934), p. 352
19. Keesing, *Modern Samoa*, p. 357
20. Meleisea, 'To whom gods and men crowded', p. 129
21. Meleisea, 'To whom gods and men crowded', p. 133
22. Keesing, *Modern Samoa*, p. 328
23. C. MacPherson, 'On the future of Samoan ethnicity in New Zealand' in Spoonley, P., MacPherson, C., Pearson, D., and Sedgewick, C. (eds), *Tauiwi: Racism and Ethnicity in New Zealand* (Palmerston North: Dunmore Press, 1986), pp. 107-126
24. MacPherson, 'On the future of Samoan ethnicity'
25. MacPherson, 'On the future of Samoan ethnicity'
26. Adrienne Kaeppler, 'Exchange patterns in goods and spouses: Fiji, Tonga and Samoa' *Mankind*, vol. 11 (1978), pp. 246-52
27. M.A. Tuimaleali'ifano, *Samoans in Fiji: migration, identity and communication* (Suva: University of the South Pacific, 1990), p35
28. N. Thomas, *Oceanic Art*, (London: Thames & Hudson Ltd., 1995), p. 36
29. V. Yarwood, 'The Backyard in History', *New Zealand Geographic*, vol. 33 (January-March 1997), pp. 124-127
30. Meleisea, 'To whom gods and men crowded', pp. 69-70
31. Bradd Shore, *Sala'ilua: A Samoan Mystery* (New York: Columbia University Press, 1982), pp. 257-262
32. R. Neich, 'Samoan figurative carvings and Samoan canoes', *Journal of the Polynesian Society*, vol. 93, (1984), pp.191-197
33. Adrienne Kaeppler, 'Art and aesthetics' in Howard, A. and Borofsky, R. (eds), *Developments in Polynesian Ethnology* (Honolulu: University of Hawai'i Press, 1989), p. 211; See also Kaeppler, A. *Poetry in motion: studies of Tongan dance* (Nuku'alofa, Tonga: Vava'u Press, 1993)
34. April K. Henderson, '*Gifted Flows: netting the imagery of hip hop across the Samoan diaspora*' (University of Hawai'i: Unpublished M.A. Thesis, 1999)

CHAPTER 2

POTTERY AND STONEWORK

Samoa's most ancient man-made articles that survive today are those made of ceramic and stone. One of the most significant discoveries related to Samoan prehistory is that of a distinctive type of pottery called Lapita ware. Named after a site in New Caledonia where the early finds were made, Lapita ware provides evidence of an ancient seagoing people who were the ancestors of present-day Samoans and other Polynesians. These travellers and explorers were the first people to settle the islands of Melanesia, rapidly moving east into the islands of west Polynesia that we now know as Fiji, Tonga and Samoa.

Lapita ware is recognised by its dentate stamped decoration. Elements of these decorations survive today in motifs of other art forms such as tattooing and siapo. The finding of this distinctive form of pottery at various archaeological sites suggests the people of the Fijian, Tongan and Samoan archipelagos share a common ancestry. In Fiji, Lapita ware has been found at several sites on Viti Levu and Lakeba in the Lau Islands. In Tonga it has now been found on Tongatapu, Ha'apai, Vava'u and Niuatoputapu.[1] In Samoa it was found at the ferry berth site at Mulifanua at the western end of Upolu.

The site at Mulifanua is estimated to be nearly 3000 years old and is submerged underwater 114 metres out into the lagoon. The site was revealed when dredging took place during the construction of the ferry berth in 1973. As the lagoon bottom was shaped and deepened sherds of broken pottery started to appear among the dredged material. Over 2500 sherds were recovered and close observations showed that they were concentrated in a narrow band parallel to the lagoon shoreline.[2] This area of excavation is believed to represent a village that became submerged due to massive land subsidence in the area.

In describing the significance of the pottery finds at Mulifanua, archaeologist Roger Green, who was working in Samoa at the time said that the sherds

Fig. 2.1 Lapita pottery sherd from ferry berth site, Mulifanua, Upolu. (Museum of New Zealand, Te Papa Tongarewa)

served to document an initial period of Samoan prehistory when people accustomed to making a fairly sophisticated variety of Lapita-style pottery elsewhere, settled in Samoa and began there the manufacture of an almost identical pottery from local materials. The result was a wide range of vessel forms using decorative devices characteristic of similar Lapita pottery from Fiji and Tonga.[3]

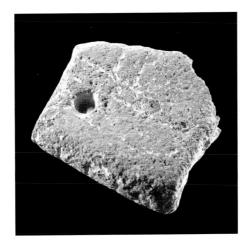

Figs. 2.2 and 2.3 Lapita pottery sherds from ferry berth site, Mulifanua, Upolu. (Museum of New Zealand, Te Papa Tongarewa)

Soon after the village at Mulifanua was established, changes occurred in pottery making that led to the disappearance of the motifs characteristic of Lapita ware. In their place came a range of bowls that were plain and undecorated except for an incised motif that occasionally appeared on odd rims.[4] This type of pottery is described by archaeologists as Samoan plainware and is found at numerous sites throughout Samoa. These include Vailele, Vaiusu, Faleasi'u and also Sasoa'a, Puna Mounds and Leuluasi in the Falefa Valley on Upolu, also To'aga and other sites in American Samoa.[5]

One of the major questions that archaeologists still have about pottery manufacture in Samoa is why it was abandoned. One suggestion is that the importance of cooking in earth ovens and the development of wooden kava bowls may have swayed Polynesians away from pottery.[6] Another is that some of the social roles where pottery played an important functional part were replaced or abandoned for other activities where pottery was no longer required.[7] From archaeological work to date, it is believed that pottery became less common in Samoa after the first centuries AD and was only made in a few regions, perhaps only on Tutuila. Between about 1300 and 1600, it dwindled in production even further and had been totally abandoned by 1600.[8] There is no evidence for pottery in Savai'i or Upolu after AD500.

STONE STRUCTURES

Archaeology has also helped reconstruct other forgotten aspects of Samoa's past. Agricultural terraces, forts, walls, roads and curious star shaped structures known as tia'ave (earth or stone mounds with one or more arms or rays) have been uncovered. Many of these ancient stone features lay for many years under the bush and rainforest, their locations known only to locals. But archaeological fieldwork since the 1960s has led to intensive investigation and speculations as to their age, origin and use.

Tia'ave were made from earth and stone and faced with rock or coral slabs. They are often referred to as star mounds because of their one or more projecting arms or rays. They range in size from 30 to 40 metres in diameter and up to five metres in height.[9] Over 140 of these stone structures have been located throughout Samoa.[10]

There has been much academic argument regarding the use and function of these mounds, with the most accepted being that they were used, at least in part, for the ancient sport of pigeon snaring.[11] There are many 19th century accounts that support this view including Turner who wrote:

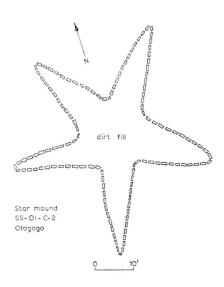

dirt fill

Star mound
SS-01-C-2
Ologogo

0   10'

Fig. 2.4 Plan of star mound SS-01-C-2, Ologogo, Savai'i. (Courtesy of Roger Green)

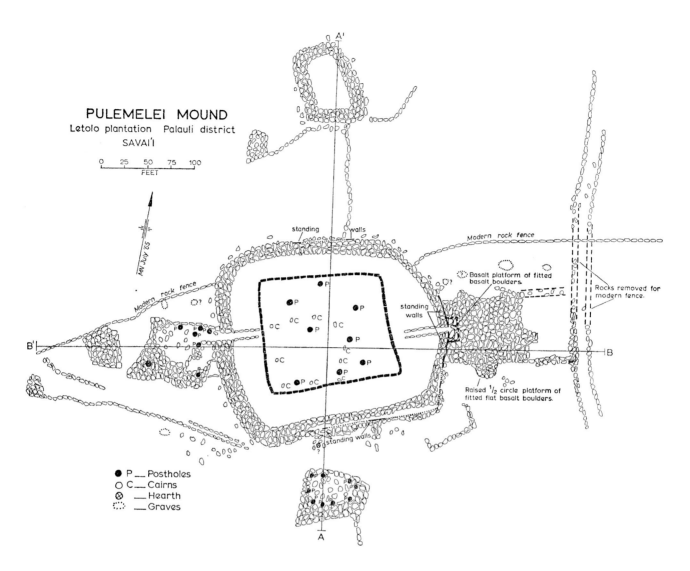

PULEMELEI MOUND
Letolo plantation   Palauli district
SAVAI'I

0   25   50   75   100
FEET

MN July 65

standing   walls
Modern rock fence
Modern rock fence

Basalt platform of fitted basalt boulders.

standing walls

Rocks removed for modern fence.

Raised 1/2 circle platform of fitted flat basalt boulders.

standing walls

● P — Postholes
○ C — Cairns
⊗ — Hearth
⣀ — Graves

Fig. 2.5 Plan of Pulemelei mound SS-Le-1, Palauli, Savai'i. (Courtesy of Roger Green)

Pigeon catching was another amusement, and one like our English falconry of other days, in which the chiefs especially delighted. The principal season set in about June. Great preparations were made for it; all the pigs of a settlement were sometimes slaughtered and baked for the occasion; and, laden with all kinds of food, the whole population of the place went off to certain pigeon grounds in the bush. There they put up huts, and remained sometimes for months at the sport.[12]

The significance of the sport of pigeon catching seems to lie in the way it served as an arena for chiefly competition for prestige, status and power.[13] Pigeon catching is also believed to have been related to ritual re-enactments of ancient stories, relating to the procurement of women and warfare.[14] The various designs of tia 'ave have been interpreted as symbolic representations of mythological entities, such as the octopus and the turtle.[15] Aspects of the sport are still alluded to in Samoan oratory and proverbial sayings. An example is *O le fogatia ua malu maunu – The catching place is full of decoy pigeons.* This saying refers to a village that boasts of many experienced orators. Another saying is *Ua numi le fau – The string (to which the decoy pigeon is tied) is entangled.* This refers to an affair that is complicated and difficult.[16]

A different type of large stone mound has been found at Pulemelei at Palauli on Savai'i. Very little is known about its purpose, but the nature of the extensive stone remains suggest that from at least the time of Christ, Samoan society must have been highly organised, in order to control the labour and manpower required to build such monuments.[17] Today, access to Pulemelei is relatively easy compared to other stone mounds. It is overgrown with ferns, but is still impressive in height and scale.

PETROGLYPHS

An example of work on stone are the petroglyphs that have been found on Tutuila. Little is known about them, but they reveal some abstract figurative forms not often seen in Samoan art. Discovered in archaeological site surveys in 1961 and 1962 the petroglyphs take the form of figurative engravings or rock carvings.[18] In a way they are like a form of prehistoric graffiti. Archaeologists have put forward several techniques that could have been used to inscribe the images on to the stone. Pre-European petroglyphs found near Leone village on Tutuila and Fitiuta village on the island of Ta'u appear to have been engraved into the stone surface by pecking (hammering the stone with a sharp pointed instrument), bruising (rubbing the surface with another stone) and abrading (a combination of pecking and bruising). The motifs take the shape of a hole or holes encircled with 5 to 20 additional holes. These are arranged among a number of carved lines that archaeologists believe represent a human figure, a paddle and an octopus.

Local Samoans questioned at the time had forgotten the petroglyphs' origin and purpose, but several chiefs suggested that they may have come from Samoa's pagan past or been made by foreigners. The archaeologists saw them as possibly signatures of individuals and groups that had been to the area.

Fig. 2.6 Petroglyphs at Leone, American Samoa. (Courtesy of the Journal of the Polynesian Society)

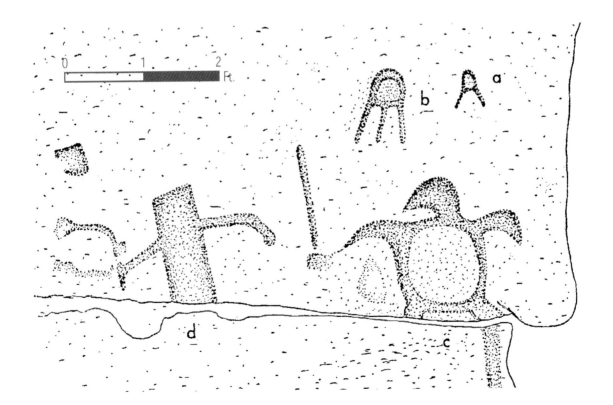

In 1966 rock previously covered with algae was exposed at the lagoon at Leone and more petroglyphs were uncovered. Four new forms were distinguishable in the stone surface. These took the shape of what appeared to be an octopus, a jellyfish, a turtle and an incomplete human figure. Once again very little could be ascertained about their origin, although the octopus points to a possible connection with an important totem of Samoan folklore.[19]

ADZES AND ADZE MAKING

The most important tool for woodworking before the arrival of metal tools was the hafted stone adze. In Samoa this was made from a piece of worked stone that was lashed with coconut fibre cord to a handle made from timber. Stone adzes were important everyday tools, and the workmanship achieved in cutting the curved rafters of fale, in shaping and fitting the planks of canoes, was due in no small part to their skilful handling. They were also used to make bowls and containers, figurative sculpture, clubs and edged weapons.

The stones for making the adze heads were taken from quarries. In the mountains of Tutuila there are quarry sites that appear to have been very important in supplying the basalt stones required for adze making. But not just for the islands in the Samoan group: investigations have indicated that Tutuila was a major supplier of basalt adzes to neighbouring archipelagos as well. Preliminary studies on a large number of adzes, using techniques of geochemical analysis, have shown that adzes of Samoan type or style found in Tokelau, Fiji and the eastern Solomons originally came from quarries in Tutuila.[20] Within the last 600 years or so Tutuila basalts were reaching the Cook Islands, and by 300 years ago they were in Tonga.[21]

What this tells us is, that despite the way in which many cultures in the Pacific seem to have developed separately and distinctly, there were still larger systems and networks of which they were a part. This is important to remember when thinking about the arts. Not only adzes flowed along these trade routes, but also people, skills, ideas and art forms.

So the preferred stone used for making the adze head, before metal tools, was a finely grained basalt, often sourced it seems from Tutuila. The stone would be roughly chipped into the desired shape by striking it with a hammer stone. It was then taken to a location near a water source, where it could be ground to produce a usable edge. Boulders used for this purpose are characterised by smooth dish-shaped concave areas and grooves where the cutting edges of the tools would have been sharpened.[22] The finished adze head was then fitted to a handle specially fashioned from a branch of a tree. Several types of adze and stone tools were made, each to fulfil different requirements and tasks. Soon after the arrival of Europeans and the introduction of metal, stone adzes quickly disappeared from the carpenter's toolkit and the quarries were soon abandoned. Steel adzes, chisels and planes are the tools for the present day woodworker.

Other small portable items were also made from stone. These include small anchors, fashioned from rocks with holes drilled through them, and also net and octopus lure sinkers.

Fig. 2.7 Hafted stone adze. To 'i ma'a. Collected by Captain J.B. Fleck when he was stationed in Samoa in 1917. (Museum of New Zealand, Te Papa Tongarewa, Ref. No: FE001543)

CHAPTER TWO

1. Janet Davidson, personal comment, (2000)
2. J.D. Jennings, 'The ferry berth site, Mulifanua district Upolu', in Green, R.C. and Davidson, J.M. (eds), *Archaeology in Western Samoa*, vol. 2, (1974), Bulletin of the Auckland Institute and Museum 7: 176-178, Auckland
3. R.C. Green, 'A review of the portable artifacts from Western Samoa', in Green, R.C. and Davidson, J.M. (eds), *Archaeology in Western Samoa*, vol. 2, (1974), Bulletin of the Auckland Institute and Museum 7: 245-275, Auckland, p. 249
4. Green, 'A review of the portable artifacts', p. 249
5. J.T. Clark, 'Samoan prehistory in review', in Davidson, J.M., Irwin, G., Leach, B.F., Pawley, A., and Brown, D. (eds), *Oceanic Culture History: Essays in Honour of Roger Green* (1996), New Zealand Journal of Archaeology Special Publication, p. 450
6. J.M. Davidson, 'Samoa and Tonga', in Jennings, J.D. (ed), *The Prehistory of Polynesia* (Cambridge, Massachusetts: Harvard University Press, 1979), pp. 82-109
7. Adrienne Kaeppler, cited in Green, R.C. 'A review of the portable artifacts', p. 253
8. Clark, 'Samoan Prehistory in Review', p. 451
9. J. Enright, and D.J. Herdich, 'Star mounds' (1998), [online] http://ashpro.org/Enright_articles.html
10. Clark, 'Samoan prehistory in review', p. 453
11. D.J. Herdich, 'Towards an understanding of Samoan star mounds', *Journal of the Polynesian Society* 100:381-435, (1991)
12. G. Turner, *Samoa A Hundred Years Ago and Long Before* (London: 1884), p. 127
13. Clark, 'Samoan prehistory in review', p. 453
14. Herdich, 'Towards an understanding', p. 424
15. Herdich, 'Towards an understanding', p. 415
16. E. Schultz, *Samoan Proverbial Expressions Alaga 'upu Fa'a - Samoa* (Auckland: Polynesian Press, 1994), p. 31
17. M. Meleisea, *Lagaga* (Suva: University of the South Pacific, 1987), p. 20
18. W.K. Kikuchi, 'Petroglyphs in American Samoa', *Journal of the Polynesian Society* (1964) 73:1 163-166
19. W.K. Kikuchi, 'Additional Petroglyphs from American Samoa', *Journal of the Polynesian Society* (1967), 76:3 372-373
20. S.P. Best, R. Sheppard, R. Green, and R. Parker, 'Necromancing the Stone: archaeologists and adzes in American Samoa', *Journal of the Polynesian Society* (1992), 101: 45-85
21. Clark, 'Samoan prehistory in review', p. 453
22. 'Culture history of American Samoa', American Samoa Historic Preservation Office (1997), [online] http://ashpro.org/Samoan_Cultural_History.html

TUFUGA FAUVA'A
THE CANOE BUILDERS

The va'a (canoe) was the means by which the ancestors of Polynesian peoples ventured beyond familiar shores, exploring and migrating to the islands and atolls of the vast Pacific Ocean. Crucial to the success of these explorations were a confidence and familiarity with the ocean environment, and this confidence rested on the seaworthiness of the vessels that carried them across the waves. These vessels were the va'a and the ancestors of the Samoans sailed in large doubled hulled va'a made by the tufuga fauva'a (master canoe builders).

The ability of these men to fashion large plank-built vessels capable of handling treacherous seas is an art on the brink of disappearing. The remaining legacy of these great artists can only be found in books and among models and the few examples of va'a that survive in museums.

The canoe was central to survival in the Pacific Ocean environment. Manufactured in a range of shapes and sizes, it played a crucial role in transport, trade, warfare and the gathering of food and resources. Some va'a were status symbols owned only by chiefs, some were owned by families or groups of families, while others were owned by villages or districts.

The building, maintenance and use of a large va'a meant that in many ways they were vessels through which the wealth, power and resources of matai and community flowed. Today the va'a, as well as still being channels for these resources, are also vessels through which knowledge and a sense of history and identity flow.

The story of the Samoan va'a is a long one that is only now being taken up and continued. As the va'a of old Samoa have disappeared, so too have the artists who made them – their special skills and knowledge being all but forgotten. Today the tufuga fauva'a are few in number but hope and enthusiasm remain for the continuation of the ancient art.

From the very first written accounts, European observers were marvelling at the workmanship and manner in which Samoan va'a were built, and the dexterity and confidence with which they were handled on the open sea. Indeed throughout the whole European era of Pacific exploration sailors and sea captains would often remark in their logs and diaries on the seamanship of the Pacific island peoples. The first written description of Samoan va'a comes from the Dutchman Jacob Roggeveen when he visited the island of Ta'u in the Manu'a group of islands in 1722:

Fig. 3.1 This 'alia, known as Fa'ainaelo was photographed at Olosega by Thomas Andrew probably in the early 1900s. (Alexander Turnbull Library, National Library of New Zealand, Te Puna Matauranga o Aotearoa. Ref. No: 115868 1/2)

Fig. 3.2 An 'alia on Apia Harbour with over 40 people on board. This 'alia is said to have been presented to German Imperial Governor Solf around the turn of the twentieth century. (Alexander Turnbull Library, National Library of New Zealand, Te Puna Matauranga o Aotearoa. Ref No: F94328 1/2).

Meanwhile there are two to three canoes—which were not hollowed-out trees, but made of planks and inner timbers and very neatly joined together, so that we supposed they must have some tools of iron...[1]

In 1787 Frenchman Jean Francois de Galaup de la Perouse noted va'a and the confidence with which they were handled:

All the canoes then came up to us, they progress fairly well with a sail but very poorly with paddles... they topple over at any moment and this happening surprises them and worries them less than a hat falling off does with us, they lift the submerged canoe on their shoulders and after emptying it of water get back in, quite sure they will have to repeat the operation within a half hour...[2]

The workmanship noticed by Roggeveen and the confidence on the sea alluded to by La Perouse are supported by another account from the missionary John Williams who was in Samoa in the 1830s:

We were running six knots an hour but the canoe played round and round us like a fish. The sail is so constructed that it lifts the whole forepart of the canoe out of the water so there is nothing to drag through the water but the hinder part of the vessel which is made so clean & tapering that it meets with no resistence.[3]

So who made these va'a of Samoa? What were the skills and customs employed to build such seaworthy craft? The answers to these questions lie in the distant past.

THE FIRST VA'A BUILDERS

An account from the 19th century records that the first tufuga fauva'a and tufuga fau fale (builders of houses) originated in heaven and were sent to earth by the god Tagaloa. On earth they formed the guild of Sa Tagaloa, the guild of carpenters and va'a builders. There are several stories that talk of the tufuga fauva'a and highlight the importance of the special customs and observances that came with them and their special art of va'a building.

In one such story, it is said that Mataiteite the daughter of Tagaloa, sent her son to his grandfather with a request to let her have some boat builders so she could build a boat for her husband on Savai'i.[4] Tagaloa granted the request, but with specific instructions saying: "Very well, but they must be taken good care of. Whenever they are to be supplied with food, the servants must not approach them quietly, but they must call out to them. Those carpenters are very particular and they might run away before their work is completed."

The carpenters came down upon the earth and started work. The people saw trees falling, but they did not see the workmen. The villagers prepared food for them and, as instructed, always made much noise when they brought it along.[5]

A story such as this highlights the respect to be shown to the tufuga fauva'a and the secrecy and protection surrounding the skills of their trade. But there were also rituals and rules that the tufuga themselves were required to follow and another story relates the importance of some of these old customs.

The story of The Sacred Trees[6] involves a young man named Lata who in pursuit of his father's enemies wrecked his va'a in stormy seas on the coast of Savai'i. Finding that his father's enemies had fled offshore, he went into the forest and set about building a new va'a so he could continue the chase. Picking out two of the best trees he could find, he set to work with woodchips flying, and by nightfall he had fashioned two beautiful hulls. Leaving these lying in the forest he retired to a nearby village for food and rest.

Just before dawn he returned to the forest to continue his work. But where the night before he had left two hulls, in their place stood two beautiful trees. In disbelief he started work again and by nightfall two beautiful hulls were once again lying in the shade of the forest. On his return to the site the next day, Lata was amazed to find not two hulls but once again two beautiful trees. In anger he set to work, working hard all through the day until the evening. This time instead of going back to the village Lata hid in some nearby bushes and watched where he had laid the hulls of the va'a.

As the moon rose the aitu (spirits of the forest) appeared, and Lata watched as they took all the chips and shavings from his work and together with the two hulls transformed them back into two beautiful trees. Noticing Lata hiding in the bushes one of the aitu challenged Lata asking why he had cut down the trees and not asked permission or made a sacrifice to the god of the forest. When Lata heard this he was ashamed, for in his rush to pursue his father's enemies he had forgotten to observe important customs. Lata left but returned later that night bringing with him a sacrifice for the god of the forest. In return the aitu made him a swift and beautiful va'a that no other tufuga could build. And in this va'a Lata continued his adventures and journeys in pursuit of his father's enemies.

As the ancient va'a building arts have changed, so too have some of the associated beliefs, rituals and customs. Fa'asamoa and early European accounts describe a series of payments and ceremonies similar to those employed when having a fale built or acquiring a tatau. The skills of the tufuga fauva'a were important and the manner in which business was conducted was not to be taken lightly. Missionary John Williams observed in the 1830s that:

...tradesmen such as canoe builders and house carpenters are both respected and rich. The chief who wants a canoe or house built will pay the principal workman who undertakes the job so many siapos or pieces of native cloth and so many fine mats ... beside feeding with the best food he can obtain during the whole time he is in his employ.[7]

Some aspects of these customs remain relevant and many others, like those outlined in the stories above, are still remembered. In recent years, some of the reasons for building va'a may have changed, as have the ways and contexts of doing business, but the old ideas live on and help shape the way things are done and the manner in which relationships undertaken in the building of va'a are managed. The details are perhaps not always the same but the principles of respecting and looking after the tufuga and his workers still apply.

The skills and customs that made this group of tufuga so important in Samoa were also actively sought and utilised offshore. In the past the vessels made by the tufuga fauva'a took not only the master sailors and fishermen abroad but also the skills of the tufuga fauva'a themselves.

Canoe building technology in parts of Fiji was once greatly influenced by two Samoan va'a builders from Manono. For some time they had been living with Ma'afutukui'aulahi, a prominent chief from Tongatapu[8], and were taken by Tongan seafarers to Lau in Fiji in the second half of the 18th century. Their expert planking skills enabled much larger va'a to be built from the Fijian vesi hardwood. One of these Samoan men was Lemaki and he 'became a master builder to the high chiefs of Lau, leading to the eventual establishment of a hereditary line of craftsmen, the mataisau, who were the carpentry, architecture and construction experts. This hereditary lineage scattered throughout Lau and as far north as Taveuni'.[9] Many of their descendants still live in these islands to this day.

It is difficult to say with any certainty just how extensive the Samoan voyaging was in the years preceding European contact, but adzes from Tutuila quarries have been found as far west as the Solomon Islands and as far south as the Cook Islands. Generally speaking, however, there was probably little motivation to venture further abroad, as the Samoan archipelago was already rich in resources such as trees, land, seafood and crops. There are many accounts of voyages by Tongans to Samoa, but it is more difficult to ascertain what voyaging was done by Samoans in the opposite direction, although there are a few Cook Island accounts, from before the 1800s.

While the missionary Reverend John Williams was in Samoa in the 1830s he saw three of a group of seven kalia (Tongan double-hulled sailing vaʻa), which had come from Tonga to purchase ʻie toga (fine mats), so we know at least that long sea voyages were taking place as recently as the early 19th century.[10] But it is likely that the Samoan ʻalia (double-hulled sailing vaʻa) of the 18th and 19th century were confined to voyages within the island group itself.

THE SAMOAN VAʻA

When discussing the seagoing vessels of the Pacific there are two basic types: double-hulled – those that have two hulls (of equal or unequal length) joined together by decking; and outriggers – those with one hull and a float attached to the hull by two or more booms. Throughout the Pacific islands there is a great range of both these types and their methods of construction vary. The two most common hull types are those made from individually fashioned planks sewn together, and those that are dugout or hollowed from the trunk of a tree.

In Samoa both double-hulled and outrigger vaʻa were made, as were plank built and dugout hulls. It is, however, the plank built vaʻa that embody the finest skills in the vaʻa building arts of Samoa.

THE VAʻA TELE

Historical accounts describe several types of plank-built vaʻa that were made in Samoa at different times. The earliest on record was a large seagoing vessel known as the vaʻa tele. This double-hulled craft had a Tongan equivalent known as a tongiaki which was essentially designed, manufactured and sailed in the same way. European explorers sailing near Tonga made the first images of these vessels. There was Schouten in 1616 off the island of Tafahi and later Abel Tasman in 1643 near Tonga. As their sketches clearly show, two hulls of equal length were joined by a deck on which a shelter and a fireplace were built. They were propelled by a large triangular sail made from pandanus and kept on course through the use of two steering paddles fixed to and

Fig. 3.3 A vaʻa tele – double-hulled plank-built voyaging canoe. (Courtesy of Herb Kane)

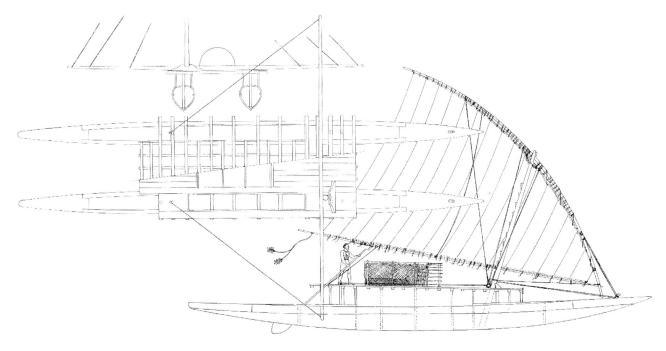

controlled from the stern.

Although large and difficult to manoeuvre, the following account from the Reverend J.B. Stair in the 1830s makes clear that the huge decking of the va'a tele made it a useful vessel for long voyages and transporting people and goods:

Upon the fishing expeditions made at certain seasons of the year to a reef midway between Wallis Island [Uvea] and Savaii they were accustomed to carry two va'a alo or large fishing canoes, on the deck, which, on reaching the reef, were used in fishing for bonito etc., the large canoe being reserved for crew and cargo.[11]

The last va'a tele was seen in Samoa around 1838[12] and was soon superseded by a type of vessel known in Fiji as the drua and in Tonga as the kalia. From at least the early 1700s when James Cook first visited Tonga, kalia already co-existed with tongiaki and would eventually replace them. The same process occurred in Samoa, the va'a tele disappearing early in the 1800s in favour of the swift and more manoeuvrable va'a known as the 'alia.[13]

THE 'ALIA

In the 19th century the most prized and finely crafted vessels in Samoan waters were the 'alia. The 'alia differed from the va'a tele in that their rigging and the shape and length of their hulls allowed them to be sailed more easily. In terms of design they were the equivalent of the Fijian drua and Tongan kalia and could be very large in size. As well as being used for transportation, they were also used in times of war, with some 'alia even carrying cannons.[14] One 'alia seen in Tutuila in 1862 was 70 feet long, five feet deep and able to transport up to 100 men. It was described as sailing 'round a vessel in which the consular agent was a passenger, going eight knots'.[15] So despite their great size they were very manoeuvrable.

At the end of the 19th century photographs of at least four Samoan 'alia can be

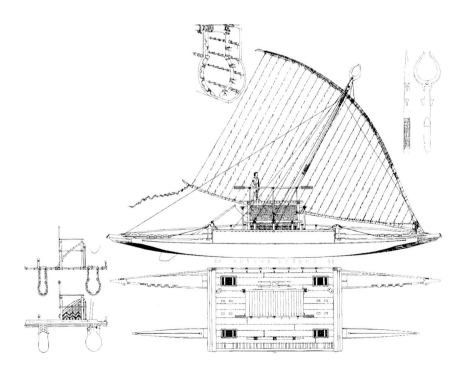

Fig. 3.4 An 'alia – double-hulled plank-built canoe. (Courtesy of Herb Kane)

verified. There is the *Fa'ainaelo* at Olosega, *Sau'aitagata* of Saleaula at Savai'i, *Fa'ataugali* of Safune[16] at Sanaitopata, near Leotele in Savai'i, and one photographed with over 40 passengers on board, said to have been presented to Imperial Governor Solf of Germany around the turn of the century.[17]

The building of large va'a such as the 'alia utilised the skills of many other specialist craftsmen such as sail makers, rope makers and paddle makers and was probably a great strain on the resources of a village or district. So the gift of an 'alia to Governor Solf would have been both costly and prestigious. Sadly, due to the high costs of transporting the vessel to Germany it rotted away on the beach at Apia. This was probably the last of the full size 'alia to be seen.

The 'alia are also interesting in that they were sometimes decorated with geometric designs and animal representations. A closer look at the four photographs reveals what appear to be carved images in relief of a pig, a dog and horses (one with rider). This decoration is quite unique as there is little documented evidence that figurative artwork of this kind was widely practised in Samoa.

THE AMATASI

Amatasi were vessels built for speed under sail. They were used to chase and hunt down the large and fast schools of surface feeding fish such as bonito and tuna, but were also used for protecting people travelling in 'alia, preparing landings[18] and for short journeys. They were similar to the va'aalo, but much bigger. Powered by an inverted triangular sail up to ten feet high[19] and elegantly plank-built, these amatasi travelled very swiftly on the open sea. The use of the suati (balancing spar) to the windward side of the sail was a distinguishing feature. A crew member would walk out on this spar in order to balance the vessel if there was a danger of capsizing during fresh winds. Those on the other side of the va'a would be ready to go out on the

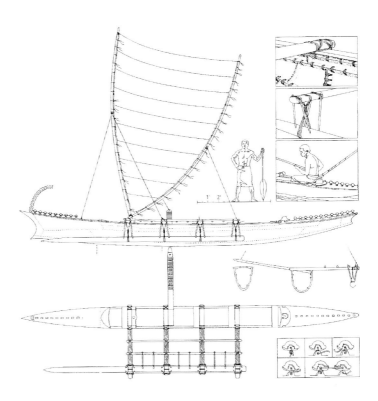

Fig. 3.5 An amatasi – single outrigger and plank-built canoe. (Courtesy of Herb Kane)

outrigger when that became necessary.[20] By the mid 19th century amatasi were rare and by the turn of the century they had gone out of use. The reasons for this are not clear, but it has been suggested that the influence of the missionaries, who in some cases restricted long sea journeys and ocean voyaging, may have contributed.

THE TAUMUALUA

Taumualua were, as their name suggests (taumua meaning bow and lua meaning two), the va'a with two bow-shaped ends. They are said to have been first introduced into Samoa in 1849 by an American, Eli Jennings, who was resident in A'ana. According to an early account,[21] Jennings built two boats of some 50 feet in length modelled on the large European whaleboat. As they were to be used by A'ana and Atua war parties, these two examples were made to accommodate bamboo palisades that protected warriors and crew from enemy missiles.

They were built in the Samoan style from planks sewn together with coconut fibre cord, although in later examples the introduced clinker-built style of construction was used. As well as warfare, they were used for transporting people and goods. Two taumualua joined together are said to have been called va'alulu if designed for battle, and faiosova'a if they were to be used as a supply ship.[22]

Another interesting feature of taumualua was the wreaths of white pule shells and carved figureheads used to ornament the vessels. These usually took the form of animals, and represented the war emblems of a particular village community. As the wars in Samoa ceased and the European influence grew, the plank-built taumualua soon evolved into what are known as fautasi. Constructed in the whaleboat style, these longboats became very popular and the main form of transport between villages. In the late 20th century they have been used recreationally by community and village groups in the annual Samoan Independence Day races on Apia harbour.

Fig. 3.6 A model of a taumualua – a plank-built canoe. It is pointed at both ends and as its Samoan name suggests, it has two bows. It comprises plank components sewn together with 'afa (coconut-fibre cord) on the inside so the outer surface of the canoe appears smooth. Purchased 1916. (Museum of New Zealand Te Papa Tongarewa, Ref. No: FE01194)

THE VA'AALO

From the earliest accounts va'aalo were another fishing va'a used to chase the large schools of surface feeding fish such as bonito. They were long and sleek, about 20 to 25 feet long and manned by two people. They were generally owned by people of status or by a group of families. They had bow and stern covers decorated with lines of white shells fixed to square wooden knobs or stands.

Like amatasi they were plank-built but smaller in size. They were seldom used with a sail, but strong arms and bodies could paddle the vessels through the water with impressive speed. Most examples had a fishing rod support built onto the outrigger and another on the stern cover to hold the long bamboo fishing rods.

Two types of late 20th century equivalent of the va'aalo still exist in Samoa today. They are made from a single tree in the dugout form, but retain the shape and lines of the plank-built va'aalo and are still described as a va'aalo. One type features decorative elaboration of the wood supports on the bow and stern covers, while in the other the covers are plain and curve upward to a point.[23] When Te Rangi Hiroa was in Samoa the dugout va'aalo was already very common throughout the archipelago, sharper steel tools no doubt making it easier to fashion a light hull of consistent thickness. Despite this the va'aalo has largely been replaced by aluminium dinghies and other double-hulled craft also known as 'alia.

THE ART OF VA'A BUILDING

Te Rangi Hiroa provides the most detailed account of the building of a va'aalo – a Samoan plank-built canoe.[24] The precise dimensions, methods of lashing, construction techniques and the local variations are painstakingly recorded, so there is no need to repeat the entire account here. What follows is an overview of the key elements of the building technique as it was in the 1920s. While focussing on the va'aalo, it also sheds some light on the techniques likely to have been used in the construction of the other types of plank-built va'a, such as the amatasi and 'alia, which by that time had long since disappeared.

So what made the plank-built va'a so special? The plank-built va'a stand apart from the dugout va'a in that they were painstakingly fashioned from individual planks that were cut, shaped and carefully sewn together with coconut fibre. While there were trees available to make one-piece hulls in a range of sizes; for example, the dugout soatau and paopao, the fastest va'a were plank built. The fashioning of individual planks allowed a consistently thin and light hull to be manufactured creating faster and lighter craft. This was especially important in the case of the va'aalo and amatasi used to chase fast moving schools of tuna and other predatory fish. The task of fashioning a consistently thin, light hull was achieved by shaping short planked sections rather than attempting to do the same work on a single dugout hull.

So in creating these planked vessels that were light, strong, fast and seaworthy, great skill and judgement were needed to exploit the available materials and make the pieces fit. And it is here that the true art form reveals itself. For this reason the building of dugout va'a such as the paopao and soatau was generally considered a lesser skill and thus a non-specialist task. As a tufuga fauva'a interviewed by Te Rangi Hiroa in the late 1920s commented 'The paopao is not a canoe'.[25]

The most important material in va'a construction is obviously the timber. There was a range of timbers available to the tufuga fauva'a and it seems that as builders they were fairly flexible and quite open to using what was available in their local area. Their flexibility was such that some parts of the va'a – for example the left and right gunwales – could be constructed from two totally different timbers. Te Rangi Hiroa explains:

In the selection, expediency plays a large part. There are always alternative timbers and if one is too far away in the forest a nearer one is used. Timbers that have been proved unsuitable were, of course, never used. The craftsmen knew the materials of their particular districts. What was used in one district might not be used in another, simply because of varying quantity in the distribution of plants, as well as the varying distribution itself.[26]

The other important material in va'a construction is 'afa (coconut fibre). This fibre comes in short lengths from the dry husk of the coconut and once separated is rolled and plaited into long cords and rope. These are of different degrees of quality and fineness depending on the use they are to be put to. There were experts who specialised solely in making this rope.

But the real art and craftsmanship in the building of a plank-built va'a lies in the shaping and fitting of the planks. The tufuga would lay a keel on the ground, usually inside a specially built house or shed, and place the planks upon it, carefully building them up in a series of tiers.

The lower planks were very important as they formed the foundation lines of the va'a. The tufuga would give the planks in this lower tier individual names so that he and his work party could refer to them more easily during the course of their work.

These planks were made to fit exactly and were held together in such a way that no lashings were visible on the outer surface of the va'a. In fact, on existing examples of va'aalo it is very often difficult to see where the planks are actually joined. What holds the va'a together is visible on the inside. The tufuga dubs out special flanges along the planks' inside edges and perforations drilled through them allow him to virtually stitch

Fig. 3.7 Two fishermen in a va'aalo (bonito fishing canoe) on Apia Harbour in the early 1900s. The bonito rod is visible and what appears to be a pandanus sail lying rolled up across the 'iato. (Alexander Turnbull Library, National Library of New Zealand, Te Puna Matauranga o Aotearoa. Ref. No: F134175 1/2)

them together. The lashings were the crucial element that kept the va'a in one piece; the whole fitting and lashing involving a lengthy process of temporarily lashing, then re-lashing, while reshaping and refitting each individual section.

The exact fittings between the different sections were made by brushing the narrow edge of one plank with a mixture of water and red volcanic earth known as sama.[27] The dry narrow edge of another plank was fitted against this edge and the areas where the sama mixture left its mark were carefully chipped off. The tufuga would repeat this process until the two plank edges were perfectly fitted. Before the planks and sections of the va'a were permanently lashed together, he applied heated breadfruit gum to the fitted surfaces. This acted as a caulking and also waterproofed the join. Sometimes barkcloth or coconut fibre would also be inserted in the join.

The ama (float) of the va'aalo gives it stability in the water and is usually made from fau – a very light wood. The ama was attached to the hull with two 'iato (booms). The general rules in making the ama were that the point should never extend beyond the cutwater of the bow and the end should never be long or sharpened. It was important that the ama pointed slightly inward toward the bow to assist with steering.

The bow and stern covers of the va'aalo were flat except for a row of raised, square projections which ran down the middle of them. These were known as the tulaga pule and acted as miniature stands upon which the valuable white shell ornaments were attached with 'afa. These white shell ornaments were pule shells, which are very rare and difficult to find in Samoa. They usually came in the way of presents to high chiefs. Sets of these shells would often remain in the possession of a chiefly family for many generations. When a va'aalo rotted and was abandoned, the shell ornamentation would be removed and transferred to the new va'a.[28] On dugout va'aalo in the 1980s it was noted that the pule shells were no longer in use; instead the tulaga pule themselves had become more elaborate and decorative and, like the va'aalo themselves, painted in colours.[29]

RECOVERING THE ARTS OF THE TUFUGA FAUVA'A

The old stories and ethnographic accounts give us clues and descriptions of the customs involved in building va'a as well as the va'a themselves. These old accounts have been crucial for the survival of the art in the 1990s. They have formed a foundation that has provided clues and rekindled memories that have allowed va'a enthusiasts to revive old skills and learn a little more about the past.

The few va'a building projects in Samoa of recent times include the building of a va'aalo and the 'alia *Tapuitea*. A small group of enthusiasts in Apia initiated the project to recover the skills employed in building a planked va'aalo. In the late 1980s through to the 1990s Muagututia Harry Paul, Nofoatolu Peter Meredith, Tauatele Fosi Levi and Folasaitu Joe Annandale were the key members in the group.

There was a perception at the time that Samoa had a very strong va'a building culture; that there were plenty of tufuga as well as plenty of va'a. But extensive enquiries on Savai'i and out to Manu'a failed to locate a tufuga fauva'a who knew the old planking skills. Rumours of old planked va'aalo existing on Savai'i turned out to be false. The last of them were said to have been destroyed by hurricanes or left to rot on the beaches. So the group had to start almost from scratch with no va'aalo and no

Fig. 3.8 A va'aalo made by Alai'a Sa of Fagaloa and his team of apprentices. Seen here at the festival village at the Seventh South Pacific Arts Festival, Apia, Samoa, 1996. (Sean Mallon)

tufuga, who knew how to do the work.

Through looking at books and journals and making enquiries overseas, a research base was built up which gave the group confidence to finance and develop plans to build a full-size va'aalo.

A search for a suitable tufuga took place and two candidates were identified to take part in the project. The first built a fourteen foot long model in 1989 which ended up in the Roma Museum in Germany. But it was the second candidate Alai'a Sa Vaelua who was selected to see the project through. Coming from the village of Sauano in Fagaloa and not strictly a tufuga fauva'a, Alai'a Sa Vaelua was a gifted woodworker and carpenter with excellent finishing skills and a knowledge of building fautasi (large whaleboat). His skills were seen as the base upon which the group could start to redevelop the va'a building arts.

Fig. 3.9 Woodworking tools. (Craig Potton)

Using the research the group had gathered, Alai'a built several small-scale prototypes to rediscover and teach himself the construction process. Starting with two foot models he progressed to a six foot and then a ten foot vessel. The group pored over Te Rangi Hiroa's 1930 publication *Samoan Material Culture* as it outlined the building of a va'aalo in great detail. This text and Alai'a Sa's practical skills helped them develop the technical knowledge required to attempt a full-size va'aalo. It was a process where both the group and tufuga were learning at the same time, but it gave all involved the necessary confidence.

Several woodworkers were chosen by the tufuga to assist with the construction of the full-size va'aalo. They were chosen for their adze skills and their empathy with the project. The group took it upon themselves to look after the workers in the customary way. The old values and customs of providing for the tufuga and his work party were negotiated in present day terms, an expensive but rewarding undertaking, and the obligations of fa'asamoa were fulfilled.

Fig. 3.10 Alai'a Sa of Fagaloa, Upolu, Samoa. (Sean Mallon)

The reward was the first plank-built va'aalo to be seen in Samoan waters for perhaps 50 years. It was publicly displayed at The Seventh South Pacific Arts Festival in Apia to great acclaim and much interest. It eventually became part of the collections of the Museum fur Volkerkunde in Frankfurt, Germany, and featured in a major exhibition of Samoan culture.

Also at the arts festival was the 'alia *Folauga o Samoa* since renamed *Tapuitea*. This project grew out of an initiative by a Tutuila-based group called 'Aiga Tautai (family of seafarers). *Folauga o Samoa* made the 80 mile crossing from Tutuila to Apia to be at the festival and was an impressive sight moored among the yachts in Apia harbour. Made from marine plywood built on a frame, this project was not focused on the va'a building arts as such, but was a starting point for further explorations into the arts and skills of Samoan seafarers.

Today va'a no longer serve the chiefs or provide transport between islands. Outboard motors and aluminium hulls provide the quickest means of chasing bonito, and cars and roads take people between villages. Va'a today have perhaps taken on a new significance and are more of a symbolic vessel, one through which new ideas and a sense of history flow.

TUFUGA FAUVA'A ALAI'A SA

Alai'a Sa lives in the village of Sauano in Fagaloa Bay. Several families in this remote village on Upolu's northern coast rely on the tourist art/souvenir trade for their income. Men, women and children participate in producing wooden tanoa (bowls), to'oto'o (orator's staffs), fue (orator's flywhisks) and model va'a for shops in Apia.

Alai'a Sa built the va'aalo that was a highlight at the festival of the arts in Samoa during 1996. 'I was the first in my family to learn to work with wood,' he says. 'I was a tufuga fau fale myself, then a builder of fale palagi. I was also one of the builders who built the fales for the Kitano Tusitala Hotel in Apia.'

He was approached to build the va'aalo by local businessman Muagututia Harry Paul. 'When I was given the plans for the va'aalo I could already picture it in my mind.' He remembered seeing a va'aalo as a young man at the nearby village of Falefa, so years later he immediately had an idea of what was required. 'I completed the work with five other workers. It was difficult at times but the answers were always found, just through doing it.'[30]

CHAPTER 3

1. A. Sharp (ed), *The Journal of Jacob Roggeveen* (Oxford: Clarendon Press, 1970), p. 151
2. J. Dunmore (ed), *The Journal of Jean-Francois de Galaup de la Perouse 1785-1788* (London: Hakluyt Society, 1995), p. 338
3. R.M. Moyle (ed), *The Samoan Journals of John Williams 1830 and 1832* (Canberra: Australian National University Press, 1984), p. 106
4. Augustin Kramer, *The Samoan Islands* vol. 2 (Auckland: Polynesian Press, 1995), p. 238
5. Brother Herman, *Tala O Le Vavau: The Myths, Legends and Customs of Old Samoa*; translations adapted from the collections of Steubel and Brother Herman (Auckland: Polynesian Press, 1987), pp. 102-103
6. F. Ma'ia'i, *Stories of Old Samoa* (Wellington: Whitcombe and Tombs Ltd, 1960), pp. 9-13
7. Moyle (ed), *The Samoan Journals of John Williams*, p. 250
8. A.C. Reid, 'The Fruit of the Rewa Oral Traditions and the growth of the pre-Christian Lakeba State', *Journal of Pacific History*, vol. 12, p. 17
9. M.A. Tuimaleali'ifano, *Samoans in Fiji: migration, identity and communication* (Suva: University of the South Pacific, 1990), p. 35
10. Moyle (ed), *The Samoan Journals of John Williams*, pp. 82-83
11. J.B. Stair, *Old Samoa; or flotsam and jetsam from the Pacific Ocean* (Papakura: Southern Reprints, 1983, first published 1897), p. 617, as quoted in Haddon, J.C. and Hornell, J., *Canoes of Oceania* (Hawai'i, Honolulu, Bishop Museum Press, 1936), p. 241
12. Stair, *Old Samoa*, in Haddon and Hornell, *Canoes of Oceania*, p.241
13. Haddon and Hornell, *Canoes of Oceania*, p. 241
14. W.J. Pritchard, in Kramer, A., *The Samoan Islands* Vol. 2, p. 302
15. T.H. Hood, *Notes of a Cruise in H.M.S. Fawn in the Western Pacific in the year 1862* (Edinburgh: Edmonston and Douglas, 1863), p. 100
16. Kramer, *The Samoan Islands*, Vol. 2, p. 300. These three were sighted and examined by Kramer who also gives a description of the building of an 'alia.
17. Haddon and Hornell, *Canoes of Oceania*, p. 242
18. Thilenius in Kramer, *The Samoan Islands*, Vol. 2, p. 304
19. C. Wilkes, *Narrative of The United States Exploring Expedition during the years 1838, 1839, 1840, 1841, 1842* (227 Strand: Ingram, Cooke and Co, 1852), p. 199
20. Wilkes, *Narrative of The United States Exploring Expedition*, p. 199
21. S. Ella, 'The Samoan "Taumualua"', *Journal of the Polynesian Society* (1898), 7, p. 247
22. Thilenius in Kramer, *The Samoan Islands*, Vol. 2, p. 315, footnote 175
23. R. Neich, 'Material culture of Western Samoa', *National Museum of New Zealand*, Bulletin 23 (1985), p. 54
24. Te Rangi Hiroa (Peter Buck), 'Samoan Material Culture', *Bernice P. Bishop Museum*, Bulletin 75 (Hawai'i, Honolulu, 1930), pp. 370-417
25. Te Rangi Hiroa (Peter Buck), 'Samoan Material Culture', p. 377
26. Te Rangi Hiroa (Peter Buck), 'Samoan Material Culture', p. 403
27. Te Rangi Hiroa (Peter Buck), 'Samoan Material Culture', p. 385
28. Te Rangi Hiroa (Peter Buck), 'Samoan Material Culture', p. 401
29. Neich, 'Material culture of Western Samoa', p. 54
30. Alai'a Sa, interview with author, (1999)

TUFUGA FAIFALE
THE MASTER HOUSE BUILDERS

The Samoan faletele (big house) has for a long time been a prominent and important feature of Samoan settlements. Usually situated near the malae (village green) it was the place where guests were received, dances and performances took place, and where meetings were held and important decisions made. These houses were built for and by people of status and in turn enhanced the status of the patron family and community.

The faletele were built by highly skilled carpenters, who were also known for their skill in constructing special types of va'a (canoes). When building va'a they were known as tufuga fauva'a, when building fale they were tufuga faifale.

Tufuga faifale drew upon specialised knowledge and skills developed through years of apprenticeship. For this they were widely respected and richly rewarded. They were organised in small family-based groups that were part of a larger guild.

Early commentators admired the Samoan fale for its beautiful lines and shape, its workmanship and its practicality. These days there are many descriptions and images of fale in printed form and for many years they have also been made as models and souvenirs for the tourist industry. The Samoan fale in the 20th century has become one of the enduring images or icons of Samoa. But its significance was established in the earliest days of Samoa's past.

Fig. 4.1 Faletele under construction, circa 1900. (Alexander Turnbull Library, National Library of New Zealand, Te Puna Matauranga o Aotearoa. Ref. No: F137653 1/2)

THE FIRST FALE BUILDERS

A 19th century Samoan song[1] tells how the god Tagaloa convened the first group of builders, who were known as the Sa Tagaloa, the family of Tagaloa. It is said that they were responsible for building the first ship and the first house. As a translation of part of the song tells us, the work was commenced with '… A class of workmen as ten thousand known, with architect in chief, but one alone …' This contingent was sent to earth and their first accomplishment was to tie the first plank va'a for the King of Manu'a. The workmen then went on to build a splendid house for the King without first consulting Tagaloa. Consequently, he descended in anger and destroyed the building and scattered the builders.[2] All the societies of builders spread throughout

Fig. 4.2 Faletele under construction, circa 1900. (Photographer, Thomas Andrew. Museum of New Zealand, Te Papa Tongarewa, Ref. No: C001446)

Samoa were said to have derived from an original member of this first group.

Accounts from the 1920s tell us that collectively the tufuga faifale were once organised in the same manner as European guilds. In this respect they shared continuity over time as a group, a firm set of internal rules, regulations and standards, and a hierarchy consisting of master craftsmen and their apprentices.[3]

When commissioned to build a fale, the tufuga would often have a group of workers with him, one or two of whom would be apprentices in training. Since it was a hereditary trade, these apprentices were usually relatives and would be attached to the tufuga's household for a long period of time. They would basically be the labourers, carrying materials and learning how to use an adze. Meanwhile they would watch and learn the finer skills of the trade. But it was not all observation. As part of the learning process, an apprentice would be encouraged by relatives to take on contracts to build smaller structures such as cookhouses and outhouses.[4] These projects would allow him to put into practice his newly acquired skills and in turn build his confidence and reputation. It was, however, the successful completion of a faletele or faleafolau (guest house) that marked the end of the apprenticeship and saw the student emerge as a tufuga faifale in his own right.

THE SAMOAN FALE

In 1797 French navigator La Perouse was the first to write down detailed observations of Samoan settlements and during his visit on Tutuila he was particularly impressed with fale that he saw there. His journal records the following:

I went into the best hut which presumably belonged to the chief and I was extremely surprised to find a vast latticed room as well and better made than any in the environs of Paris. The best architect could not have given a more elegant curve to the ellipse ending this hut, a row of columns five feet from each other ran along the edge, these columns were only tree trunks very elaborately worked...[5]

Fig. 4.3 Two faletele, circa 1930s. (Alexander Turnbull Library, National Library of New Zealand, Te Puna Matauranga o Aotearoa. Ref. No: 900mnz 1/4)

Much later in 1832 the Reverend John Williams, an early missionary to Samoa, also commented on the Samoan fale:

In the construction of their houses they display considerable ingenuity. The spacious houses erected for public entertainment are firm & neatly put together. They are between a round & oval...they are from forty to fifty feet long & and about thirty or five & thirty feet wide. The dwelling houses of the natives are of the same shape but much smaller & lower.[6]

From these and other comments we know that the most prestigious and important fale in Samoa in the last 200 years were the faleafolau and the faletele.

The faleafolau was the long guest house with two rounded ends separated by two long straight sides. It had a steep thatched roof supported by a double row of posts that ran the same length as the sides of the fale.

The faletele was the big house, the meeting or community house of the village. It also had two rounded ends, but separated by very short straight sides. This gave the impression that the fale was completely round or slightly oval in shape and floor plan. The high thatched roof was supported by between one and three central posts. The roof of each fale type dropped down to within 1.5 metres of the ground, where the eaves were supported all around by a line of short posts.

Between these posts were positioned sets of pola (coconut leaf blinds). These were pulled up during the day to keep the air circulating and the interior cool. But they could also be lowered to keep out the wind or enclose the fale at night.

In the early 19th century the faletele was believed to be the more ancient and original Samoan house form, and the faleafolau was considered a recent introduction which had come from Tonga.[7] One oral account from eastern Samoa seems to dispute this,[8] but archaeological excavations of fale sites in Western Samoa only reveal evidence of the central row of supporting posts typical of the faletele.[9]

From some of the earliest written records of the 1830s we know that the faletele played a significant role in village life. Most settlements at this time had one or two faletele according to the number of matai who lived there.[10] They were used for important fono (meetings), for the reception of visitors, for dances and were usually built in close proximity to the malae (village green).

In these early days of European presence, the faletele was also utilised by the missionaries to hold meetings and spread the gospel message. Their location was certainly convenient and some of them could apparently hold a great gathering of potential converts. The measurements given in John Williams' account seem small when we consider that one house at Lealatele on Savai'i, which appears to have been the most magnificent house in Samoa in the 1830s, could allegedly accommodate 1,000 people.[11]

THE BUILDING OF A FALETELE

The construction of a Samoan fale has been described at length in several studies made last century.[12] They detail the different parts of the fale, how they are put together and the ceremonials involved. These should be consulted for a full and detailed account of the fale building process. The following is only a summary of the main stages of construction.

To match the status of the matai who owned them and the occasions held within, the faleafolau and the faletele were made from the best materials available. A great deal of time went into gathering materials and preparing for the arrival of the tufuga and his workers. The Samoan fale had no nails: it was completely lashed and held together by cords made from coconut fibre, which had been gathered, twisted, rolled and plaited into hundreds of metres of 'afa (sennit). Sugar cane leaf was collected and dried to make the thatch. And then there was the timber to make the posts, rafters and various supports.

According to Te Rangi Hiroa, the preferred timber for the main posts was that of the ulu (breadfruit tree) although trees such as the ifilele or pou muli were sometimes used. Breadfruit timber has a good colour and was said to be very durable as long as it didn't get wet. It was also resistant to borer. In fact most of the fale was constructed from ulu, with the exception of the long rafters where the more flexible timber of the coconut tree was selected.[13]

Commissioning the building of a fale was a big undertaking. It required good negotiation skills, understanding of correct protocol and access to a lot of resources. Two types of contract could be entered into spelling out the respective obligations of the tufuga and the taufale (the prospective house owner). One only specified the obligations of the tufuga and the amount of payment. It was a commitment of mutual

Fig. 4.4 Interior of faleafolau with black and white lashings, circa 1900s. (Alexander Turnbull Library, National Library of New Zealand, Te Puna Matauranga o Aotearoa, Ref. No: C16989)

Fig. 4.5 Faleafolau under construction, 1914. (Alexander Turnbull Library, National Library of New Zealand, Te Puna Matauranga o Aotearoa, Ref. No: 1/2-148820, PAColl-1682)

Fig. 4.6 Fale interior at the Sinalei
Reef Resort, Upolu, 1999. Built under
the direction of Talamaivao Masoe
Niko and Likisoni Lelua Talamaivao.
(Craig Potton)

respect, where little on-site negotiation was entered into, although the rules, customs
and decisions of the fale builders were closely observed. The other was different in that
the taufale could have a greater say in the work, give direction and keep an eye on
quality and productivity. Under these terms the taufale could be quite specific and
demanding in his instructions. Te Rangi Hiroa records that:

*If he does not approve of the lashing patterns or the lack of neatness of the turns, he can draw the
head builder's attention to them. He can insist on the right timber being used, such as breadfruit
wood for the thatched rafters. Any slovenly or poor work he can condemn and have rectified.*[14]

The tufuga would happily work to please the taufale, but if the taufale had a lot
of input into the building process then the tufuga could insist on being extremely well
looked after – which could put great pressure on the resources of the taufale. He
would have to ensure that the best food was obtained and prepared, and that it was
served to the tufuga and his party in the correct way. Pigs would have to be slaughtered and cooked, and fish and crops harvested. How the taufale managed his side of
the contract would determine the quality of the house he received. If the tufuga was

not satisfied that the taufale was meeting his obligations he could abandon the project and put notice on the site ensuring no other tufuga would complete the work. This would bring great shame on the taufale and his family. The offence could only be rectified with the humbling of the taufale before the tufuga and the presentation of 'ie toga (fine mats).[15]

THE FALETELE STRUCTURE

The faletele was built around a frame of scaffolding, which would eventually become enclosed as the roof was built above and around it. The central supporting posts were then put into the ground using the scaffold as a brace to support them. A ridge pole would be fixed across the top of the posts. The construction of the straight centre-sections of the fale would then follow. Rafters and thatch support would go in and then work would stop as the taufale and his family thatched the centre section.

The collecting, drying and manufacture of the thatch was done by the taufale's women relatives and friends. Sugar cane leaf was the material of choice.[16] To make a sheet of thatch the women would fold the sugar cane leaves over each other on a cane or reed rod at least 3 feet in length, pinning the leaves into position using coconut leaf midribs. These sheets were then lashed to the house frame, starting at the eaves and working up towards the ridge of the roof. For some faletele between 2000 and 4000 reeds were required.[17]

Once this was completed attention would be turned towards the curved ends of the fale. The centre arches and posts that made up the ends were installed on each end in turn, so one end would be completed before the other was started. The arches acted as a guide to the curve the roof should take. From here additional arches and thatch rafters would be added, the builders using the scaffold still in the fale interior to complete the work.

With the framework of the ends finished, the taufale and his family could begin to gather and place loose stones on the fale floor to build up a paepae (living platform). This would continue for several months, well after the builders had gone. But in the meantime the finished ends of the fale would be covered in thatch, with the final piece being placed by the tufuga himself. This would officially mark the house's completion.[18]

As part of the process, important ceremonies and feasts would be held at the completion of key stages, and these marked periods when part payment could be made to the tufuga.[19] Typically, the contract to build a fale was initiated with the presentation of an 'ie toga to the tufuga by the taufale. Once the terms of the contract had been negotiated they were sealed with the drinking of kava. From this point on special ceremonies and feasts marked the raising of the central house posts, the setting of the ridge pole, the installation of the centre end arches and posts, and the completion of the house. They were important because as well as marking key events they reinforced the roles and social relationships amongst the participants and between the tufuga and taufale.

Fig. 4.7 Fale interior at the Sinalei Reef Resort, Upolu, 1999. Built under the direction of Talamaivao Masoe Niko and Likisoni Lelua Talamaivao. (Craig Potton)

THE BINDINGS

Samoan houses were given as presents, paid as fines and dowries, and also used as articles of barter. So on occasion they had to be moved or transported to other locations. Fortunately this was made easier in that not a single nail was used to build a fale, because when Samoans moved house, they *really* moved house. Writing in 1853, Captain John E. Erskine of the Royal Navy tells us:

Fig. 4.8 Rafter lashing, Sinalei Reef Resort, Upolu, 1999. (Craig Potton)

When built, however, they [fale] are easily moved from one situation to another, the three compartments of the roof, which may be considered the chief part of the house, forming a load for two canoes, the two ends placed together occupying one, and the centre the other.[20]

The Reverend George Turner records that the roofs were constructed in such a way that they could be lifted straight off the posts they were resting on. Particular joints in the fale could be quickly untied and re-lashed, enabling the separate parts of the roof to be transported to another location quite easily by land or water.[21]

As well as holding the structure of the fale together and allowing for portability or reuse, the lashings were also in a sense the final touch, the important detailing of the project. There was a skill, a patience and an appreciation involved in tying a lashing. As the Hawai'ian illustrator and canoe designer Herb Kawainui Kane recalled:

The complexity of lashings used in the assembly of houses and canoes imparts an aesthetics which is not lost on the builders. I remember watching a Samoan craftsman weaving an intricate lashing to connect the rafters of a house. Suddenly struck with the beauty of what he had wrought, the man burst into tears.[22]

To accentuate their beauty, the coconut fibre cords were arranged in strong geometric lines and patterns, and were sometimes artificially coloured. One account from 1923 describes the practice, further enhanced with the availability of commercial paints and dyes:

The ornamental sennit ('afa) lashings, colored the natural brown, yellow, red, purple and black (much of it nowadays with commercial paint or dyes) are very beautiful and are put on in patterns with the greatest precision, the sennit strands used in this fine work being made with care to produce regularity and smoothness.[23]

Some of the skills and care taken with lashings in former times lie dormant or have disappeared with dwindling opportunities to build fale in the present day. In 1980 a comparison of lashings from old fale with those in new fale showed that the recent lashings had become sparser (with more bare timber showing), and used a more irregular thinner braid.[24] But the same study also highlighted the appearance of figurative art in the decoration of some fale. This was a development that was to catch on and is discussed further in Chapter 9, Painting and Folk-Art.

The decline in constructing old-style fale using lashings is due in part to the availability of nails, milled timbers, roofing iron and other more resilient materials. The

use of these ready-made materials saves valuable time. This is an important considera-
tion today, when the building of a fully-lashed fale can be a long and expensive project,
especially when people are paid an hourly wage and materials have to be milled and
processed manually.

Another small but important decorative element present among the bindings of
the fale was the unique marks of the guilds who did the work. The tufuga faifale had
special trademark signatures that identified their work. These were incorporated into
the patterns of the lashings or consisted of a characteristic mark or technical detail in
the lattice framework of the roof interior. Known as 'aso maga lua, they represent the
'Aiga sa le Malama of Tutuila and were seen on Tutuila in 1927.[25] These types of
trademarks are still used today. The mark of Tuataga Levao, a present day expert in
the art of lashing, reveals itself in the bindings of the fale he worked on at the Sinalei
Reef Resort in 1996. (See fig. 4.8).

FALE AND TUFUGA FAIFALE IN THE PRESENT

Today there are very few faleafolau and faletele of the old style in Samoan villages. But
the familiar form of the fale lives on, albeit in modified forms.

Faleafolau and faletele are now made in many different styles and in more durable
materials, but they still retain recognisable Samoan attributes such as open sides and a
single room under one roof.[26] These days housing structures can be built in a week if
necessary, and builders make full use of mill-sawn timbers, nails and corrugated iron.
The stone paepae of former days have now been replaced by concrete slabs. In many
villages the old paepae are still visible under masses of weeds, their position given away
by rotten and lonely-looking house posts. Some paepae remain standing in the interests of historic preservation. Each paepae has a name and the remnants of the old
structures will only be removed if the family who owns them are ready to put a new

faletele in its place.[27] In some of the remote villages, however,
you will still see thatched roofs and posts milled by hand,
although more often than not these too are set into foundations of concrete.

Today a typical guest or meeting house consists of a
concrete house platform with a square or rectangular floor plan.
Upon this sits an open-sided house structure with a perimeter
of square wall-posts, supporting a corrugated iron roof on a
milled timber frame. Nearby you will probably find the owner's
dwelling house built in a European style with enclosed walls
and windows. This adjacency would appear to be a development of recent decades, but as early as the 1890s, Samoan
chiefs near Apia were living in houses built from planks, with a
second Samoan-style house nearby.[28] Although the Samoan-
style houses are of a different generation, this arrangement has
become a characteristic feature of many contemporary Samoan

Fig. 4.9 Faleafolau, National University
of Samoa, Apia, Upolu. Built under the
direction of Likisone Lelua Talamaivao.
(Sean Mallon)

villages.

There is some evidence that the special knowledge of the tufuga faifale still
survives. Many of the old men are no longer alive, but it is thought that their families
may retain some knowledge. As already mentioned, due to the changing system of
economic exchange and the availability of new ready-made materials, there are few
opportunities to build fale. Unfortunately, this means that old skills and knowledge are

being lost and replaced with more modern techniques. Nevertheless there have been a few large-scale projects outside the village context that have provided occasions for the use and preservation of the tufuga's skills.

Some high profile examples of the last few decades include the fale-styled house at Aggie Greys Hotel built in 1968[29] and the Hotel Kitano Tusitala which opened in 1974. Both of these projects demonstrate the adaptation of Samoan architecture to meet other roles and uses outside the customary village environment. In both cases the fale were made to accommodate dining areas and performance spaces. The Tusitala fale were built to very large dimensions and were considered a massive undertaking at the time. When the hotel was opened it was described by the board chairman as being a 'showcase for Samoan architecture', its great structure and fine detailing a testimony to the work of a group of skilled tufuga.[30]

Over twenty years later the appeal of the Tusitala fale encouraged the owners of the soon to be built Sinalei Reef Resort to also seek out someone who could build old-style fale. Their enquiries turned up the original tufuga who built the Tusitala, Talamaivao Niko. He and his team from Fagaloa went on to build three fale for the Sinalei over a period of eight months.

Since the completion of this project in 1996, members of the same building team have worked on other business or government-assisted fale projects. The largest of these was the fale built for The National University of Samoa; it is even longer and higher than the Tusitala fale. Then there were the House of Worship and another large fale built for the Houses of Parliament. Each of these projects has helped to ensure that the old skills live on, but they also presented new challenges for the builders. The scarcity of materials and the incorporation of new ones meant that different skills and techniques had to be devised. It was a process where long established methods or conventions were changed and adapted to meet new circumstances. This is a situation that Samoan communities overseas have also faced.

FALE-INSPIRED BUILDINGS OVERSEAS

Samoan communities overseas have used elements of Samoan fale design in buildings such as churches and community centres. Somewhat restricted by more changeable climates and rigid building codes, the most prominent or recognisable feature of Samoan-inspired architecture in New Zealand is the domed roof. An example of this can be seen in the design of the Congregational Church of Western Samoa in Wellington, New Zealand. Its arching rafters and references to siapo motifs make an understated and successful amalgam of Samoan and western building styles.

Another example is Samoa House in Auckland. Opened in 1971, the project was instigated by Samoa Inc, an organisation created by a group of Auckland-based Samoans, with the intention of bringing the community together, creating a focal point and keeping their culture alive. The president of Samoa Inc at the time, Tofa Mau'u Alofi Pereira, said the project would help all Samoans living in New Zealand: 'We are from a communal life, always wanting to do things together … for the last 20 years, since Samoans have been coming to New Zealand, we have had this in mind'.[31] Samoa House has certainly fulfilled this role over the last 30 years, providing a place for meetings, ceremonies and celebrations. Designed in the form of the old faletele, it mediates new networks and relationships for the Samoan community living abroad. It is an important symbol for the enduring culture and community that built it.

FOLASAITU JOE ANNANDALE

One of the most successful fale building projects of the 1990s has been the three fale (two faletele and one faleafolau) built as part of the Sinalei Reef Resort. A long and expensive project spanning 12 months, it took eight months to build the three fale. Folasaitu Joe Annandale, a supporter and enthusiast of Samoan and Pacific island arts, commissioned the fale in 1995 and takes a great deal of pride in what the tufuga and his workers achieved:

The head tufuga on our project was Talamaivao Niko, who had worked on the Hotel Kitano Tusitala. He was a former Member of Parliament from the Fagaloa district and is still a very prominent chief from that area. I spoke to him early on about the project and as he happens to be a member of my family he was fairly pleased to get involved. When he started he brought about nine builders from Fagaloa, people who had proven themselves to him. And they came across and camped here. They were joined by seven men from Siumu and together they built the three fale.

There was not too much fa'asamoa involved in this project, if you're talking ceremonies. It was a strictly commercial transaction, the workers got paid by the hour and that's all there was to it. But the method of construction was very much traditional to a large extent, in the way they handled and stood the posts up, that was all done traditionally, we did not have cranes and all that sort of stuff. The way they lined up and levelled beams was all done by eye, using the horizon as a level, and because all these posts were huge logs they had to use metal axes and adzes to shape them.

We used asi toa for the main posts. It's a very, very hard wood and we got it from the forests quite close to here. And that's one area where we deviated from tradition. We could not find enough breadfruit timber for the beams. We are talking about 1995 when we started building and we had the cyclone in 1991, so a lot of the breadfruit trees had been destroyed. And when we went looking for breadfruit there were only young trees coming up, and a lot of the older trees had rotted away since the cyclone. So we had to find a substitute. Talamaivao and I came up with the idea of laminating the timber and it worked. Other projects have since followed the same style of construction.

There was a lot of excitement, particularly for me, in seeing those traditional structures go up. Sure, I had seen the Tusitala go up, but I didn't really pay much attention to the details. It wasn't until I had my own built and I was there every day looking at it. It's fascinating when you come up and see the pattern of scaffolding and it looks quite chaotic and you think, how is this all going to come together? It's just amazing how all of a sudden the scaffolding starts to be peeled off and there it is, you blink and open your eyes and it's all there finished. You take the props away and everything just stands there and it doesn't fall. It's just unbelievable.

TUFUGA FAIFALE: TALAMAIVAO MASOE NIKO

My father's family is from Asau Village in Savai'i and were traditional builders, as were my mother's family from Fagaloa. They were builders as well. My father's name was Masoe Tulele – Masoe being a chief title at our village in Savai'i.

But my father was never involved with any building in all his life. What happened was I had learnt a bit of carpentry in New Zealand and when I came back to Samoa there was a company who wanted to set up a hotel building incorporating a Samoan fale. I was in Savai'i at the time and they came looking for a supply of local timber to build a house. I talked to these people and they asked me if I would be interested in building them a fale. So we started to look at some sketches and I told them that I could. They showed me what they wanted to do and I could see that I could do it, so I just went along and I found it was more or less just in me. So I came

Fig. 4.10 Talamaivao Masoe Niko.
(Sean Mallon)

down and built the first fale, the lighting room of the Kitano Tusitala Hotel and after that I went on to build the whole lot. There were eight fale altogether and the very last one I built was a very large one right in front. They took about 18 months to two years to complete. I had about 60 men working at the time and then another gang of 12 in Savai'i shifting the trees over to Apia.

When the Sinalei Reef Resort came up Joe Annandale kept coming to me so I went and built the main fale for him. Then I left my boys to complete the rest and I trained my young nephew to carry on with the project. His name is Likisoni Lelua Talamaivao. The reason why I chose him is because I could see that he liked it. He had an interest in it and that's the reason why I encouraged him to go ahead with it. He went on to complete the work and I more or less guided him along. After that he was just like me, he just carried on. He then built the House of Worship and another fale near Parliament.

The tufuga has to like what he is doing, the art of putting things together. I think that's most important, you've got to like building the thing first and then all the other things should fall into place. You have to like to build them and make them look nice, do good finishing and make them strong. You see the Tusitala building, it's been hit by several cyclones and it's still standing. It's very strong because of the way the thing is constructed. So I think that's an important thing too. And you have to have something in your blood to get the feeling of what things you should have to make it look nice. It's an art.

ARCHITECT: ALBERT REFITI

Albert Refiti was born in Samoa in 1963 and travelled to New Zealand at age 14 where he finished college and attended university, studying architecture for five years. Currently, he is lecturing in architecture at Unitec and design at the Manukau School of Fine Arts, and he has also worked as an architect for Noel Lane Architects (Auckland) and Feary and Heron (London). Among his many research interests is the Samoan fale. In the late 1990s he had an opportunity to visit some tufuga faifale living in Samoa, some who are now deceased. He shares some of the insight he gained from his discussions and observations:

My main impression of the tufuga that I visited is they are very wily characters. They have a body of knowledge and they know they have that body of knowledge. One that I called in to visit named Tutufaiga has passed on now, but when I arrived he was sitting there playing a Gameboy![32] I was going to visit this man who was supposedly an important man who knew all the fa'asamoa and it was a complete surprise when I arrived to see him playing space invaders on a little Gameboy. After a while I realised a lot of these guys are thinking people, and they are always involved in a mode of operation. The way to make buildings the professional way is one form of knowledge that they use, but I suspect that they have a wide range of things that they draw from, not just traditional and working.

After seeing some of the houses, especially this certain one, the way the curve was done on the roof made it slightly different to all the other ones. There was a subtleness about the curvature and then kind of a pregnant pause at the top. That was his, if you like, his kind of own little eye. Often the way they [the tufuga] used to determine the shape of the roof is they'd have someone holding a stick up and have an assistant bowing the stick until I guess this chap would have said yep right, and then they would have fixed the position of the stick in mid-air. The way I'm trained in architecture now is often with models and we often detach the making of something from the real thing. We make it in bits and pieces and then maybe we scale them up and make the real thing. The thing about the tufuga is they didn't have drawings or models, they actually

Fig. 4.11 Albert Refiti. (Jeff Evans)

modelled the thing in full size. On a one to one scale. When I asked this tufuga to draw me a picture of how he constructed the house he said no I'm not allowed to draw, that would be giving away the secrets. To him the notion of representing these things was kind of a knowledge that is not to be.

So tufuga faifale are often given that title Sa le Malama because the knowledge they had were often secrets and you had to be ordained into the guild five or six years before you were eligible to become a tufuga yourself. It's very different to what we do nowadays where it's more about representation, we try to detach an image of everything so we can manipulate it before we make the thing reality. In the old days there was no detachment, the thing was it.

SAMOAN CHURCHES

Churches are another form of building that have come to dominate the Samoan village landscape and are a focus for community life – especially among Samoan communities overseas. In many cases Samoan church architecture combines religious symbolism with images and styles reflective of Samoan culture and values. These churches are receptacles for both community pride and a Samoan aesthetic, though each is manifest in different ways.

The first churches in Samoa were built very early in the 19th century. In many villages they replaced special structures known as faleaitu (spirit houses). By as early as 1835, the church structures in Samoa included buildings made in a purely Samoan style and others that were lime plastered. In 1834 there were at least two plastered

Fig. 4.12 Congregational Christian Church, Tuasivi, Savai'i, 2001. (Sean Mallon)

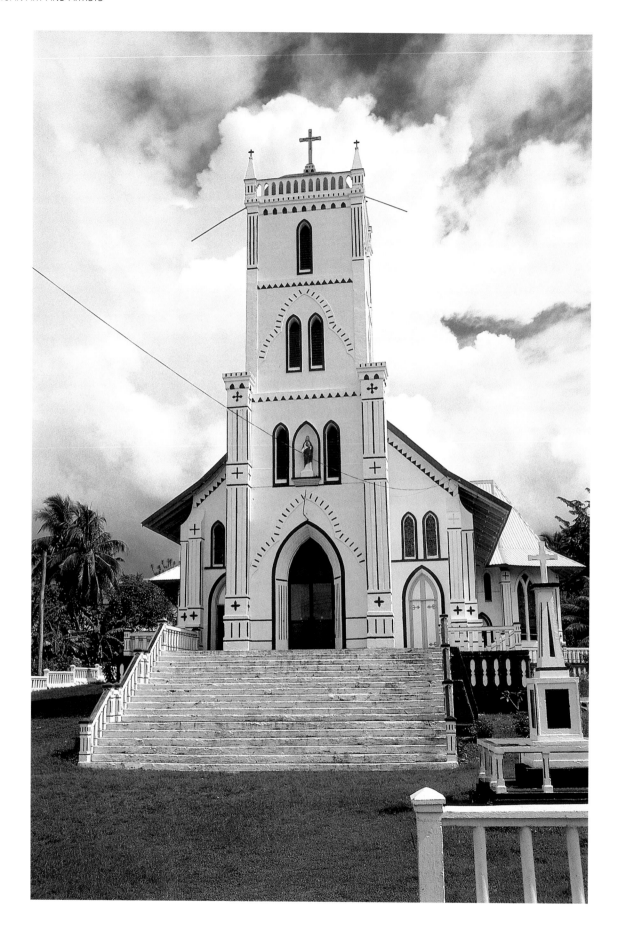

churches – one on Manono and the other on Upolu.[33] By 1835 there were at least seven plastered chapels, some of which had been built under the direction of a sailor. In addition to this, several villages had established prayer houses. Stone chapels began to be built soon after, with the first two stone chapels being constructed at Solosolo around 1841.[34]

Churches quickly became a dominant feature of the Samoan landscape. Some were extremely well made, as William Churchward noted in 1883 when he visited a church in Falefa:

…we came to the Roman Catholic church, whose spire we had noticed on first arriving – a really good building, constructed of blocks of white coral cut from the reef spanning the bay, and boasting stained glass windows. A peep inside revealed the scene common to all churches of this denomination, the only difference being that there were no chairs, their substitutes appearing in the form of mats strewn all over the floor. It was truly a very creditable building. Many worse are to be seen in Europe any day…[35]

Another interesting aspect of church building in the 19th century was its competitive nature. Churches were such a dominant feature in the village that, as R.J. Crawford suggests in a thesis, 'the introduction of plastered chapels probably first provided a mark of status … which a village would attempt to acquire'.[36] And one of the causes of the 1847 war was said to be 'Manono's jealousy of A'ana's superior buildings and chapels'.[37]

Churches are still very prominent in the Samoan landscape today. They incorporate many different architectural ideas, styles and colours. Their magnificent ceilings and looming towers are as dominating as their white walls, which are often decorated with geometric patterns, delicate symbols and script. They are a reminder that European churches were probably the model for the first Samoan churches and subsequently became the established style. As Albert Refiti notes:

The Samoan churches are an interesting phenomena to me because they reveal a cross-cultural mix between the Christian religion culture and Samoan values. They for me talk about a very

Fig. 4.13 (opposite) Church, near Falefa, Upolu, 1999. (Craig Potton)

Fig. 4.14 Church interior with European architectural features and painted decoration, near Falefa, Upolu, 1999. (Craig Potton)

Fig. 4.15 Church interior. (Craig Potton)

interesting hybrid. The churches are often like little fantasies, leftovers from memories of what a church would look like in Rome or other places in the world. They are kind of like a reversal of what people in Europe and other places think of the Pacific of these palm trees and huts. Perhaps the churches reflect for us a kind of fascination with the fantasy we have about Europe and those other places.[38]

In contrast to this, present day Samoan communities in New Zealand cities such as Auckland and Wellington have drawn on aspects of the Samoan fale in their church design.[39] There are still churches built in the classic European style, but many predominantly Samoan congregations have built churches in a 'Samoan style'. The most familiar design element to be found is the domed fale roof, clad in corrugated steel or tiling. In some cases a classic almost oval floorplan is retained along with furnishings decorated with siapo, carving motifs and passages from Scripture. A sense of Samoan aesthetic is maintained in their design and appearance, and within their walls Samoan custom and values are nurtured.

Fig. 4.16 Church door, Savai'i. (Craig Potton)

CHAPTER 4

1. A. Kramer, 'O le Solo o le Va o le Foafoaga o le Lalolagi', *The Samoan Islands*, vol. 1 (Auckland: Polynesian Press, 1995), pp. 539-544
2. M. Meleisea, *Lagaga A Short History of Samoa* (Suva: University of the South Pacific, 1987b), pp. 9-10
3. I. Goldman, *Ancient Polynesian Society* (Chicago and London: University of Chicago Press, 1970), p. 255
4. M. Mead, 'Social organisation of Manu'a', *Bernice P. Bishop Museum*, Bulletin 76 (Hawai'i, Honolulu, 1969), p. 39
5. J. Dunmore (ed), *The Journal of Jean Francois de Galaup de la Perouse 1785-1788*, vol. 2 (London: Hakluyt Society, 1995), p. 39
6. R. M. Moyle (ed), *The Samoan Journals of John Williams 1830 and 1832* (Canberra: Australian National University Press, 1984), p. 251
7. J.M. Davidson, 'Settlement patterns in Samoa before 1840', *Journal of the Polynesian Society* (1969), p. 70
8. Te Rangi Hiroa (Peter Buck), 'Samoan Material Culture', *Bernice P. Bishop Museum*, Bulletin 75 (Hawai'i, Honolulu, 1930), p. 20. In 1927 some older men of Ta'u told Te Rangi Hiroa that the first house built by the Sa Tagaloa was a long house.

9. Davidson, 'Settlement patterns in Samoa', p. 17

10. Buzacott, in J.M. Davidson, 'Settlement patterns in Samoa', p. 63

11. Davidson, 'Settlement patterns in Samoa', p. 64

12. E.S.C. and W.C. Handy, 'Samoan housebuilding, cooking and tattooing', *Bernice P. Bishop Museum*, Bulletin 15 (Hawai'i, Honolulu, 1924); Augustin Kramer, *The Samoan Islands*, vol. 2 (Auckland: Polynesian Press, 1995); Te Rangi Hiroa (Peter Buck), 'Samoan Material Culture', *Bernice P Bishop Museum*, Bulletin 75 (Hawai'i, Honolulu, 1930); Roger Neich, 'Material culture of Western Samoa', *National Museum of New Zealand*, Bulletin 23 (1985); See also J.B. Stair, *Old Samoa; or flotsam and jetsam from the Pacific Ocean* (Papakura: Southern Reprints, 1983, first published 1897) for some differing details in terms of customs.

13. Te Rangi Hiroa, 'Samoan Material Culture', p. 22. Kramer indicates that a greater variety of timbers were used.

14. Te Rangi Hiroa, 'Samoan Material Culture', pp. 88-89

15. Te Rangi Hiroa, 'Samoan Material Culture', pp. 88-89

16. Up until the 1970s sugar cane was grown in most villages and used as a ready source of thatching material. But by the 1980s these groves had been largely replaced by groves of sago palms, the leaves of which lasted twice as long as a sugar cane leaf thatch. R. Neich, 'Material culture of Western Samoa', p. 20

17. G. Turner, *Nineteen years in Polynesia: missionary life, travels, and researches in the islands of the Pacific* (London: John Snow, 1861), p. 258

18. A.E. Geurnsey Allen, 'The Ritual of Architecture: the creation of Samoan guest fale', *Pacific Arts* No. 9 and 10 (1994), p. 81

19. Geurnsey, 'The Ritual of Architecture', p. 79

20. J.E. Erskine, *Journal of a cruise among the islands of the Western Pacific including The Feejees and others inhabited by the Polynesian Negro races in Her Majesty's ship Havannah* (London: John Murry, 1853 [reprinted 1967]), p. 47. A photograph of part of a house being carried during the war in 1899 appears in Kramer, 'The Samoan Islands', p. 271

21. Turner, *Nineteen years in Polynesia*, p. 258-259

22. H.K. Kane, *Voyage, The Discovery of Hawai'i*, Knowlton, William (ed), (Hawai'i: Island Heritage Ltd, 1976), p. 100

23. E.S.C. and W.C. Handy, 'Samoan housebuilding, cooking, and tattooing', p. 13

24. Neich, 'Material culture of Western Samoa', p. 19

25. Te Rangi Hiroa, 'Samoan Material Culture', p. 19

26. Te Rangi Hiroa, 'Samoan Material Culture', p. 19

27. Folasaitu Joe Annandale, Personal comment, (January, 2000)

28. Kramer, *The Samoan Islands*, p. 260

29. N. Eustis, *Aggie Grey of Samoa* (Adelaide, Australia: Hobby Investments PTY Ltd, 1980), p. 182

30. *Pacific Islands Monthly* (May, 1974), p. 118

31. *Pacific Islands Monthly* (June, 1971), pp. 22-23

32. A handheld electronic game with a visual display screen.

33. Barff and Buzacott, cited in J.M. Davidson, 'Settlement patterns in Samoa', p. 66

34. M.S. Buchanan, 1841, cited in Davidson, 'Settlement Patterns in Samoa', p. 68

35. W. Churchward, *My Consulate in Samoa: A record of four years sojourn in the Navigators Islands, with personal experiences of King Malietoa Laupepa, his country, and his men*, (London: Richard Bentley and Son, 1887), p. 233

36. R.J. Crawford, 'The Lotu and the Fa'asamoa: Church and Society in Samoa, 1830-1880', unpublished PhD thesis (New Zealand: University of Otago, 1977), p. 291

37. Erskine, *Journal of a cruise among the islands of the Western Pacific*, pp. 64-65

38. Albert Refiti, personal comment, (23 March, 2000)

39. Albert C. Moore, *Arts in the Religions of the Pacific: Symbols of Life* (London: Pinter, 1995), p. 134

CHAPTER 5

SIAPO MAKERS

The making of tapa (barkcloth) was once widespread throughout the islands of the Pacific. From parts of South East Asia, as far south as New Zealand, east out to Rapanui and northward to Hawaï'i, each island group or culture had its own special techniques, motifs, designs and uses for the cloth.

Today the art of tapa making is still practised in the Pacific, but it is in the west Polynesian island groups of Fiji, Tonga and Samoa that it is strongest. In Fiji decorated tapa is called masi, in Tonga it is ngatu and in Samoa it is siapo. In all three cultures tapa retains some of its value as a cloth that is presented and exchanged at ceremonies, weddings and funerals. The great numbers of siapo that survive in museum collections, in people's homes as heirlooms, and in books and photographs are testimony to the industry and creativity of generations of Samoan women artists. From a few shared motifs and elements taken from nature, they make beautiful works of balance, style, colour and individuality.

There is one old 19th century story that tells us that the plants to make tapa cloth came to Samoa by way of a Fijian chief. He had come to Samoa to find a husband-chief for his daughter. On arrival he found that the Samoans had no mats in their houses and slept only on dried grass. So he returned to Fiji and made up a present as if it was a dowry for his daughter, and as part of this gift he included

Fig. 5.1 Siapo on display at an agricultural show and fair circa 1930. (Alexander Turnbull Library, National Library of New Zealand, Te Puna Matauranga o Aotearoa, Ref. No: F56039 1/2)

Fig. 5.2 Siapo mamanu (freehand painted tapa) collected by Alexander Horsburgh Turnbull. Late 1800s. 'Laumua seiotu' is written on the tapa. (Museum of New Zealand, Te Papa Tongarewa, Ref. No: FE000825)

pandanus and paper mulberry plants. Returning to Samoa, he presented the gift, knowing that in time it would provide the essential materials for making mats and cloth.[1]

PREPARATION

Samoan barkcloth is made from the bark of the u'a (paper mulberry) tree (*Broussonetia papyrifera*), although in the past it was occasionally made from the inner bark of the breadfruit or banyan tree.[2] It is decorated using dyes made from a variety of trees and plants. The brown dyes come from several sources, the first being the bark of the 'o'a

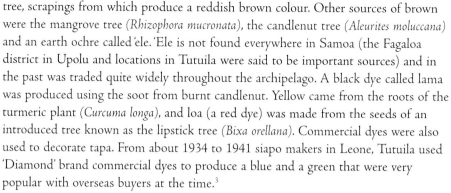

Figs. 5.3 Tools and dyes used in siapo manufacture, Palauli, Savai'i, 1999. (Craig Potton)

Figs. 5.4-8 Va'amuli Moli-Salu demonstrates the manufacture of a siapo, Palauli, Savai'i, 1999. (Craig Potton)

tree, scrapings from which produce a reddish brown colour. Other sources of brown were the mangrove tree (*Rhizophora mucronata*), the candlenut tree (*Aleurites moluccana*) and an earth ochre called 'ele. 'Ele is not found everywhere in Samoa (the Fagaloa district in Upolu and locations in Tutuila were said to be important sources) and in the past was traded quite widely throughout the archipelago. A black dye called lama was produced using the soot from burnt candlenut. Yellow came from the roots of the turmeric plant (*Curcuma longa*), and loa (a red dye) was made from the seeds of an introduced tree known as the lipstick tree (*Bixa orellana*). Commercial dyes were also used to decorate tapa. From about 1934 to 1941 siapo makers in Leone, Tutuila used 'Diamond' brand commercial dyes to produce a blue and a green that were very popular with overseas buyers at the time.[3]

Before the colouring or dyeing begins there are several stages involved in the making of the tapa cloth itself. The siapo maker first selects and cuts a long straight plant from her stand of u'a. She makes a cut at the base of the selected stick and pulls the bark back in one long and continuous strip. The strip is then rolled up so that the inner surface is facing outward. A knife is used to separate this inner surface or bast from the rough outer bark layer, which is thrown away.

The long strip of inner bark is then laid on a sloping wooden board. At this point, the bast is kept wet, and the siapo maker scrapes the bark with a shell in order to remove any small fragments and other imperfections that might spoil the cloth's appearance. This process also helps to break down and spread the fibres of the bast. Once the scraping is complete, the excess water is carefully squeezed out of the now clean bast pieces.

The next stage is to lay the bast on the tutua (anvil) where it is beaten with an i'e (a small heavy hand-held wooden beater), spreading it out and widening it into a larger size. The tutua is a smooth suitably-sized section of cut timber or tree trunk on which the bast is beaten. It is usually laid on the ground and the siapo maker will sit behind it. Several pieces of bast will often be beaten on the tutua at the same time.

The i'e are usually grooved on two or three sides and smooth on the fourth. The grooved side does the initial work and is followed by the smooth side to finish off the beating process. In the 19th century, separate smooth and grooved beaters were made.

The siapo maker beats the bast until it meets the required

thickness and size. The bast pieces are then folded into a small bundle and struck with the beater several times. This makes it possible to separate the individual sheets without them tearing in the process.[4] Once the sheets are opened, they are laid out on mats for drying.

There are two methods used to decorate the cloth. The first produces siapo mamanu and involves the freehand painting of patterns onto the barkcloth. The range of motifs used in this process is taken directly from plants and animals. These are painted on with a little brush made from a dried pandanus fruit or something similar. In the making of a siapo mamanu, motifs are arranged in an infinite number of ways to create very distinctive and individual decorations.

In contrast to siapo mamanu, there are the siapo tasina or siapo 'elei. Both are names given to siapo that are decorated using an 'upeti; a relief pattern either carved into a plank of timber or made from leaves. The 'upeti made from leaves was called an 'upeti fala, and incorporated pieces of coconut fibre cord, bamboo strips, pandanus leaves and coconut midrib sewn onto pandanus leaves with bast fibre from the fau tree (*Hibiscus spp*). This created a raised pattern that would transfer onto the cloth during the dyeing process. 'Upeti fala appear to have been used only up until the 1930s, with the more durable and quickly made wooden 'upeti replacing them almost entirely from this time on.[5]

In creating a siapo tasina or siapo 'elei, a plain piece of u'a is placed over the relief pattern of the 'upeti and rubbed over with 'o'a dye. The pattern of the underlying board comes through and marks both sides of the cloth. It is a simple process that works in much the same way as a pencil rubbing of a coin or other raised or indented pattern.

The joining of other pieces of cloth is also done at this stage, as are any repairs and patching of holes, using glue called masoa made from boiled arrowroot tuber. During this stage more 'o'a is also rubbed in with a cloth swab, along with a powdered red ochre 'ele that is grated and thinly spread over the cloth. Once the siapo is dry, a small brush is used to do freehand infilling work, elaborating on the lines and shades of the rubbed through patterns. This freehand work can give very different appearances to two siapo created from the same 'upeti.

Siapo have been put to many different uses, such as curtains, mosquito nets, garments and belts. An account from 1838 describes the use of siapo as a pupuni (curtain) to partition a fale into different 'apartments':

…an awning of native tappa is arranged which lets down from nearly the top of the house to the floor, forms an arch overhead and curtains all around. These are arranged according to the family

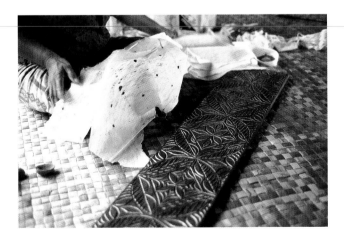

Fig. 5.9 Siapo collected between 1887 and 1902 by Reverend A.E. Hunt. Donated to the museum by Mrs Lorna A. Crawford. (Museum of New Zealand, Te Papa Tongarewa, Ref. No: FE003511/1)

in the house, commonly having one large awning sufficient for the family, and a small one for the accommodation of visitors, sufficiently large to cover 2 or 3 persons.[6]

A longtime common use for the siapo is as a lavalava worn by both men and women. But as another account indicates, this wasn't always the case:

Before the arrival of the Europeans and indeed for some time after, the use of the siapo as an article of dress was confined to a few unmarried females of the highest rank … all others being prohibited from wearing it upon pain of heavy chastisement…[7]

Things changed a great deal with the arrival of European styles and ideas. In the 19th century siapo went on to be adapted and used in many forms of dress – a trend that continues to this day. Men sometimes wrapped barkcloth around their heads in the form of a turban, or around their waist as a malo (loincloth). Long strips of barkcloth were also used as a belt or girdle, or for holding fine mats in position. An interesting 19th century manifestation of the barkcloth was as a tiputa (poncho).

Barkcloth ponchos were introduced into Samoa by Tahitian missionary teachers who arrived with the Reverend John Williams in the 1830s. Worn by the first Christian Samoans, tiputa complied with missionary ideas of personal modesty, but also became what we would now regard as a form of Sunday best. The wearing of tiputa was a way in which Christian Samoans could distinguish themselves from those who had not embraced the Christian faith. It helped them build a sense of identity and collectivity. As anthropologist Nicholas Thomas suggests, the wearing of tiputa gave the new Christian calendar visibility and practical meaning in Samoa: '…they were not part of a repressive missionary law, as much as a productive effort to teach people that their sense of self-worth and pride might be invested in their self-presentation on Sundays, on the path to church'.[8]

It is an interesting point to make, because the legacy of this pride of self-presentation continues in Samoa. While the wearing of tapa ponchos has stopped altogether, the wearing of white or Sunday best is still common in Samoan Christian churches, as is the wearing of distinctive choir and church youth group uniforms.

Another 19th century introduction was patterned printed cloth, the new images and styles of which may have been an influence on local siapo designers, particularly those who made siapo mamanu. It is probable that local siapo patterns and compositions may have been inspired by the patterns of this imported cloth – as was the case with some indigenous textiles in Tahiti.[9]

SIAPO OF LEONE

One of the most interesting periods in the development of siapo decoration occurred long after the early missionary period, from the 1920s until just after World War II. During this time, the village of Leone on Tutuila gained a reputation for its siapo mamanu. In her book *Siapo: Barkcloth Art of Samoa*, Samoan artist and teacher Mary J. Pritchard wrote of her experiences learning the art form from the talented women of this village around this time.

Pritchard was originally from Pago Pago and joined the Leone siapo group in the late 1920s. By this time their distinctive work was already well known and admired. One woman in the group, Kolone Fai'ivae Leoso, was to emerge as an influential figure and a prolific designer. In her book, Pritchard describes Kolone's influence and role

5.10 Siapo 'elei, collected in 1949 by Dr T. T. Barrow. (Museum of New Zealand, Te Papa Tongarewa, Ref. No: FE010552)

Fig. 5.11 Siapo made by Kolone Fai'ivae Leoso. Presented to Lady Bird Johnson. (Photo courtesy of Marilyn Walker)

5.12 Siapo mamanu attributed to American Samoa, Tutuila, probably Leone. Collected 1937-1939 by Mrs R. Miller and presented to the museum by Mrs R. Miller. (Museum of New Zealand, Te Papa Tongarewa, Ref. No: FE008126)

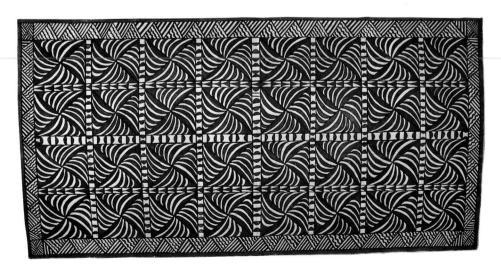

5.13 Siapo mamanu made by Mary Pritchard, 1974. Private collection. (Photo courtesy of Marilyn Walker)

among the siapo makers at this time:

She was a stately woman, seldom speaking unnecessarily except to direct those working with her... Surrounded by adult women, Kolone sat designing one siapo after another. Some of these were her own pieces, to be completed by young girls who would learn about siapo... Some designs were for women who would complete them for their own use, or to give as gifts or to sell ... masterpieces of siapo were being produced under the direction of Kolone.[10]

Kolone's compositions were often inspired by the stained glass windows of the Leone Congregational Christian Church. Pritchard notes that the patterns and colours which are said to have influenced her work on barkcloth also led to a localised but significant innovation in siapo design:

I can remember watching her, lost in thought, staring at the church windows. Turning to her blank barkcloth, she would divide the space into sections similar to those in the windows and then start to place her symbols within these spaces. It is my opinion that the church windows also were the source for Kolone originating the use, all in the same siapo, of multiple colours – that is brown, black, yellow and red used together at the same time.[11]

People constantly requested of Kolone siapo and designs, and since there was a steady flow of supplies in payment it was unnecessary for her to grow or gather materials. An indication of her recognition is that some people brought fine mats as payment for work requested.[12]

Figs. 5.14 Siapo artist Mary Pritchard. (Photo F. Sutter, courtesy of University of Hawai'i Press)

Kolone Fai'ivae Leoso died in 1970, but under her guidance and that of her sister-in-law Tui'uli, Mary Pritchard had developed into a talented artist herself. Her work continued through the 1960s and 70s and later she became an inspiring teacher in the art of siapo. Her own extensive body of work illustrates her skills in the use of a limited colour palette and also her compositional and design abilities. She has also made great efforts to share her knowledge, conducting workshops and finding time to write her landmark book, and her siapo designs and influence have encouraged many young Samoans to explore the techniques and heritage of the art form.

As well as Pritchard's work teaching and promoting the art, the 1960s and 70s saw siapo marketed overseas by the South Pacific Commission in a series of handicraft catalogues.[13] These publications indicate that although artists in American Samoa were still producing siapo mamanu it was easier to acquire siapo tasina and siapo 'elei. As well as the standard rectangular pieces, circular and undecorated siapo were also available. The rectangular siapo could be very small or up to four by six feet in size.

In contrast siapo from Western Samoa were much larger, an average piece reported at nine by six feet. The colours used in decoration tended to be browns, yellows and blacks.[14] From the catalogues of this time, the use of colour appears to be more conservative, as do the patterns and designs. In fact between 1958 and 1970 it appears that siapo production had greatly reduced in Western Samoa. One report from 1958 states that siapo were produced in not more than three or four dozen villages in the country.[15]

This conservatism in design and reduced production seem to have continued and by the 1980s and into the early 1990s there had been an even more noticeable decline in the production of siapo right across the archipelago.

Neich's study of Samoan material culture in 1980 found that siapo were made in only a few villages on Savai'i and only in small sizes. However, the same study also described an extraordinary exception to this general trend in the form of a special event held later that year. It was the 150th anniversary of the arrival of the Reverend John Williams, which was commemorated at Sapapali'i on Savai'i. The event increased local siapo production for a short time as people met the requirements of the gift giving, ceremonies and presentations associated with the celebrations. The occasion also provided an opportunity to review a great number of siapo from a number of different artists around the island.

In assessing the qualities of the individual cloths, local Samoans who were questioned were most interested in pieces with good variation and intricate designs, and particularly noted siapo that made use of two 'upeti rather than one. This was interesting because the prevailing ideas about what was considered 'good' seemed to mirror tastes from earlier in the century. When examples of siapo from the 1920s and 30s are compared to examples photographed in the 1980s, the differences are obvious.[16] The freehand work and elaborate compositions of earlier years are certainly missing, as are the diversity and complexity in patterning. A photograph from a 1930s agricultural show illustrates this distinction clearly (see fig. 5.1). So while the appreciation of a finely decorated siapo was evident at the 1980 celebration, either the desire, knowledge or ability to reproduce such standards was not.

CONTEMPORARY SIAPO

The last decade of the millennium saw the decline of siapo continue throughout Samoa. Developments that were noted at the eastern end of the archipelago, highlight some of the issues that have affected not just siapo manufacture but Samoan women's arts in general.

The contemporary production of siapo on Tutuila has been studied by long-time Samoa resident and folklorist John Enright. Initially it was thought that the decline in siapo production was due to the disappearance of the u'a, but Enright discovered that farmers were cutting stands of the plant back, thinking it was a weed.[17] He then identified the increasing westernisation of time as a potent agent in the decline of several local art practices, but in particular the arts of weaving and siapo making. At the time of his study, women in Tutuila were engaged in employment and business that took them away from the home and village for greater periods. Tasks and responsibilities had become organised around a western concept of time, leaving little opportunity to prepare materials and manufacture articles.

Today not much has changed, with siapo production still centred in only a few villages, mainly on Savai'i. It is most often made in the form of small swatches for the tourist trade, but larger pieces suitable for wearing or presentations are made on request. These are usually commissioned for events such as church openings and title bestowals, although from at least the 1980s Tongan tapa has also been imported to meet the demands of these social and customary occasions.

The siapo-making arts today may be a mere shadow of former times, but the creative spirit of the Samoan

Fig. 5.15 Siapo vala made by Lausolo Segafili circa 1980 at Fualuga village, Salelologa, Savai'i. (Museum of New Zealand, Te Papa Tongarewa, Ref. No: FE007719)

women who have produced these cloths lives on. In Apia in 1999 there were signs that there was a revival of sorts occurring, at least in terms of siapo decoration. Images of crabs and other animals were seen on siapo for sale in markets, and in the Samoan Museum there was a siapo with rose motifs. It appears that new and lavishly illustrated publications on Pacific tapa had generated a new interest in old and forgotten designs. In the Museum of Samoa and the handicraft store Kava and Kavings in particular, there was evidence of siapo being produced with crisper lines, cleaner workmanship and more complex compositions, features reminiscent of earlier styles.

Today the distinctive patterns of siapo and other Polynesian barkcloths are recognised far and wide, even if they are not so much seen on the textured surface of the u'a. The balanced compositions, patterns and lines have been applied in many different ways to all kinds of media. Tapa designs and prints from throughout the Pacific appear on shirts, ceramics, stationery, uniforms and are constantly referenced in other art forms. As well as being a form of decoration they have become bold and striking symbols of community and identity. In many ways the few simple motifs and patterns are saying as much, and perhaps even more, than they ever have. Mary Pritchard eloquently summed it up:

There are 12 different notes in an octave, if you count all the half notes, 26 letters in the English alphabet; three primary colours plus black and white. From such limited resources, great music, literature, and art has been created. Siapo too has a small repertoire of stylized motifs taken from nature; patterns which suggest a net; the midrib of a coconut leaf, the trochus shell, pandanus and breadfruit leaves, the sandpiper and starfish. When repeated, rearranged, reversed, inverted the result is an intricately balanced mosaic, a Samoan siapo.[18]

SIAPO ARTIST: VA'AMULI MOLI-SALU

Va'amuli Moli-Salu works in a fale in the village of Palauli on the south coast of Savai'i. In the large house close to the road Va'amuli spends most days of the week scraping, beating and decorating barkcloth. Nearby, not far from her tools and dyes is a small stand of u'a and it is from the bark of these plants that she makes siapo. It's a skill she learnt as a young woman from her mother Fa'auliuli Vaipua and one she now passes on to her own five daughters.

Siapo making on Savai'i underwent something of a revival in recent times. An outbreak of taro blight has forced women like Va'amuli Moli-Salu in villages like Palauli, Sala'ilua and Siutu to look for other sources of income. 'I can make between two and three hundred small tapa in a week; some ladies can make up to 80 tapa in one day. Most of my work is siapo 'elei, but sometimes I make siapo mamanu.'

The two wooden 'upeti she uses were purchased at the markets in Apia, and interestingly they came from different ends of the western islands. One was made in Falealupo on Savai'i, the other in Fagaloa Bay on Upolu. Both areas are well known for their woodworkers. The 'upeti from Fagaloa Bay is carved on both sides with different patterns that give her more options in varying her decorations.

Most of Va'amuli Moli-Salu's work consists of small pieces made for tourists and

Fig. 5.16 Siapo 'elei made by Va'amuli Moli-Salu, Palauli, Savai'i, 2000. (Museum of New Zealand, Te Papa Tongarewa, Ref. No: FE011577)

some of the large hotels. Occasionally local tour operators will arrange a demonstration and this gives her another opportunity to sell her work. But she also makes siapo for her local community and friends and relatives overseas. Sometimes the production of small siapo pieces is interrupted with a special order for larger siapo. These are used for presentations and ceremonies such as title bestowals. In 1999 she made and sold four very large pieces for the opening of a local church. She said she also prints 'ie palagi (decorated cloth) and sells the decorated fabric at the flea market in Apia.

Reluctant to state outright what the qualities of a good siapo are, Va'amuli Moli-Salu takes the middle ground and says that 'people will have their own ideas about what they will look for in a siapo and what they will like…' From her own point of view she draws the most satisfaction from overpainting and elaborating on the carved, 'upeti designs 'making good patterns'. Working from the basic outlines of only one or two 'upeti at a time, it is this aspect that allows her to be creative and demonstrate her skill.

Figs. 5.17 Siapo 'elei made by Va'amuli Moli-Salu, Palauli, Savai'i, 2000. (Museum of New Zealand, Te Papa Tongarewa, Ref No: FE011576)

CHAPTER 5

1. Adapted from the story in Turner, G., *Samoa A Hundred Years Ago and Long Before* (London: 1884), p. 123
2. R. Neich and M. Pendergrast, *Pacific Tapa* (Auckland: David Bateman Ltd, 1997), p. 13
3. M.J. Pritchard, *Siapo: Barkcloth Art of Samoa* (Honolulu: University of Hawai'i Press in association with American Samoa Council on Culture Arts and Humanities, 1984), p. 40
4. Pritchard, *Siapo: Barkcloth Art of Samoa*, pp. 29-30
5. Pritchard, *Siapo: Barkcloth Art of Samoa*, p. 48
6. D. McKenzie, MS Journal of Daniel McKenzie jnr, 1838, on board the ship Samuel Robertson of New Bedford, 1837-1840. Cited in Richards, R., *Samoa's Forgotten Whaling Heritage: American Whaling in Samoan Waters 1824-1878* (Wellington: The Western Samoa Historical and Cultural Trust Wellington Lithographic Services Ltd, 1993)
7. J.B. Stair, *Old Samoa; or flotsam and jetsam from the Pacific Ocean* (Papakura: Southern Reprints, 1983, first published 1897), p. 115
8. N. Thomas, 'The case of the misplaced ponchos: speculations concerning the history of cloth in Polynesia', *Journal of Material Culture* Vol. 4 (1999), p. 115
9. L. Jones, 'The Pareu: persistence and revival in a French Polynesian folk art', in Dark, Philip J.C. and Rose, R.G. (eds), *Artistic Heritage in a Changing Pacific* (Honolulu: University of Hawai'i Press, 1993)
10. Pritchard, *Siapo: Barkcloth Art of Samoa*, p. 13
11. Pritchard, *Siapo: Barkcloth Art of Samoa*, p. 15
12. Pritchard, *Siapo: Barkcloth Art of Samoa*, p. 19
13. A. McBean, *Handicrafts of the South Seas* (Noumea, New Caledonia: South Pacific Commission; Sydney: Bridge Printery Pty. Ltd., 1964)
14. McBean, *Handicrafts of the South Seas*, pp. 9-11 and pp. 84-87
15. I.J. Fairburn, cited in Neich, R., 'Material culture of Western Samoa', *National Museum of New Zealand*, Bulletin 23 (1985)
16. R. Neich, personal comment 1999. Neich had the opportunity to survey a great range of siapo at this time. Images that appear in his article were very typical of those seen at the time.
17. J. Enright, 'The Westernisation of time and Samoan folk arts', in Dark P.J.C. and Rose, R.G. (eds), *Artistic Heritage in a Changing Pacific* (Honolulu: University of Hawai'i Press, 1993), p. 119
18. Mary Pritchard, quoted in F.K. Sutter, *The Samoans: A Global Family* (Honolulu: University of Hawai'i Press, 1989), p. 210

CHAPTER 6

WEAVING

Weaving is the most widely practised art form in Samoa. Women are the weavers in the Samoan community and they make a range of woven plant fibre items, the most important being mats. This chapter discusses Samoan mat weaving, the different types and their uses with a particular focus on the 'ie toga, the most important Samoan mat.

A significant feature of Samoan mat weaving in the last hundred years or so has been the innovative use of both structural (decoration of the core material of the woven fabric, like a stripe in a knitted jersey) and applied decoration (material applied to the woven fabric once it is complete, like tassels) in certain types of mats. The decorations on Samoan mats have included dyes, feathers, wool, paint and even tinsel. Some applied elements such as feathers have important historical origins and relate to rank and status. Others contribute a visual aesthetic appeal. But the value and appre-

Fig. 6.1 'Ie toga (fine mat) made in 1800s from pandanus leaves and feathers. (Museum of New Zealand, Te Papa Tongarewa, Ref. No: FE010379)

ciation of Samoan weaving can run much deeper. The intrinsic value of the highest-ranking Samoan mat, the 'ie toga, moves beyond the aesthetics of tactile or applied decoration, and through its use mediates important aspects of the relationships and values of fa'asamoa.

MATERIALS

In the last 200 years the most widely used plant fibres in weaving have been the coconut leaf and pandanus. Mats made from the leaves of the coconut tree are more disposable and less valuable than those made from pandanus, which are generally more highly processed and finely woven.

Pandanus is usually planted in groves and is carefully tended so that the plants produce healthy leaves suitable for the weaving process. Three different varieties are used for weaving: the paogo used to make the coarse brown floor mats seen in most homes; the fala used to make the finer floor and sleeping mats; the 'ie used for making the very fine 'ie toga.

The pandanus is processed and prepared differently depending on the type of mat being made. With laupaogo (leaves of paogo), the leaves are stripped of their short sharp spines and left to dry on the ground for several days. They are then rolled and stored away ready for use. The same is done with laufala (leaves of fala), although the drying process sometimes lasts a bit longer to let the leaves bleach in the sun. The leaves are also sometimes split into narrower strips before weaving.

The lau'ie (leaves of 'ie) require more thorough processing to get them to the highest standard of preparation. Once the spines are removed, the leaves are made into parcel-like lots and placed in a container of boiling water for five to ten minutes. The top layer of the leaf is carefully peeled away from the dull underside, which is discarded. The leaves are then tied to a stick in bundles and bleached in the sea for three to five days until they turn a lighter colour and take on a smooth shiny appearance. They are then washed in cold water and dried in the sun before being split down the midrib and rolled.

When required for weaving the leaves are split again into extremely thin strips. During the weaving process they are woven together so that the smooth side of the leaf appears on both sides of the mat. The fineness of the woven strips and the shiny and highly processed appearance of the mat add greatly to its value. Needless to say, mats made of this material take a great deal of time to manufacture and so are rare and difficult to acquire. The following descriptions list the mats from lowest to highest, as told to the author in 1999 during an interview with Peka Malo, a weaver from Manase, Savai'i.

POLAVAI

Polavai are mats made from coconut leaves. They were once used directly on the gravel floor of the house to protect other pandanus mats that would be laid on top of them. Now that these floors have been replaced with concrete slabs, papa mats (see below) are often laid down instead, making polavai less common.[1] These days papa mats are often laid directly on the floor. Te Rangi Hiroa noted that polavai were also called the polataufale (pola within the house) as distinct from the polataufafo, the wall screen that hangs to the outside.[2]

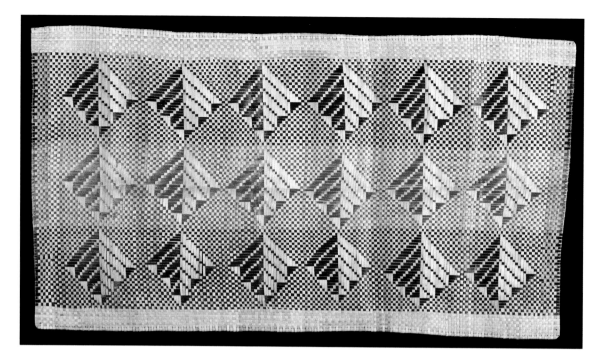

Fig. 6.2 Fale tapito (sleeping mat) made by Foaluga Moe, Salani, Upolu, 2000. (Museum of New Zealand, Te Papa Tongarewa, Ref. No: FE011524)

Fig. 6.3 Papa laufala

PAPA

Papa laupaogo and papa laufala are floor mats made from varieties of pandanus. With papa laupaogo the wefts or strips of pandanus material are cut to a size of 20 – 25 mm making them the widest strips used in Samoan mats. They are also double-wefted meaning that two weft strips are placed together and woven as if they were one. This technique gives papa mats a similar appearance on both sides. The mats can be quite large, up to two metres in length and up to one metre wide. The edges of the mat are straight and the thick construction makes them heavy and durable and not prone to curling while on the floor. In the past women would sometimes mark these mats with two or three nicks, or steps, at a corner, or by putting in a short row of twill some-where, to distinguish their property.[3] Apart from material, papa laufala are very similar to laupaogo, except they are made with a smaller weft and have a softer texture.

FALA MOE

Fala moe are sleeping mats or floor mats also made from pandanus but more elaborate than those just described in that they incorporate structural or applied decoration. Unlike the double-wefted papa mats they are made from a single weft that is much narrower in width. For this reason they are sometimes referred to as fala lili'i or fala nini'i. In some fala moe weft elements are dyed black using natural dyes, or red and purple using commercial dyes.[4] Coloured wool fringing is also a feature and is applied along the mats' edges. In 1928 Te Rangi Hiroa considered both these aspects of coloured decoration as being fairly modern, and perhaps encouraged by increasing tourist traffic.[5] It remains a feature of contemporary fala moe.

Fala moe can be broken down into three types of mat. The lowest ranked is the afeafe, the term referring to a finishing technique used along the edge of the mats' shorter sides. The afeafe is also distinguished by a fringe of wool decoration that appears only along the edges of the two longest sides. The tu'u laufala also has a fringe of wool decoration, except it appears along all four edges of the mat. Although not

Fig. 6.4 Tu'u laufala made by Olailagi Leaitua, Lotofaga, Upolu, 2000. (Museum of New Zealand, Te Papa Tongarewa, Ref. No: FE011525)

often made today, it is higher ranked than the afeafe.[6] The highest ranking of the fala moe is the fala tapito. It differs from the afeafe and tu'u laufala in that it usually has no wool fringing and is unique among Samoan mats in that the wefts run parallel to the sides instead of obliquely.[7] As with other fala moe however, it is decorated with dyed structural wefts interwoven with the natural coloured wefts.

FALA SU'I

Fala su'i are mats where the surface is decorated with designs and images stitched in coloured wool. The mat is made from the lower ranking laufala and the wefts are about 100 mm in width. Onto this laufala mat, words, shapes and images such as flowers, fale (houses), birds and flags are needle-stitched. Fala su'i were designed to fit the frame of a bed. Two-thirds of the mat's surface is plain and one-third decorated. The plain part would sit under the mattress, and the wool decorated portion would hang over the side of the bed frame like a valance. According to Neich, fala su'i are 'an important item among the mats presented at weddings and at the fa'afailelega-tama ceremony when a new baby is brought home to its father's village from the village of its mother'.[8]

Fig. 6.5 Fala su'i (embroidered mat used as a bed cover) made by Lepetia Toa, Moata'a, Upolu, 2000. (Museum of New Zealand, Te Papa Tongarewa, Ref. No: FE011522)

Fala su'i different to those just described feature decoration over the entire surface of the laufala mat. In such cases the mat is used to decorate the top of a bed or the top of a pile of mats. But the decoration also makes other display opportunities possible. In the exhibition Mata o te Pasifika at the Dowse Art Gallery in Lower Hutt, New Zealand in 1995, fala su'i featuring images covering the entire surface of the mat were displayed. Made by a local women's group specialising in fala su'i, they featured very local but also international references in their work. One example incorporated an American bald eagle, the Maori greeting 'kia ora' the English greeting 'hello' and the Samoan greeting 'talofa'.

Fig. 6.6 Fala lau 'ie (mat made from lau 'ie used as a bed cover) made by Vilealava Vaipae, Lepuiai, Manono, 2000. (Museum of New Zealand, Te Papa Tongarewa, Ref. No: FE011520)

Fig. 6.7 Fala vali (painted mat used as a bed cover) made by Pemiata Leiataua, Lepuiai, Manono, 2000. (Museum of New Zealand, Te Papa Tongarewa, Ref. No: FE011521)

FALA UFI MOEGA

The fala su'i developed from older higher-ranking sleeping mats known as fala ufi moega. Like the fala su'i they were used to hang down the side of the bed. Presently there are two types of fala ufi moega: the fala lau'ie and the fala vali.

The fala lau'ie is probably the present-day version of what was formerly known as the 'ie moega.[9] Te Rangi Hiroa noted the existence of this plain, largely undecorated sleeping mat in the late 1920s. Used by matai, it was made from a variety of pandanus known as lau'ie that was used mainly for making 'ie toga. The difference was the wefts were not as thin as those used in 'ie toga. The fala lau'ie that was to follow and replace the 'ie moega typically featured '…soft, well prepared, narrow, double layered wefts of lau'ie; a fringe and/or flaps or tags at the bottom edge; restrained geometric designs stitched or laced through the mat with wool of a limited range of colours'.[10] One old fala lau'ie measured in 1980 had wefts 6 mm wide.[11] These old fala lau'ie are quite rare with Peka Malo, a weaver from Manase, saying that any good fala lau'ie in use today were likely to be at least five to ten years old.[12] This comment is supported by Neich who noted in 1980 that modern fala lau'ie were much thicker and coarser and not processed or made as carefully as they were in former times.[13]

Fala vali are another type of fala ufi moega. Made to hang over the side of the bed, decorations are painted directly onto the fala rather than stitched on using wool. The range of images, patterns and motifs seem to be unrestricted, and in the past stencils were made from leaves and used to create a repeating motif or pattern. As in the case of the fala su'i, there are examples of fala vali where the decoration or images cover the entire mat. Again it is likely that these mats were specially made for presentation or display purposes.

'IE TOGA

Of the several types of mats that have already been discussed, the 'ie toga, also commonly referred to as the fine mat, is the highest ranking and the most finely made. Used as an item of ceremonial dress or for presentation, the 'ie toga is never left to lie flat on the floor. Its significance in Samoan society has attracted the attention of many anthropological writers, who have commented on its role as an article of exchange as well as the many stories, customs and histories associated with its use.[14]

As we have seen, some of the value of an 'ie toga is found in the preparation and quality of the materials used to make it. The important tactile qualities are manifest in an 'ie toga's softness, shine and fineness. The softness depends on how thin and well prepared the materials are. One reference to old 'ie toga compares the thinness of the strips to the hair on the head.[15] The shine has been described as being like that of silk. Today the highly processed type of 'ie toga is distinguished from those not so highly processed by the term 'ie sae.[16] This term refers to the stripping of the dull underside of the leaf and the retention of the shiny side.

Penelope Schoeffel has done the most recent research into the history and significance of the 'ie toga. She highlights two accounts that tell the story of its origin.

Fig. 6.8 'Ie sae (fine mat) without feather fringe dressing. Made by Gataiala Leiataua, Lepuiai, Manono, 2000. (Museum of New Zealand, Te Papa Tongarewa, Ref. No: FE011519)

One says that the subspecies of pandanus from which 'ie toga are made was first planted at Falealupo by the goddess Nafanua, near the entrance to Pulotu (the Samoan Hades). Another traces the origin of the 'ie toga to Pulotu itself, where it was carried into the world of the living by Savea Si'ule'o, father of Nafanua. The hands of the lady who wove it were said to have been rendered so sacred by her task that she had to be fed by an attendant.[17]

The 'ie toga is largely undecorated except for a row of feathers usually in from and along its bottom edge. Historically the 'ie toga was decorated with a fringe of rare and valuable red parakeet feathers usually obtained from Fiji. In fact for many years a trade in parrot feathers was carried out between Tonga, Samoa and Fiji. Feathers were often transported to Samoa by Tongan seafarers, who would return to their own islands with 'ie toga bordered with some of the same feathers.[18] In some cases people skirmished, raided and lost their lives in pursuit of a supply. However, the trade in feathers was banned early in the 20th century by colonial authorities in the interests of conservation.

In the past young women would often commence their own mats or complete ones left by older female family members. The finer the mat the more skill was required and the greater the investment in time. The weaving of an 'ie toga could take months or years to complete. Preserved with great care, some 'ie toga would pass through several generations, and as their age increased and more people or events became associated with them, so too did their intrinsic value.

The 'ie toga is the highest ranking item in the Samoan exchange system, as the most prestigious item in a category of valuables known as toga. In marriage ceremonies 'ie toga are presented to the husband's family by the bride's family and as 'toga' they are viewed in much the same way as dowry property. In the past the toga exchange

Fig. 6.9 'ie toga, without feather fringe dressing, made by Atagai Simone, Tufutafoe, Upolu, 2000. (Museum of New Zealand, Te Papa Tongarewa, Ref. No: FE011518)

valuables included siapo, other lower ranking varieties of mat, grass skirts, coconut oil, turmeric and other dyes. The greater the number of 'ie toga presented and the more history or associations attributed to them, the more clearly a bride's family presented their status and worthiness. In return the husband's family would present bride price property known as 'oloa. This consisted mainly of food, such as pigs and chickens, but could also include canoes, houses, weapons, tools, ornaments and foreign property.[19]

For very important weddings the number of 'ie toga exchanged could total in the hundreds. The exchanged 'ie toga would be redistributed later to the husband's extended family as a display of respect and recognition, and to provide assistance in preparing the 'oloa. These redistributed 'ie toga would then be redistributed in the next ceremonial occasion and in this way circulate through Samoan society, accumulating history, associations and value.

Besides weddings the 'ie toga can also be used in a ritual form of apology known as ifoga or fa'asifoga, a type of ritual that acts as a plea for atonement and forgiveness.

If a Samoan commits a sin, like adultery, manslaughter through a motor accident, through a public fight, through a jealous rage, the abduction of someone's wife, publicly insulting another matai, there is only one recourse open to him…the fa'asifoga requires the matai of the offender's aiga to cover himself with fine mats, then kneel and humbles [sic] himself before the house of the wronged family, and usually before sunrise.[20]

In the past this ritual self-humiliation could also involve the offender taking stones and firewood from which an oven would be made, and offering fine mats in reparation. The offender would be offering himself as a pig to be cooked and eaten. As anthropologist Derek Freeman notes, 'such a gesture, which to Samoans is deeply moving, almost always leads to reconciliation'.[21]

The significance of the 'ie toga used in the context of a formal apology is further illustrated in a unique case from 1976. On this occasion a matai who had broken New Zealand immigration laws offered an 'ie toga in an act of contrition to the then New Zealand Prime Minister, Robert Muldoon. The matai was conscious that he had broken the New Zealand law and to enable him to return with dignity to Samoa wanted to bestow the fine mat on the Prime Minister and the government.[22] The gesture was accepted.

Other important exchanges involving 'ie toga include presentations made during house building, canoe building, tattooing and the opening and dedications of schools and churches. The 'ie toga bring formality and dignity to the occasion and honour the status of the event as well as those involved.

As mentioned earlier, some 'ie toga pass through several generations, gaining value as their age and associations accumulate. Such 'ie toga often acquire a sentimental value far in excess of their intrinsic value. Some 'ie toga are named, and the most important could be given a series of names. Others are named depending on their use for specific occasions.[23]

The associations attributed to an 'ie toga often relate to stories, histories, events and changes of name given to it. Te Rangi Hiroa observes, 'Some changes of name were recorded in song and often these songs and the historical value would give the 'ie toga a value that exceeded the fineness of plait, though where both existed the value was naturally enhanced'.[24]

Generally, the older an 'ie toga the more it is valued especially if it is of fine weft and manufacture. Tears, a general state of disrepair or even evidence of patching do not make an 'ie toga any less valuable; as C.C. Marsack, a former Chief Justice of Samoa commented:

Very often the mat occupying the place of honour on some dignified occasion will be one which in European eyes would appear almost valueless because of its poor state of repair. When one of the political leaders of Western Samoa, Tamasese, went with his wife at the invitation of the New Zealand Government to the Coronation of Queen Elizabeth, he took a storied fine mat which in Samoa was regarded as a magnificent gift, thoroughly worthy of the purpose it was to fulfil; to the untutored recipient it would no doubt have appeared as dreadfully second hand.[25]

The ʻie toga are so important in the Pacific context that many very old (some of them dating back to the 17th century) and significant examples are held by the Tongan Royal Family as their most valuable heirlooms.[26] The practice of exchanging Samoan ʻie toga as valuables in the weddings of high-ranking Tongan chiefs was certainly well established by the early 1800s and continues to this day.[27]

Today ʻie toga retain an important position in the Samoan exchange system, despite a manufacturing process that has been streamlined and simplified. In 1980 Neich noted that where previously an ʻie toga would take months or years to make, ʻie toga were being made in just a few days. The process of carefully preparing the fibre and slowly weaving it, with double layers and fine elements has been almost totally discarded. The use of dyed feathers in decoration and in some cases tinsel has become common. These days feathers are often glued on and come in a range of colours including red, purple, pink, green and blue.

It is only recently that the finer style of ʻie toga, referred to as ʻie sae, has undergone a revival. Another change is that with the simplification of techniques and loss of fineness there has been a corresponding increase in size. To display the best ʻie toga during a presentation three people, one at each end and a third in the middle, are often needed, sometimes with supporting poles.

Neich has also noted that the use and contexts for ʻie toga have been expanded upon: 'Previously, ʻie toga were only presented for the funeral of titled chiefs, but within the last ten years their presentation has been extended to the funerals of untitled adults and even children.'[28] Other changes include the selling of ʻie toga in markets, the raffling and auctioning of them, and even the establishment of a company that recycles and repairs them.[29]

This change in the tactile elements of ʻie toga, the fineness of wefts, the types of feathers, does not seem to have altered their value as an exchange item. It has been suggested that perhaps today the value and appreciation of ʻie toga lies not so much in these qualities alone but the way in which they are used and presented. While less obvious as an aesthetic and artistic quality, the performance aspect and the occasions and relationships ʻie toga mediate are perhaps just as or more important than the cloth itself. The formalised handling of ʻie toga is, according to Neich, one of the most artistic performances apart from dance.[30] When displayed or paraded in ceremonies or formal occasions, the incorrect handling of ʻie toga provokes strong criticism. A general convention is that ʻie toga should be laid on top of, or covering other less prestigious mats, not directly on the floor. They must also be carried and displayed in a flowing and graceful manner.

OTHER WEAVING AND FIBRE ARTS

Another type of mat usually worn as a garment but also used as a wedding bed are the ʻie sina and ʻie fau. These mats were made entirely from fau bast and distinguished by their shaggy fleece-like appearance. The shaggy look was achieved through long string-like tags attached to a woven mat base. See also Chapter 15, Costume and Clothing.

These mats are a curious part of Samoan material culture. They were not ranked or seen as part of the standard classification of mats by Te Rangi Hiroa or Neich, but obviously figured highly in Samoan culture for many years. Their use by women of status is fairly well documented and Te Rangi Hiroa does mention them under a chapter on clothing. By the time of Neich's study they had completely disappeared and only survived as family heirlooms.

Fig. 6.10 Basket made from coconut leaves. (Sean Mallon)

Baskets are another item made from woven plant fibres, the most common being those made from coconut leaf. These are still used every day in Samoa, with some of the simpler ones made by both women and men. They are used to carry goods and items around the home, to the markets in the towns, or between plantations and villages.

Older styles of coconut leaf baskets varied in design and manufacture and were made for a range of purposes and functions. Naturally some of these basket types no longer exist as the activities they were made for have become less frequent or disappeared from everyday village life. As described by Te Rangi Hiroa in the 1920s, the range of coconut baskets included the ola malu, a small deep basket to carry small fish and shellfish from the lagoon, the ola tu, a basket used by women to catch fish driven out of the piles of stones in the lagoon that had been erected to attract them as resting places, and the si'u ola, a basket named after a type of fish and used for collecting it either on the canoe or when it was brought to shore. According to recent research by Wendy Arbeit on Polynesian baskets, the si'u ola was still being used in the 1980s but not as much as in the past. She notes that 'the generic names ola fagota (fishing basket), malu and malu fagota are now used interchangeably by the younger generation to describe the various sorts of fishing baskets'.[31]

The coconut leaf basket was the working bag or convenient carryall used by people throughout their working week and quickly replaced when lost or dried and withered. Other types of basket made from this leaf were the ato 'afa, a small hand-held basket used by matai for storing 'afa, the coconut shell fibre that they would sometimes roll and plait into cord while listening to long meetings. There was also the 'ato lavalava, now known as the ola lapotopoto,[32] a round basket used for storing garments or laundry.

Also used for storing articles of cloth such as siapo and costume were large baskets made from pandanus called taga. These are no longer made in Samoa and probably disappeared in the mid 19th century with the introduction of wooden chests and coiled baskets.[33] In 1861 George Turner illustrated a basket supposedly of the taga type and a miniature version later became popular and was made for sale to tourists. Another type of pandanus basket took the form of a small loop-handled bag that was sometimes decorated. In the 1920s these were considered a modern development and were used to carry around small articles.

Coiled baskets, made from the coils of split coconut leaf midrib covered with thin strips of pandanus were also made in Samoa. The technique is believed to have been introduced, but the exact origin of this type of basket is difficult to pinpoint. Some accounts say it was introduced into Pukapuka from Samoa, while others say into Samoa from Niue and still others say from Samoa into the Tuamotus.[34] From wherever it originated, the coil style of basket spread quickly throughout Samoa and is still occasionally made there.

Very rare and used for holding tools or fishing equipment, was a basket made from 'afa (coconut fibre cord). Only two examples of this satchel-like bag are known to exist. The special technique used to knot the fibre and braid it together is the same as that used to make a type of small fishing scoop.[35]

Fig. 6.11 Square basket made from pandanus and coconut leaf. Purchased from W.H. Denton, 1943. (Museum of New Zealand, Te Papa Tongarewa, Ref. No: FE011245)

There is also a great variety of decorative baskets made primarily for the tourist and only occasionally purchased or used by the locals. Some are imported from places such as Vanuatu and Fiji and sold in the larger souvenir and craft shops. Locally made baskets sometimes incorporate printed cloth sealed beneath a protective sheet of clear plastic built into the basket's structure.

WEAVING IN SAMOA TODAY

Weaving in Samoa is still widely practised, and mats, baskets, hats and fans find markets, uses and roles that ensure their ongoing production. Many 'ie toga and other classes of mat are made for export overseas to help families abroad in meeting their fa'asamoa commitments for weddings, funerals and church openings.

One recently established programme is run by the Samoan Women in Business Foundation based in Apia. This organisation looked at the opportunities available for Samoan women and saw that the art of weaving fine, well processed 'ie toga was becoming a thing of the past. Part of the organisation's aim is to empower women in the village society and help bring them into the cash economy where they can make a small income for themselves. Through the weaving programme they hope to retain the skills of weaving and promote its preciousness at the same time. The response of Samoan women to this initiative has been mixed. Nonetheless, core groups of weavers have been established in Manono, Aleipata, Tufitafoe, Lotofaga, Falefa, Tufulele, Satoalepai and Salesatele. As the programme has progressed, people overseas have placed orders for fine mats. By May 2000 three people in Hawai'i had placed orders, as well as people in New Zealand including New Zealand's Governor General and members of Samoa's parliament, and some 109 fine mats had been completed.

WEAVER: VIVEALAVA VAEPAE

Vivealava Vaepae, now in her seventies, works with the Samoan Women in Business Foundation on the programme to maintain the art of weaving in Samoa. She is the first woman in recent years to return to weaving the very fine variety of 'ie toga called 'ie sae. The term 'ie sae refers to the preparation process of the pandanus material used in making fine mats. In the recent past there have always been a few villages making 'ie sae in the customary way, but they haven't been incorporating the quality of fine weave characteristic of older 'ie toga. By May 2000 Vivealava's first fine mat on the Women in Business Programme was completed and displayed at a mother's day ceremony. Vivealava is considered a role model for Samoan women and has convinced another woman, Gataiala, from the island of Manono to return to the old style of weaving. She is very proud of the fact that she no longer needs to ask her children for money as she earns her own, and she often jokes about the fact that she finally found a job when she turned 70. Here she shares her thoughts on the importance of the weaving arts for Samoan women today:

My name is Vivealava Vaepae, and I live at Lepuiai at Manono. I began weaving when I married my husband. My mother died when I was very young, so I taught myself after watching other women weave, because I wanted to improve my family.

I love to weave. I will weave anything. I really started weaving because when I got married, having no mother, I didn't have any mats to bring with me to my husband's family. Samoan women should know how to weave. It's an art that belongs to them. It's their purpose in life.

Fig. 6.12 Weaver Vivealava Vaepae. (Photo courtesy of Samoan Women in Business Foundation)

Mothers should teach their daughters how to weave. It's their purpose.

Nowadays many weavers don't take their weaving seriously. They have no pride in their work and are only interested in completing the mat so that they can get some money for it. Children follow their mothers' habits. If this is what their mothers do, then the children will do the same.

I think that weaving is still very important in Samoan society today. It's the matafaioi [duty, purpose] of the Samoan woman to weave. It's the only way that women can earn money in the villages. I think it's very difficult for women to revive the art of weaving. Women are not teaching their children how to weave. We are becoming very lazy. People don't work on the land any more, they just wait for their families to send money from overseas.

WEAVERS IN NEW ZEALAND

Very little weaving is done by Samoan women in New Zealand. If an individual or family requires mats, they are imported or brought over from Samoa by visiting relatives. There have been some efforts, however, to practise the art form in New Zealand and bring Samoan weavers together. As mentioned earlier, in the early 1990s there was a fala sui group established near Wellington who decorated mats with embroidered wool. And since 1995 a Wellington-based programme known as Mafutaga a Tama ma Tina Matitua Samoa I Ueligitone has been organised. In this group Samoan elders meet weekly at a local church and as part of their art programme some of the women weave mats using materials imported from Samoa.[36] But generally the pressures of time and the difficulty in acquiring materials make Samoan weaving in New Zealand difficult to maintain. One exception to this is the Samoan weavers involved in the Multicultural Weavers Association based in Christchurch. As part of this group they have managed to make an ongoing effort to maintain the weaving arts. They produce work that utilises techniques from the many cultures represented in their group and incorporates New Zealand materials such as native flax or harakeke. Emma Kesha was a leading figure in getting this association started. She talks about her interest and work in weaving.

WEAVER: EMMA KESHA

I was born in Samoa and came to live in New Zealand in 1958 when I was only 18 years old. My mother is Apaua from the village of Fale Apuna and my father is Fuatavai from the village of Fusi Salofata. I learnt to weave from my mother and grandmother.

Weaving is an everyday thing that goes on in the village life and I remember when I was a little girl going to school and coming home to see my mother or grandmother weaving. That is when I first started. I used to come home from school and play around with the leftover bits and pieces of mum and grandma's weaving. I would try to make something and sometimes I would receive lessons from my mother and grandmother. Sometimes I would go off and carry on weaving the mats that were already started by my mum or grandmother.

In 1983 I set up my own Multicultural Weavers Association and started teaching weaving. My aim is to preserve the art of weaving and share my knowledge with others. Weaving is an art, that's what I started to feel and that's why I felt it was really important that I set up a weaving organisation, so I could get others to share their skills.

I wanted to learn from other weavers like the Cook Island weavers, the Maori and the Fijians. I wanted this so I could work with them, not only learn from them, but share what I knew as well. The sharing of our techniques was really important. I just believed in sharing

Fig. 6.13 Weaver Emma Kesha. (Photo courtesy of Creative New Zealand)

instead of keeping my own Samoan styles to myself. I wanted to work with others and learn other people's way of weaving.

They were really pleased to come together. It wasn't only weaving the fibres or the materials, but weaving together the people. We started off with 18 but now we've got over 50. We usually meet every month just to get together and weave.

Every time I go to Samoa I bring back my own pandanus. It is very expensive to send money over there for people to send it back. I also use bread wraps to make some experimental things. If I enjoy the things I experiment with then I will go back and use them. I use pandanus, harakeke and kiekie mostly.[37]

I took my multicultural weavers to the South Pacific Arts Festival in Samoa in1996. I went there the year before to organise the women and daughters of my village to have workshops with my weavers from New Zealand. The women in my village were so proud, they'd never experienced anything like that before: people from overseas coming to work with them. We took Maori weaving materials to share with them and we also had the privilege of showing my weavers from New Zealand how we prepared and boiled the materials in Samoa. The men, the children, just everyone from the village were so pleased because it was good for the village to have something happening.

They didn't want to come back when it was time. Some had never travelled anywhere before and to go there during the Arts Festival was great. I felt good that I took them there and my family looked after them. That's been the highlight of my weaving. Being able to take the weavers from New Zealand to my village in Samoa and for them to see and understand my way of life and to enjoy the company of the other women.

Fig. 6.14 Fala afeafe (sleeping mat) made by Tafa Lealaiauloto, Vavau, Upolu, 2000. (Museum of New Zealand, Te Papa Tongarewa, Ref. No: FE011526)

CHAPTER 6

1. R. Neich, 'Material culture of Western Samoa', *National Museum of New Zealand* Bulletin 23 (1985), p. 32

2. Te Rangi Hiroa (Peter Buck), 'Samoan Material Culture', *Bernice P. Bishop Museum*, Bulletin 75 (Hawai'i, Honolulu: 1930), p. 209

3. Te Rangi Hiroa, 'Samoan Material Culture', p. 216

4. Neich, 'Material culture of Western Samoa', p. 32

5. Te Rangi Hiroa, 'Samoan Material Culture', p. 216

6. Peka Malo, Interview: June, 1999, a weaver from Manase, Savai'i

7. Neich, 'Material culture of Western Samoa', p. 32

8. Neich, 'Material culture of Western Samoa', p. 36

9. Neich, 'Material culture of Western Samoa', p. 34

10. Neich, 'Material culture of Western Samoa', p. 34

11. Neich, 'Material culture of Western Samoa', p. 35

12. Peka Malo, Interview, (June, 1999)

13. Neich, 'Material culture of Western Samoa', p. 34

14. A.B. Weiner, *Inalienable Possessions: The Paradox of Keeping While Giving* (Berkeley: University of California Press, 1992); See also, A. Kaeppler, 'Exchange patterns in goods and spouses: Fiji, Tonga and Samoa', *Mankind*, vol. 11 (1978), pp. 246-52

15. F.J.H. Gratton, *An Introduction to Samoan Custom* (Papakura: MacMillan, 1948), p. 167

16. Adi Tafuna'i, from Samoan Women in Business Foundation, Apia, personal comment, (March, 2000)

17. A. Kramer, referenced in Schoeffel, P. 'Samoan exchange and fine mats', *The Journal of the Polynesian Society*, vol. 108 (2) (1999), pp. 117-148

18. F. Clunie, *Yalo i Viti*, A Fiji Museum Catalogue (Suva: Fiji Museum, 1986), p. 150

19. M. Mead, 'Social organisation of Manu'a', *Bernice P. Bishop Museum* Bulletin 76 (Honolulu, Hawai'i: 1969), p. 74

20. Aiono, Fana'afi Le Tagaloa, *Confessions of a Bat* (Savali: July 1984), p. 27

21. D. Freeman, *Margaret Mead and Samoa, The Making and Unmaking of an Anthropological Myth* (Canberra: Australian National University Press, 1983), p. 189

22. *Evening Post* (December 2, 1976)

23. A. Kaeppler, 'Kie hingoa: Mats of Power; Rank; Prestige and History', *Journal of the Polynesian Society* vol. 108 (2) (1999), p. 176.

24. Te Rangi Hiroa, 'Samoan Material Culture', p. 185

25. C.C. Marsack, *Samoan Medley* (London: Robert Hale Ltd, 1961)

26. A. Kaeppler, 'Kie hingoa', p. 224. Kaeppler has compiled a list of Samoan 'ie toga/Tongan kie hingoa held at the Tongan royal palace.

27. Kaeppler, 'Kie hingoa', p. 185

28. Neich, 'Material culture of Western Samoa', p. 40

29. Fine Mats Ltd, Auckland

30. R. Neich, 'Processes of change in Samoan arts and crafts', in Dark, P.J.C. (ed), *Development of the Arts in the Pacific*, Pacific Arts Association, Occassional Papers No. 1 (New Zealand: Government Printer, 1984), p. 45

31. W. Arbeit, *Baskets in Polynesia* (Honolulu: University of Hawai'i Press, 1990), p. 58

32. Arbeit, *Baskets in Polynesia*, p. 60

33. Te Rangi Hiroa, 'Samoan Material Culture' p. 206

34. Arbeit, *Baskets in Polynesia*, p. 14

35. Te Rangi Hiroa, 'Samoan Material Culture', p. 441

36. N. Harvey, 'Craft Revival' *City Voice*, (Wellington: 15 March 1996)

37. Pandanus, harakeke and kiekie are plants used for weaving.

WOODWORK AND SCULPTURE

Adze-making technology provided a means to make the most of materials offered in Samoa's rich forest environment. Wood was an important resource: it provided fuel, shelter, and transportation, as well as utensils, tools, weapons and ornaments. Shape, and function are the values revealed in the curves of elegant bowls and the form and decorations of weapons. From the early to mid-19th century examples of figurative sculpture and relief woodcarving began to appear. These represent a little-known aspect of Samoa's artistic heritage which has only recently been documented. They don't reveal the same concern with aesthetics as other articles, but at present there are too few illustrations and surviving pieces to base any solid assessments on.

The 20th century, however, has seen a great deal of woodwork and sculpture in many styles and reflecting many influences. In the present day, work produced for a village context must sit alongside that made in or for the art studio or gallery, yet each require similar artistic skills beyond the prerequisite of manual dexterity. These include imagination, an appreciation of form, and an ability to see and conceptualise the world in three dimensions and in a range of materials.

FIGURATIVE SCULPTURE

The earliest written records and examples of Samoan figurative sculpture come from the 19th century. From the early 1830s through to the late 1890s it appears that the production of figurative sculpture was well established and primarily associated with the use and decoration of certain types of canoes.[1]

The earliest examples of Samoan figurative sculpture are human in form. Unfortunately only two examples collected in the early days of European contact exist today.

The first of these images is currently in the British Museum in London. This rare example of human sculpture was collected between 1836 and 1839 and given to the museum by Queen Victoria in 1841, and since that time the image has attracted the curious interest of several writers (Fig. 7.1).

Te Rangi Hiroa's assessment from his 1935 study *Material Representatives of Tongan and Samoan Gods* was that the image was made locally in Samoa by either a Tongan or someone acquainted with the appearance of Tongan images. Some aspects of the design that differentiate the image from Tongan examples include the addition of shells

Fig. 7.1 (opposite) Wooden figure, attributed to village of Amaile in the Aleipata district of Upolu, possibly in the early 1800s. (British Museum, Ref. No. 010294)

to form eyeballs and the retention of edge marks from the adzing process. Tongan wooden images are smooth and highly polished and have no shell elements used to represent eyes.[2]

A detailed documentation of the image has been made by archaeologist Janet Davidson.[3] In her 1975 article she notes that writers who have discussed the image have looked to its shape and form in order to understand something of its origins. In particular they ' …point to its resemblance to Tongan examples, particularly those from Ha'apai, and suggest manufacture in Samoa by a Tongan, or by a Samoan familiar with the Tongan style'.[4] While not discounting these suggestions, Davidson focused on reconstructing the context in which the figure was found and how it made its way into the British Museum collections. Her close reading of early missionary correspondence and journals revealed a fascinating story.

First seen in 1836 the image attracted the interest of two separate early missionary parties travelling through the village of Amaile in the Aleipata district of Upolu. In both missionary accounts, the image was seen in association with the preserved bodies of two important chiefs that were lying in state. It is believed that these chiefs were of the Mata'afa line and if so one of them may have been Mata'afa Filisounu'u, who was killed in battle in 1829.[5] In his journal entry of August 31, 1836 the first of the missionaries, Aaron Buzacott of the London Missionary Society, described seeing the chiefs' preserved bodies and the curious human image:

We also saw here a rudely carved image which had also been worshipped by them but now it was lying down disgraced. This was the first image we had seen & we tried to purchase it but were informed that the chief to whom it belonged was not at home and therefore they could not sell it.[6]

Two months later Matthew Wilson and Peter Turner, both Methodist missionaries also saw the bodies of the two chiefs. Wilson made the following notes:

At that place we saw the corps of two old chiefs, father and son; the elder had been dead about twenty years and the other ten. As to the manner in which they were laid, there is a house built for them, and a stand made for them like a double canoe, on [this] there are [boards] fixed which rise gradual up to the head, & on that they are by each other's Side with a stone under their heads; they are covered with native cloth and tied together with native string; at their feet there is a wooden image which is the hight (sic) of the Stand on which they lie, its arms hanging down by its Sides and its eyes made of white shells, being about the size of a child a year old.[7]

Despite being initially refused possession, the existence of the image was noted and it was eventually acquired three years later in 1839 by Reverend Thomas Heath of the London Missionary

Fig. 7.2 Wooden figure said to have been obtained in Samoa in 1846. 69 cm high. (Courtesy of Peabody Essex Museum, Salem, MA. Neg. No: A10296, Acc No: ES309)

Society. His correspondence indicates that he realised it was the only example of a human sculpture found in Samoa, so it was sent on to Queen Victoria in England in 1840 with a small number of other 'curiosities'.

The second example of human sculpture can be found among the South Pacific Collection of the Peabody Museum of Salem, Massachusetts, USA (Fig. 7.2). This work was collected between 1844 and 1849 during a 52-month circumnavigational whaling voyage by Captain Selah Youngs, commander of the Connecticut whaler *Stieglitz*. [8] More naturalistic in style than the British Museum image, there are only a few small pieces of evidence to connect the Salem work to Samoa. A label on the figure itself and two brief log entries are the only clues as to its origin. Part of the now faded and handwritten label identifies the image as a 'Figure Head of Canoe – Navigator's Islands'. A map reference following this gives a position that turns out to be a few kilometres inland from the coast of eastern Upolu in the Falealili district.[9] Interestingly, and in contrast to this, the *Stieglitz* log entries indicate that Manu'a or Tutuila were the only places in Samoa the *Stieglitz* visited, and while there '…some vegetables and a raft of matter' were taken aboard. Although no other records of ethnographic objects collected in Samoa by the *Stieglitz* have been found, it has been suggested that the Salem figure could have been in this 'raft of matter'.[10]

Interesting features of the figure include a typically notched Samoan base plate and the use of red pigment about the head and black pigment around the ears. A bird-shaped figurehead in the Linden Museum, Stuttgart, Germany[11] has also been documented as painted in this way. Despite these clues there is still some doubt over the Salem figure's origin, with one suggestion being that the figure, likely to have been made after initial European contact, reflects the influence of a 'culture contact' situation.[12] So it is possible that a sailor, Pacific islander or European, may have made it after seeing similar pieces elsewhere and to pass the time at sea.

Without a larger sample of well-documented pieces we can only speculate on the explanations and stories offered in connection with these two carved human figures. The two have very little in common stylistically and are anomalies in terms of what is known about Samoan material culture at that point in time. Both predate the use of the carved figureheads associated with taumualua canoes, but Neich suggests that the British Museum figure may have been cut from an earlier type of canoe such as an 'alia or amatasi. As canoes of this type were likely to belong to a chief, the figure would have been placed with his body after his death. This suggestion makes sense, although the evidence for a connection between the British Museum figure and canoes remains tenuous and is based solely on the references to a double canoe made in Wilson's account. Neich goes on to suggest that the use of carved human figureheads in this period may have transferred to taumualua several years later, and that once that style of canoe had become established, the carving and use of animal and bird figureheads may have become more common.[13]

Apart from these speculations, the research into the origins and use of the two carved human figures gives us small but valuable glimpses into change in Samoa. In regard to the circumstances surrounding the collection of the British Museum figure, Davidson notes that:

They provide only the most tantalising glimpse of the concepts involved…[and] The fact that the image was allegedly lying down in disgrace in 1836 and was obtained by Heath shortly thereafter is one of many indications of the decline of the Samoan religious system at the very beginning of the missionary period.

So in the case of the British Museum figure we have perhaps a last portable relic from an era of indigenous religion that was about to undergo great change. Similarly, the Salem figure is also a marker of change. As a likely manifestation of culture contact, it is perhaps an early example of carved figurative art from a period that was to extend from the 1830s to the end of the 19th century and during which carved animal figureheads became well established as decorative fixtures on the prows of canoes.[14] It was a period characterised by great diversity, not only in carving and woodwork, but also in the arts in general.

CARVED ANIMAL FIGUREHEADS

Just as examples of human figurative sculpture from Samoa are rare, so too are examples of animal figurative sculpture, although from the mid to late 19th century they were quite common. For a full discussion of 19th century Samoan figurative carvings and canoes Roger Neich's short but detailed studies should be consulted.[15] Carved figureheads were made in the form of human figures, dogs, birds and other animals and decorated the prows of a type of 19th century canoe called taumualua. They were believed to be 'the armorial bearing of the village to which the canoe belonged' and were fixed to the bow usually with some form of white shell adornment.[16] Only two full-size examples of these figureheads seem to have been collected (and today survive in museum collections) despite being encountered quite frequently by 19th century visitors to Samoa. A possible reason for this is at the time they would probably have been considered 'non traditional' and therefore not worthy of preservation.[17]

One of these surviving figureheads is in the collection of the Linden Museum in Stuttgart, Germany. Taking the shape of a roosting bird, its form is very stylised and it is painted in plain colours. Interestingly, its eyes are represented by two small blue glass beads and a type of commercial paint has been used to decorate the body. From its tail feathers three diamond-shaped pieces of wood are suspended by string. In the underbody is a square-shaped attachment to facilitate its attachment to a canoe. When it was collected by Augustin Kramer from a taumualua from Falefa[18] the figurehead was initially identified as being a fua'o. But further investigations by Neich suggest that it is more likely a manuali'i or purple swamp hen (*Porphyrio porphyrio*).

Fig. 7.3 Figurehead for taumualua (two-bowed va'a). Collected by Augustin Kramer circa 1900. (Linden Museum, Stuttgart)

Another example of a full-size taumualua figurehead can be found in the Ubersee Museum in Bremen, Germany, and was collected in Apia by Admiral Wilhelm Souchon during his service there in 1888-89. Apparently sawn off a taumualua, it is almost abstract in form and made from a four-branched tree trunk which has been very roughly carved. Neich had an opportunity to view the figure and wrote the following description:

…the prow features a rudimentary animal head facing forward along the central axis of the canoe, two more rudimentary animal heads facing left and right from the central axis, and an upright human head facing back into the canoe along the central axis. The eyes of each head are roughly indicated by small drill holes. All of these heads are roughly carved with big deep metal tool cuts left showing on the unpainted prow. Around the neck of the human head, several large white ovulum shells (Samoan pule) are attached by Samoan-made cords.[19]

Carved animals have also appeared in models of taumualua canoes and as wood relief carvings as documented in a photograph of an ʻalia taken by Thomas Andrew at the turn of the century (Fig. 3.1).

In the area of tourist art, carved wooden figures have re-emerged in the 20th century in several different forms and display a range of local and overseas influences. An interesting local development has been the production of the now familiar figures of tulafale and taupou. These appeared in the late 1960s and were the result of an effort to broaden the range of wooden articles available for sale to tourists. Samoan carver Sven Ordquist, who was working in Apia at the time, trained a small group of carvers to make these, and other items such as storyboards, out of wood. Books and magazines have been another source of inspiration for carvers, with pseudo Marquesan tiki and Hawaiʻian-style images becoming popular and sold as ʻauthentic' Samoan carving from at least the 1960s.[20] Many items of this kind continue to be made in the present day.

Fig. 7.4 Tanoa faiʻava (kava bowl). Collected by Reverend J. Collier circa 1912 and presented to the museum by Mrs Tighe. (Museum of New Zealand, Te Papa Tongarewa, Ref. No: FE002624)

WOODEN CONTAINERS

Samoan woodworking specialists also made bowls and containers for everyday domestic and ceremonial use. In the 1920s wooden bowls were known as 'umete and tanoa and were used for food and kava preparation respectively. But even then this distinction in terms was beginning to disappear, and today both types of bowl are commonly known as tanoa. However, in formal meetings and at other ceremonial functions, a kava bowl will still be distinguished by referring to it as a tanoa fai'ava (bowl for making kava).[21]

In the late 1920s 'umete were made in a range of sizes, but the main types were either elliptical or round in shape, with a third type comprising an acutely elliptical bowl with grooved and spouted ends for pouring liquids.[22] Today, despite being primarily made for the tourist trade, 'umete are still found in some Samoan households and are generally used to prepare soft foods such as taufolo[23] and fa'ausi.[24]

To make an 'umete the woodworker selects a solid piece of timber, which he then hews into the approximate dimensions of the bowl he requires. This gives him the basic shape and allows him to judge precisely where the 'umete cavity should be. The inside of the 'umete is removed carefully and precisely, the artist creating a thin, flat rim with sides that gradually thicken, until the desired depth is reached. Once finished the 'umete is soaked in water. This helps to season the wood and prevents it from splitting. In the past this was done in local waterholes. Te Rangi Hiroa describes large numbers of 'umete at Asau in Savai'i, lying at the bottom of pools used for bathing.[25]

Fig. 7.5 Tanoa fai'ava (kava bowl). Collected by W.J. Crowther, 1936. (Museum of New Zealand, Te Papa Tongarewa, Ref. No: FE007830)

Tanoa fai'ava are made in much the same way as 'umete, and although round or elliptical in shape they are made with four or more legs. Their manufacture was a specialised task and certain villages had a reputation for producing quality work. For example, in the late 1890s the villages of Falealupo, Asau and Tufutafoe produced artists recognised for their skills in making kava bowls.[26] Today the villages of Falealupo, Fagaloa Bay and Uafato are known for making these items.

Tanoa fai'ava are used in the preparation and serving of a beverage made from the roots of the kava plant, which has been crushed into a coarse powder and mixed with water. The preparation and serving of 'ava is an art form in itself and so the significance of the tanoa fai'ava goes well beyond its shape and form. Its role on formal occasions and the discussions and relationships it mediates are just as important as any visual aesthetic qualities implicit in its design.

In the early 1980s a new development was noted in kava bowl design. In contrast to the kava bowls described by Te Rangi Hiroa in the late 1920s, there had been a change from cylindrical legs to flat, wide legs following the circumferential curve of the bowl. These legs were variously elaborated with notches, grooves and stepped shoulders.[27] This change from cylindrical legs to flat and wide legs may have been made to shorten production time and perhaps to strengthen the legs, which in their cylindrical form are very prone to breaking.

The oldest forms of tanoa fai'ava have four legs and are generally distinguished from Fijian and Tongan kava bowls by the flat horizontal rim between the inner and outer surfaces of the bowl. Most tanoa fai'ava seen today have many legs, either round or square and usually set very close together. These have subsequently become the

Fig. 7.6 Kava bowl. (Museum of New Zealand, Te Papa Tongarewa, Ref No: FE010512)

distinguishing characteristic of a Samoan bowl, although it can also still be identified by a flat horizontal rim. In the late 1920s when Te Rangi Hiroa questioned Samoans about the number of legs on tanoa fai'ava, they considered this style of bowl as very modern. It seems that bowls with many legs were made for tourists who were charged so much per leg.[28] Over time they became the standard type of bowl available and were used by locals as much as they were purchased by visitors.

Although wooden bowls have been largely replaced by inexpensive and durable enamel and plastic containers, wooden tanoa fai'ava and 'umete are still made today. Sold mostly to visiting tourists they are the same shape as their earlier predecessors, but in some cases are extensively decorated with incised or engraved lines and patterns. Often they are totally blackened, revealing the incised elements that are free of colour in contrast. The few examples of 'umete seen in villages in the 1990s were undecorated. But the use of decoration is not an altogether new practice. There are examples of bowls from the early 20th century decorated in the same way, but the incisions are in-filled with white and powdery coral lime. Today tanoa come in a range of sizes, big enough to serve large formal gatherings and just small enough to be portable and popular with the tourist.

WEAPONS

Some of the same patterns that are applied to the present day tanoa and 'umete were also once applied to Samoan weapons. Triangles and incised decorative elements are found on many clubs and weapons, although not to the same extent as those from Fiji and Tonga. In Samoa the few incised elements are often inlaid with coral lime.

Samoans engaged in spear throwing and club fighting contests but weapons were most often used in battle. In the 19th century most battles were small-scale skirmishes or ambushes, but fighting could be vicious and the injuries, if not fatal, very serious. Battles were fought over major chiefly titles and to settle disputes or avenge insults. It has been noted that firearms were not widely used in this period and no one side had a monopoly on them.[29] Clubs seem to have had some importance as heirlooms and were passed down, and in some cases even named.[30] The family war club was known as the 'anava, and it would be brandished on the malae of the village when a troop of warriors was setting out to march. One such club called Faitasi was owned by Ama ia Matoto of Lotofaga in Safata. It can be seen in a photograph in *The Samoan Islands, Volume 1*, page 307 by Augustin Kramer.

All clubs were cut from solid pieces of wood, with hardwoods such as pau and toa being preferred. The smooth surface was acquired by rubbing with pieces of nullipore. It was then polished using a smooth piece of stone or shell. If patterns were to be made, a shark tooth was used to make incisions in the wood.

Surface decoration on Samoan clubs seems to have been quite restricted in comparison to examples from Tonga where human figures, fish, birds and dogs were common. The standard decorative motif on Samoan clubs was the fa'amuli'ali'ao, a small triangle which was representative of the trochus shell. Small incised squares, wavy lines and chevrons were also used.

A number of different types of club are recorded as being made in Samoa. But

Fig. 7.7 Selected examples of wooden clubs. Left to right: fa'alaufa'i, povai, uatogi, anave (dance club), nifo'oti (wooden blade with inlay), nifo'oti (metal blade). Below: fa'alautalinga, (Museum of New Zealand, Te Papa Tongarewa)

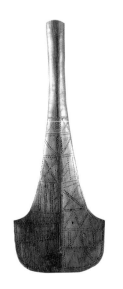

even in 1927 Te Rangi Hiroa considered that most of the old clubs had left Samoa for private and museum collections.[31] There are believed to have been six basic club forms. These could have numerous slight variations depending on who made them. Curves, lengths and decorations were executed at the discretion of the artist, with some artists specialising in decorating only. But amongst this variation several distinguishable club types can be identified.

Based on the detailed work of Te Rangi Hiroa and William Churchill the following summary of the different types of Samoan club can be made. Several are still made today, but in modified forms for the tourist market.

The povai was a long slender club with a domed end. It could be either round in section or hexagonal. Examples of this club often have decorative bands of carved motifs spaced at intervals along its length. It is a type of club also commonly found in Tonga and Fiji.

The fa'aaufala was a short mace-like club, covered in numerous stud-like projections or spikes. Most were very short but some were long enough to be two-handed.

The uatogi was a club made in the shape of a coconut stalk or midrib. It was made so the wide end formed a blade, which sometimes had raised ribs carved into it, to help strengthen it. The technique of carving these ribs gives the weapon its name, although in some texts it is called lapalapa, after the midrib of the coconut tree. There were many variations of this club and Te Rangi Hiroa depicts eight of them.

The talavalu was characterised by the eight spikes, four either side, that projected from its narrow blade. Its top end was wide and concave and formed a distinctive crutch-like shape.

The fa'alaufa'i, as its name suggests, was structured on the shape of the banana leaf. The pointed end and shoulders of the blade formed its leaf-like attributes. The many teeth or nicks set close together along either side of the blade set this weapon apart from the talavalu where the same projections were further apart.

'Amu'amu is the name given to clubs said to be paddle shaped. A feature of most 'amu'amu was cross-ribbing running across the width of the club, which gave the flat paddle blade extra strength. This style of club was also made in Tonga and Fiji.

The fa'alautalinga was shaped like two ears placed close together. These clubs appear to have always been decorated across the blades and were made with slight variations in shape. Depending on its length, the fa'alautalinga could be either a single or two-handed weapon. Small triangle motifs often decorated the surface and in some examples coral lime filled the incision.

The nifo'oti was a wooden club characterised by long teeth along one side and a single curved hook projecting at the end of the other. Possibly modelled on the blubber knife of English and American whalers, a mid to late 19th century Samoan version was made from steel and proved a popular weapon in the Samoan civil wars. In 1927 Te Rangi Hiroa considered the wooden nifo'oti a modern development most likely made for show and ceremonial purposes. However, in the Peabody Museum in Salem, there is an example of a wooden nifo'oti given to the museum in 1821, very early in terms of European contact with Samoa, but perhaps late enough to have been influenced by the blubber knives of the whalers.[32]

Another club called 'olo is described by Te Rangi Hiroa as being a throwing club, and is very similar in style to the Fijian throwing clubs known as i ula.

One of the points of difference between Samoan clubs from the 19th century and those of the present day is the restrained use of carved or inlaid decoration. But given what we know about other forms of Samoan figurative carving and its rarity, this is not surprising. Carved figurative decoration is common in Tongan clubs and to a lesser extent in Fijian clubs. It is only in the late 20th century that it has appeared as a dominant feature of Samoan clubs made for the tourist art market.

There is scope for further research in regard to the clubs and weapons of Samoa. The connections and shared styles between the nearby archipelagos of Tonga and Fiji could to some extent be revealed through a study of the various club forms and decorations. A comprehensive study of Fijian weaponry has been made by Fergus Clunie in his book *Fijian Weapons and Warfare*,[33] but there is no comparable study for Samoa or Tonga. Some general stylistic features have been identified between the different island groups, but remain unverified due to the unclear provenance of many weapons in museums and private collections.

SPEARS

Known as tao, spears were made in one piece from either pau wood or mature coconut wood. They ranged in length from 1.8 metres to over three metres. Some were pointed at one end, while others had single rows of barbs cut into them. One particular type had multiple barbs consisting of three points projecting from the same base cut into the spear shaft. These spears were termed tala o le lo (the spine of the lo fish), and they were the most prized, due to the amount of work that was invested in making them.

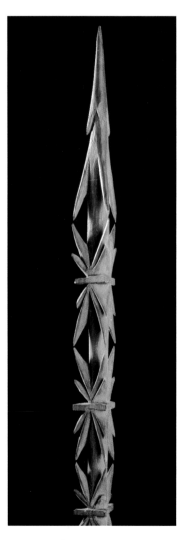

Fig. 7.8 Tao (spear). (Museum of New Zealand, Te Papa Tongarewa, Ref. No: FE005866)

OTHER WOODEN OBJECTS

Other wooden objects of note made in former times include three-legged stools and fans. The pigeon-snaring stool is another anomaly in Samoan material culture, as the 19th century Samoan household generally did not have stools or chairs of any description. The stool consisted of a dubbed-out seat with three legs, stabilised with crossbars. The legs were lashed with coconut fibre cord to lugs projecting from the underside of the seat. Like the sport for which it was used, the stool is no longer found in Samoa. But an early reference to stools, not directly related to pigeon snaring, comes from the missionary Reverend J.B. Stair who resided in Samoa between 1838 and 1845. He noted the use of three-legged stools in a description of events at an assembly in the village of Leulumoega in the early 19th century:

In A'ana the nine speakers of Leulumoega were privileged to sit on seats or three legged stools, which were placed at a little distance in front of their party, while the rest of the assembly, high and low, sat cross-legged upon the turf. [34]

Stair doesn't elaborate on the use of the stools except to say that their use in this way was unusual.

More common was the sport of pigeon hunting, where the stool was used in the faleseu (pigeon-netting house). Built on large stone tia'ave deep in the forest and usually on a ridge-line, these temporary shelters made from vines were like hides where the pigeon catcher could sit and await his prey. Decoy pigeons attached to cords and trained to land on a hand-held perch were used by the catcher to attract wild pigeons out of the trees. The stool placed in the faleseu would allow the pigeon catcher to stand up quickly, sweeping his net to catch the wild pigeons flying within range of his camouflaged hide.

Fig. 7.9 Nofoaga seu lupe (pigeon netting stool). Collected early 1900s. (Museum of New Zealand, Te Papa Tongarewa, Ref. No: FE005617)

Fig. 7.10 Ili pau (wooden fans). (Museum für Völkerkunde zu Leipzig. Neg Oc Obj 2347. Photographer Ingrid Hanse)

Up until the early 20th century, fans, as described in Chapter 14, Adornments, were also made from wood, and no doubt utilised the greater control offered by introduced metal tools in their construction. Made from a single thin wafer of timber with a thick handle, shapes and patterns were cut through the body of the fan forming an ornamental openwork body. Long, slender combs with the same delicate open patterning, cut from the solid wood were also made.

CONTEMPORARY SCULPTURE AND MIXED MEDIA

There are many situations in Samoa today where skills with the adze can be important for everyday living. But beyond the village context and the historic and more functional uses of stone and wood, new creativity continues to emerge. Contemporary Samoan artists continue to experiment and push the boundaries of three-dimensional work using sound, space and light as well as a range of mixed media. The following artists demonstrate the range of styles, materials and expressions that are part of the contemporary Samoan artist's world.

JOHN IOANE

John Ioane works in mixed media as well as sound, light, video and performance. Trained at Elam School of Fine Arts in New Zealand and formerly an art teacher, until recently John was mostly known for his paintings. A return to postgraduate study, however, resulted in new work bringing together sculpture, mixed media, sound, video and light. These installations incorporate what he describes as 'an ancient concept of dialogue between a number of different disciplines into one space and time...trying to a create space for magic to happen'. A major work, *Fale Sa* (Sacred space) (1999), captures some of this magic as well as highlighting some of the possibilities for contemporary Samoan installation art. *Fale Sa* was the result of a process of recovery from an upheaval in John's personal life. In a sense it was a therapeutic exercise. 'I was after some form of celestial affirmation that I was not fucked up, and *Fale Sa* was that for me ... a sacred space where magic occurs of itself.'[35] *Fale Sa* was a large installation incorporating several spaces of rippled light, looming carved forms and dozens of cowrie shells carved in wood. Art historian Caroline Vercoe suggested that the work '...encourages the viewer to react on more emotive levels, using as a point of departure the idea of *Fale Sa* as both a sacred place and a more internalised site of contemplation and redress'.[36] A more accessible side of John's work can be seen in his clever contribution to a group exhibition called *Romantic Notions* (2000) where he looked to demystify some of the romantic notions of the Pacific. Work such as *Easylei.com.Pi* (1999) faced up to Edwardian perceptions of the Pacific that still linger and provided a humorous but critical commentary. John sees the confronting of romantic or stereotypical notions of Pacific-ness or Samoan-ness as an ongoing challenge in his work:

To be Samoan is to be human, my flesh belongs to a certain society of the world ... I am proud of the cultural platform to which I was born, but I don't want to limit myself to that platform. It's a springboard, and I evolve with the spirit of tradition and certain ideas of Samoan-ness.[37]

Fig. 7.11 *Fale Sa*, John Ioane, 1999. Mixed media. (Auckland Art Gallery Toi o Tamaki)

Fig. 7.12 *Asiasi II*, Michel Tuffery, 2000. Made from fish tins and recycled copper. (Museum of New Zealand, Te Papa Tongawera, Ref. No. 2001-0032-1)

Fig. 7.13 (above) *Corned Beef 2000 (Pisupo Lua Afe)*, Michael Tuffery, 1994. Made from tin cans and rivets. (Museum of New Zealand, Te Papa Tongawera, Ref. No. FE010516.)

Fig. 7.14 *Matai*, Iosefa Leo Tupuana'i, 1992. Made from Hinuera stone. Collection of artist. (Norman Heke)

MICHEL TUFFERY

Michel Tuffery is a New Zealand-based artist of Samoan, Rarotongan and Tahitian heritage and has worked for many years in printmaking and drawing. But he has also had great success with his sculpture and performance art. Over the years his work has touched upon many themes and issues central to the environment and people of the Pacific, including religion, mythology, pollution and recycling, as well as the customs and changing nature of life in the Pacific region. Creatures such as fish, turtles, lizards, dogs and cattle all find a place in Michel's unique interpretations of the natural world and how man interacts with it. He is probably most well known for his corned beef tin steers, two of which were robotic and used in dynamic performance pieces both in New Zealand and overseas. These sculptures comment on the impact of global trade and the effect that colonial economies have had on Pacific island cultures by showing how an imported commodity has become an integral part of the Polynesian customs of feasting and gift giving.[38] His sculptural work has also seen him examine the forms and colours of the 'upeti – the carved printing board made by men and used by women artists for decorating siapo. In these works Michel created collages of wood images, interwoven and layered in three dimensions, giving a new life and meaning to worn pattern boards.

IOSEFA ILIAIA LEO TUPUANA'I

Iosefa Iliaia Leo Tupuana'i was born in the village of Letogo in the district of Vaimauga, Apia and now lives and works with his wife and family in Blenheim, New Zealand. Iosefa is self-taught and works primarily with Mount Somers limestone because of its beautiful, clean finish, which, combined with the soft and rounded lines of his craftsmanship, offers a range of subtle shades and curves. Some of his most recent work has been in wood, and he has also sculpted in marble. The themes and subjects of Iosefa's sculptures generally reflect aspects of fa'asamoa: its history, legends and relationships, as well as stories from the Bible. More recently, however, he has made observations on Pacific life, people's attitudes and the way they interact and hold themselves. From the sombre countenance of a matai to the loving embrace of a father and son, it is the faces and hands of the figures that capture the gentle and expressive nature of the people and relationships he figures.

JOHNNY PENISULA

Johnny Penisula painted his first mural in a church in Fatuvalu, Savai'i when he was 13 years old. It was the beginning of a lifelong interest and dedication to the arts that has seen him develop his own skills and talents and pass them on to a new generation. He remembers having his 21st birthday on the banana boat when he travelled to New Zealand in 1962 to realise his dream of attending art school. But once he found a job it was 'blow the art school, I'll be a millionaire in a few years!' Despite this initial distraction the creative urge stayed with him, and he eventually achieved his long sought-after art qualification by correspondence. While he focused for a time on painting, he remembers that he 'learnt to hold the chisel and the adze before the paintbrush' so it has been in sculpture and carving where his strength and reputation have developed. His first exhibition was in Bluff in 1974 and since then he has worked full-time as an artist, probably one of the first Samoans in New Zealand to do so. His most recent work has been in hard stone (argillite) but he has also worked in soft stone, wood, steel and fibreglass. It ranges in scale from earrings and pendants, to sculptures up to a tonne in weight. The themes in his work have focused mainly on Samoan legends and culture. Johnny currently tutors carving and sculpture in Invercargill, New Zealand.

Fig. 7.15 *Matai*, Johnny Penisula, 1994. Made from wood and stone. Collection of artist. (Photo courtesy of artist)

JEWEL CASTRO

Jewel Castro is a multimedia installation artist who lives and works in the United States. Born in Chicago, Illinois, Jewel spent the first year of her life in American Samoa, but was raised in San Diego, California in the United States. Her Samoan heritage links her to the village of Fitiuta, where her grandparents originally migrated from, but she also has strong Danish and Irish connections through her father. She has many years experience as an illustrator and fine artist and completed postgraduate training at University of California at San Diego. Her work is influenced by the Samoan art forms of weaving and siapo, but also often features the colours of Mexican muralists and of Chicano and Native American art. Jewel filters these influences through sculpture, sound and lights to make all-encompassing storytelling installations. The installations are layered environments that speak of Samoan identity and history. For Jewel they capture

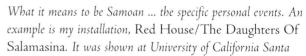

Fig. 7.16 *Red House/The Daughters of Salamasina*, Jewel Castro, 2000. Mixed media. View of back section of the installation. (Photo courtesy of artist)

What it means to be Samoan ... the specific personal events. An example is my installation, Red House/The Daughters Of Salamasina. *It was shown at University of California Santa Cruz in February 2000 and at the ARC Gallery, Chicago later that same year. It was a multimedia installation inspired by the history and traditions of Samoan women, and their persistent presence in contemporary Samoan culture.*

SVEN ORDQUIST

Sven Ordquist is a Tutuila-based artist who works in a variety of materials but is probably most well known for his woodcarving and reliefs. For many years he has passed on his artistic skills as well as his love for Samoan history and culture. Here he talks a little about his lifelong interest in art and some of his recent work.

Originally I am from Samoa, I was born in Tifitoala, Safata, but I migrated to American Samoa in 1975. My father is Swedish, his name is Sven Orquist, and of course my mother is Samoan. I remember as a young boy that the beaches near Safata were so beautiful and the sand so firm and that there used to be big stretches of sand and I used to love drawing on the sand, I think my

Fig. 7.17 Sculpture of Christ, Catholic Cathedral, Pago Pago, American Samoa, Sven Ordquist (Sean Shadbolt)

interest in art started way back then. Even when I was in elementary school I was already doing illustrations for the teachers. And I used to get lunch by drawing things for the other students. Those were the days of the cowboys, and when a movie came out everyone wanted a drawing of it so I would do this, I would draw something and pass it around and soon everyone would want something for themselves. So I would do it for a sandwich.

An early influence was my dad, he was a very able gentleman and he could create things from nothing. He was very creative and I think I inherited something from him. I was also inspired by one of my brothers, John. Like my father he was a jack-of-all-trades. He could whittle things in wood and he could paint and sew… heck, I didn't know what he couldn't do! I remember he taught me to draw. When he wanted to punish me he would take a piece of stick and he would whittle something and give it to one of my friends. That's how he used to punish me. So one day I decided that I was going to show him that I too could carve. So I started carving my mum's soaps and she didn't mind, because it provided good suds when you threw the chips into the bucket. From there I went on to pieces of wood; I found a pocket knife and joined the Scouts and then it continued there, carving woggles and totem stuff.

When I was about 20 or 21, I was running workshops in Apia. I introduced and taught my students to carve the little tulafale and taupou. It was something new. I taught them to add to the kava bowls and the pates and the little canoes that were flooding the market then, they needed something new that was also Samoan. I introduced these in the early 1960s through my work in Togafu'afu'a, the Catholic settlement in Apia. One of the other things we made was storyboards, I showed them how to carve relief, we had Samoan stories and legends, tropical scenery and pictures of canoes. They were not exactly like the Micronesian storyboards, they were not as busy, but they told a story.

Those were bad times, just before the 1966 hurricane that destroyed most of the plantations and crops, with many people getting laid off their jobs. So these old boys having nothing to do would stroll over to my little fale at Togafu'afu'a and they would sit down and watch us carve. The advantage in this for me was they would sit around the kava bowl and they would start talking about culture, traditions, the arts. They had nothing else to do so all these things would start to come out. Through these conversations I came to appreciate my mother's culture, that of Samoa. I learnt how rich our culture and traditions were.

After these encounters with the matai at my workshop I didn't want to be or do anything

else but Samoan work. So everything I do is Samoan, and through this association with the older folks I have come to learn a lot more of the history attached to other artifacts. After all art is the signature of the nation.

My reliefs are mostly of Samoan legends and things connected to the culture. I also designed some stained glass windows; they were made by a guy in Chicago for the Holy Family Cathedral in Pago Pago. I also made a lot of the other artwork inside. The stations of the cross, for example, are depicted with Samoan characters. I have the Holy Family sitting under the shadow of the cross, and Jesus is not drinking from a chalice, instead he is holding a kava cup. His mother is a Samoan woman, his father, St Joseph, is a Samoan man. I often take tours down there and I explain the artworks. It's not the conventional stuff, it's a little different. I have a strong conviction that Christian religion is Samoan, by that I mean it has matured in Samoa, God is Samoan as much as he is English, American, German, French or Chinese. I find it very hard to make copies of the other stuff [religious art] so I am a little controversial on that side. Some people don't appreciate my work very much, they are so convinced that Christ should look this way and Mary should look this way, and here I am coming up with something different.

Fig. 7.18 Sven Ordquist at work. (F. Sutter, courtesy of University of Hawai'i Press)

CHAPTER 7

1. R. Neich, 'Samoan figurative carvings and taumualua canoes - A further note', *Journal of the Polynesian Society* vol. 100 (1991), p. 327
2. Te Rangi Hiroa (Peter Buck) (1935), 'Material representatives of Tongan and Samoan gods' in Fraser, D. (ed), *The Many Faces of Primitive Art, A Critical Anthology* (New Jersey: Prentice Hall, 1996), pp. 110-111
3. J. Davidson, 'The wooden image from Samoa in the British Museum: A note on its context', *The Journal of the Polynesian Society* vol. 84 (1975), pp. 352-355
4. Davidson, 'The wooden image from Samoa', on p. 352 cites Buck [Te Rangi Hiroa] 1935: 93-5; Barrow 1956m 1972: 77 and Archey 1974: 40 and also notes that Buck wrongly stated that the image was presented to Malietoa and that this error was later repeated by Barrow.
5. Davidson, 'The wooden image from Samoa', p. 354
6. Buzacott MS (1836-37); cited in Davidson, 'The wooden image from Samoa', p. 353
7. Wilson M.S. (1836), entry dated October 17, cited in Davidson, 'The wooden image from Samoa', p. 353
8. S.D. Scott, 'A human image from Samoa - some observations' *Journal of the Polynesian Society* vol. 91 (1982), p. 591
9. R. Neich, 'Samoan figurative carvings and Samoan canoes' *Journal of the Polynesian Society* vol. 93 (1984), p. 193
10. Scott, 'A human image from Samoa', p. 591
11. Neich, 'Samoan figurative carvings and taumualua canoes', p. 327
12. K.E. Larsson, 'Fijian Studies' *Etnologiska Studier* vol. 25 (Goteborg: Etnografiska Museet, 1960), p. 109
13. Neich, 'Samoan figurative carvings and Samoan canoes', p. 196
14. Neich, 'Samoan figurative carvings and taumualua canoes', p. 327
15. Neich, 'Samoan figurative carvings and Samoan canoes', p. 591
16. T.H. Hood, *Notes of a Cruise in H.M.S. Fawn in the Western Pacific in the year 1862* (Edinburgh: Edmonston & Douglas, 1863), p. 47
17. Neich, 'Samoan figurative carvings and taumualua canoes', p. 317
18. A. Kramer, *The Samoan Islands* vol. 2 (Auckland: Polynesian Press, 1995), p. 304
19. Neich, 'Samoan figurative carvings and taumualua canoes', p. 322
20. P.J.C. Dark, 'Tomorrow's heritage is today's art and yesteryear's identity', in Hanson, A. and Hanson, L. (eds), *Art and Identity in Oceania* (Australia: Crawford House Press, 1990)
21. Neich, 'Material culture of Western Samoa' *National Museum of New Zealand* Bulletin 23 (1985), p. 57
22. Te Rangi Hiroa (Peter Buck), 'Samoan Material Culture' *Bernice P. Bishop Museum* Bulletin 75 (Hawai'i: 1930), p. 587
23. Taufolo is a dish made with breadfruit paste and coconut sauce.
24. Fa'ausi is a dish consisting of cooked grated taro cut into cubes and served with warm coconut cream.
25. Te Rangi Hiroa, 'Samoan Material Culture', p. 150
26. Friedlander, quote in Kramer, *The Samoan Islands* vol. 2, p. 244

27. Neich, 'Material culture of Western Samoa', p. 587
28. Te Rangi Hiroa, 'Samoan Material Culture', p. 57
29. K.R. Howe, *Where the Waves Fall* (Sydney: George Allen & Unwin, 1984), p. 245
30. Kramer, *The Samoan Islands* vol. 2, p. 256
31. Te Rangi Hiroa, 'Samoan Material Culture', p. 587
32. Peabody Essex Museum, Salem Cat no: 7121A12/2 Donor: B.V Johnson. Date received 1821.
33. F. Clunie, 'Fijian weapons and warfare', *Bulletin of the Fiji Museum* No. 2 (Suva: 1977)
34. J.B. Stair, *Old Samoa; or flotsam and jetsam from the Pacific Ocean* (Papakura: Southern Reprints, 1983, First published in 1897), p. 87
35. Interview with author, (21 May 2000)
36. C. Vercoe, *John Ioane Fale Sa* (Auckland: Auckland Art Gallery, Toi O Tamaki, 1999)
37. Interview with author, (21 May 2000)
38. Exhibition label, Museum of New Zealand Te Papa Tongarewa, (2000)

CHAPTER 8

TUFUGA TATATAU
THE MASTER TATTOOISTS

The art of tattooing is widespread throughout Polynesia, but it is in Samoa that the art form has remained strong, despite a period of missionary censure in some regions. In Samoa the process of tattooing is known as tatatau; tatau are the tattooed lines and motifs that appear on the body, and the tatau artist is known as tufuga tatatau.

Tatau has often been recognised as a necessary rite of passage for young men. After being tattooed, the young man is not only accepted as a full member of the 'aumaga (the association of young men), but is also allowed to serve the matai.[1] The tatau also symbolises ideas connected with the wrapping, sealing and defence of the body, as well as with decorating it and making it beautiful.[2] So it is seen as both a treasure and a stepping stone to manhood, something that garners respect for the wearer by speaking of his inner strength and resilience.

These values generally remain central to the process and ritual of tatatau today. But in migrant Samoan communities overseas, tatau has also become an identity marker, a way of signifying Samoan heritage and an important link to what can sometimes seem like a distant heritage and way of life. Tatau is such a strong image of Samoan identity that its symbols and motifs appear on clothing and apparel, and have been reinterpreted and re-presented by artists in new media and art forms.

In an account recorded in the 19th century, it is said that two sisters, Taema and Tilafaiga, who were Siamese twins, brought the first tattooing tools to Samoa. They acquired the tools and the instructions on how to use them from the tattooists Filelei and Tufou in Fiji. They were told to 'tattoo the women and not the men', and they sang this instruction over and over as they paddled their canoe to Samoa. On the way they saw a large and beautiful shell glistening in the waters below and they stopped singing in order to swim down and fetch it. On returning to the surface they tried to remember what they were singing and got the song mixed up. 'Tattoo the men and not the women' they sang, and this was the message they took on to Samoa.[3]

One of the earliest descriptions of what could be Samoan tatau comes from the journal of Jacob Roggeveen, a Dutch seafarer who in 1721-22 voyaged across the Pacific from Cape Horn to New Ireland. On 13 June 1722 his three ships sighted the easternmost islands of Samoa. The next day, as they passed by the islands of Olosega and Ofu, Roggeveen described the people sighted there:

The Indians of this first island are like the Paaschlanders in sturdiness and robustness of body,

Fig. 8.1 *Self-portrait with back of pe'a, Basque Road, Newton Gully, 1995.* (Photograph Greg Semu. Collection of Auckland City Art Gallery)

Fig. 8.2 *Self-portrait with front of pe'a, Basque Road, Newton Gully, 1995.* (Photograph Greg Semu. Collection of Auckland City Art Gallery)

also in painting themselves, but not so much and abundantly, as their colouring commences from the thighs downward to the legs. Furthermore we did not see anything as covering for their nakedness, except a girdle round the waist to which a lot of long broad leaves or rushes, or of another plant, was fastened.[4]

This glimpse of 'colouring … from the thighs downward to the legs' is probably the first written description of Samoan tatau.

Samoan men receive a heavy tatau from the waist down to the knee which is known as pe'a. It is made up of fine parallel line-work, areas of shade and a wide range of motifs and geometric patterns. The word pe'a refers both to the tatau and to the fruit-eating bat known as the flying fox. Untitled young men with the tatau are called soga'imiti and as such they responsible for serving and performing duties for the matai.

Women's tatau appears on the legs, starting at the knee and finishing at the top of the thigh. Sometimes the lower abdomen and right hand are also tattooed.[5] Called malu, women's tatau is less elaborate than the pe'a and its structure is less well defined. The malu perhaps takes its name from the malu motif itself, usually placed behind the knee, and one of the key motifs not seen on men.

Ethnologists have tended to make a strong distinction between the malu and the pe'a. Te Rangi Hiroa, for instance, pointed out that as well as being less elaborate and involving less ceremony 'the tattooing of a girl is often used as an opportunity for a student to try his prentice hand', although 'For the daughter of a high chief, … an expert artist would be requisitioned…'.[6] This may have been the case in the 1920s, but in the 1990s attitudes seem to have shifted and malu may now be more significant than ever before.

THE ARTIST

In the 19th century and into the early 20th century, artists who specialised in tatau belonged to a special guild which had two family branches, Su'a and Tulou'ena. The hereditary nature of the occupation has meant that descendants of these families still work today as tufuga tatatau, and the skills continue to be passed from generation to generation, father to son.

Tufuga tatatau have been much sought after. In the 1700s, certain classes of Tongan nobles travelled to Samoa specifically to be tattooed. Tufuga tatatau also visited Tonga or became part of the Tongan royal court. Some Samoans, known as matapule, became part of an intermediate class of ceremonial attendants who played important roles in the Tongan social system. Tongan commoners were forbidden to touch the royal person, yet these Samoan matapule 'could tattoo Tongan chiefs with immunity, cut their hair (the head of a Tongan chief is extremely tapu) and prepare their bodies for burial'.[7]

THE TOOLS

The tool kit of the tufuga tatatau is made up of several small hand-held tools and a selection of accessories. They are finely crafted for precision. The form and function of these tools have changed little over time, but conservation and hygiene concerns have led to changes in the materials from which they are made.

The basic tool kit comprises a set of 'au (tattoo combs), sausau (a short wooden rod or mallet), a mortar and pestle, and a palette for mixing the pigment.

The 'au are made of three components: a small bone comb (or chisel), a shell plate and a wooden handle to which they are attached. The comb, which perforates the skin and delivers the pigment, is made from small sections of boar's tusk. These sections have a row of very fine sharp teeth cut into them. In earlier times human bone is said to have been used to make these combs[8] and they were fixed with strands of coconut fibre to a turtle shell plate, which in turn was fastened to a thin stick which formed a handle. Today, this turtle shell is sometimes replaced with a piece of perspex or metal and the coconut fibre with nylon fishing line. Restrictions on turtle fishing in the islands have made it difficult (but not impossible) to acquire shell, and the use of nylon fishing line allows the tools to be boiled and sterilised between uses.

The 'au come in different widths, each designed to render a different quality of line. Some are used for filling in large dark areas while others are used to make very fine lines and dots. When not in use, the 'au are stored in a tube-like container called a tunuma. Made from the hollowed out trunk of the pandanus tree, it is open at both ends, with one end slightly wider than the other. Inside, a piece of barkcloth or rag holds the 'au in place, pointing inwards so the teeth of the combs are not damaged.

Tunuma that survive in museum collections today are generally plain and without applied decoration. However, an example made in 1996 has a different shape, carved elements and a decorative fibre binding around its top edge. The form of decoration is similar to that on a tunuma seen by Te Rangi Hiroa in Samoa in the 1920s, which he describes as being 'covered on its outer side by a close check plaiting of the single thick coconut husk fibres…'[9] At the time he considered this form of decoration to be unique. Another tunuma thought to be from Tonga, now in the British Museum, is similar to the Samoan tunuma in shape but intricately carved, possibly by a matapule in the Tongan court.

The sausau is used to strike the 'au so that pigment is deposited from the bone-toothed comb into the skin. The pigment is mixed in a half coconut shell and spread on a palette made from a freshly picked taro leaf stretched across the top of an empty tin can or half coconut shell. The tufuga draws the pigment from this palette before it is applied to the skin.

The pigment used to be made from the soot of the candlenut. In the 19th century this was collected in a small, specially constructed shed made from coconut leaves, woven closely together to stop wind penetrating. A small fireplace of three stones, two upright with one across the top, was built inside. Candlenuts strung on lengths of coconut midrib were burnt between these stones with the soot collecting on the underside of the top stone. This was scraped off when a sufficient amount had collected and stored in a coconut shell for later use.[10] When required the soot was ground up with a wooden pestle in a mortar made from a coconut shell; water was then added to produce a pigment of suitable consistency. Nowadays commercial inks are used and, not so long ago, a mixture of kerosene, soot and water was employed.[11]

Fig. 8.3 Tattooing set including tunuma (container) and 'au (tools). Made by Su'a Suluape Petelo, Faleasiu, Samoa. Acquired, Samoa, 1996. (Museum of New Zealand, Te Papa Tongarewa, Ref. No: FE010596)

THE PROCESS

There are several historical accounts of the tatatau process in Samoa at different times over the last 200 years. These describe the customs, stories and songs, and transformations in style and meaning that are part of the history of tatau. They also highlight the Samoan community's attitudes and responses to the growing influence of the outside world and new ideas within the community itself.

An early and detailed account comes from the missionary J.B. Stair, who lived in Samoa from 1838 to 1845. He stated that all males from the age of 12 upwards were tattooed and specifically describes the tattooing of a young chief. According to the custom, sons of the tulafale (orators) of the district were expected to receive their tatau at the same time as the young chief. They were expected to share in his sufferings. There was usually great interest in the occasion and a large shed was usually erected in the malae (village open space) where the tattooing would be performed. The young chief's family and people from all over the district would come to observe the proceedings and help to support the young men:

Fig. 8.4 Tattooing set that belonged to Su'a Sulu'ape Paulo I. Collection of Rotorua Museum of Art and History Te Whare Taonga Te Arawa. (Mark Adams)

...when all was ready the opening scene commenced, a kind of military parade or sham fight – which was followed by the first distribution of property to the operators [tufuga], this first instalment consisting of seven or eight good mats and twenty pieces of siapo.

The young chief then advanced, and, having laid himself down, the tattooers gathered around him, some holding his arms, others straining tightly the skin upon the small of his back, on which part the most skilful operator commenced the first part of the design. The instrument selected was dipped into the pigment provided, and then struck sharply into the skin by a blow from the stick, the instrument being shifted for each blow. The punctures were made rapidly, and the incisions placed as close as possible together, so that the marking might be dark, depth of colour and every part being well covered forming the chief beauty in tattooing...

The operation was continued as long as the patient was able to bear the pain, some continuing the operation for several days in succession, while others were compelled to allow days to intervene before the inflammation had subsided, so as to enable the operation to be resumed...[12]

The time taken to tattoo a young chief and his supporters could be anything from four to six weeks. During this period, friends, family and well-wishers staged evening entertainment in the form of dancing, sham fights and wrestling matches. When all the tattoos were complete, the tufuga would receive his final payment. The amount varied, but in Stair's account the payment is recorded as:

... consisting of a large number of valuable mats, sometimes to the extent of 600 or 700, and even at times to 1000, besides large quantities of native cloth.

The next day the families of the lads who had been the sharers of their chief's sufferings came to receive the payment allotted to them. Property was also distributed to those connected in any way with the family of the chief, and also in recognition of the large quantities of food they had supplied to the visitors during the ceremony.

The distribution of goods was followed by o le lulu'uge o le tatau (the sprinkling of the tattooed) a ritual in which coconut milk was sprinkled over all the men who had been tattooed, ritually cleansing them. Seventy-five years later, Te Rangi Hiroa's account of tattooing in the late 1920s describes a ceremony and process that had changed a great deal and were still in transition.

Fig. 8.5 Back view of man with pe'a photographed by Thomas Andrew, 1890s. (Alexander Turnbull Library, National Library of New Zealand, Te Puna Matauranga o Aotearoa. Ref. No: PA1-0-469-67)

At the time of Te Rangi Hiroa's research, tatatau was still practised on all the islands of the archipelago except Manu'a. This had been the case from at least the 1860s, when the matai of Manu'a had banned tatatau for religious reasons. Despite this ban, many of the young men of Manu'a travelled to Savai'i to get their tatau, although they were forbidden by law to return home.[13] By the 1890s it seems that this law had been revoked and young men were allowed to return to Manu'a on condition they paid a fine to the church.[14] Young Tongan men also came to Savai'i to receive tatau, the missionary influence being just as strong in the Tongan islands to the south.[15]

Te Rangi Hiroa's remarks also hint that some design innovations were emerging from the tufuga of the time. He makes reference to a younger school of tufuga tatatau and a move towards a breaking up of the dark areas of the pe'a with the introduction of more ornamentation. This took the form of fa'aila, window-like design elements that framed motifs and skin imperfections such as birthmarks. This was in contrast to the work of the older school, which preferred a greater proportion of plain bands and dark areas.[16]

The tattoo operation itself, as described by Te Rangi Hiroa, does not seem to have changed a great deal, but the festivities that accompanied it seem to be less elaborate. The sham fights and wrestling had been replaced by music: young men with modern musical instruments and 'melodies ... diffused from foreign music halls' would sit around their friend who was being tattooed, singing to distract him from his pain.[17]

TATAU SINCE 1980

Tim O'Meara gives an account of tattooing in the 1980s in his book *Samoan Planters*. He discusses why Samoan men get tattooed as well as the renewed interest in the tatau. Several reasons are given, including cultural and family pride, but for many young men the pain of tattooing itself is reason enough to receive the pe'a. In making this statement O'Meara offers the following remarks.

In addition to personal testimony, my evidence for this conclusion is that the young men eschew the use of any sort of pain killer or antibiotic during the tattooing even though these are readily available just down the road at the district clinic. The young men I talked to also had the devil-may-care pride in taking only minimal sanitary precautions during the operation. When one young man's tattoo became infected, he would not hear of taking an antibiotic, even though I offered to supply it privately so he would not have to approach the nurses at the clinic...

Men explicitly compare the pain of their tattooing (which they note, continues for days or even weeks) with women's pain during childbirth. As one man told me proudly, 'Women give birth, but men are tattooed'.[18]

During the time O'Meara was in Samoa he recalled seeing no men and only one woman over the age of 40 with a tattoo. He suggests that the resurgence of tatatau among young men probably began around the time of Samoan Independence in 1962.

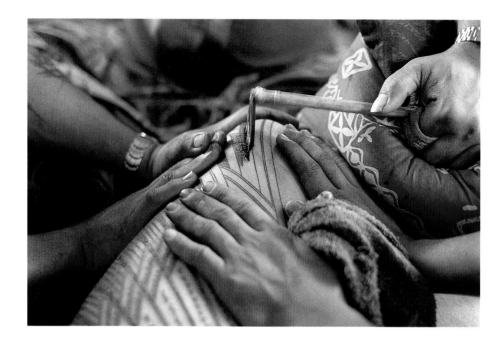

Fig. 8.6 Su'a Suluape Petelo at work on the pe'a of Robert Roebeck in Leone village, Apia, Upolu, 1999. (Craig Potton)

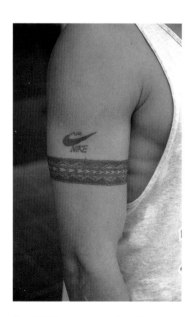

Fig. 8.7 Nike symbol and taulima, Apia, Upolu, 2000. (Sean Mallon)

At this time people were refused admittance into chiefly assemblies unless they were tattooed.[19] And more recently, in 1990, one village on Savai'i made it compulsory for all men to have the pe'a.[20]

This resurgence has continued. As Samoans have migrated to cities such as Honolulu, Los Angeles, Sydney and Auckland, so too have their culture and customs. Today, among migrant Samoan communities, the tatau is seen as a strong statement of Samoan heritage and identity.

Among the Samoan community in Auckland, New Zealand, tufuga tatatau have been at work since the 1970s. The steady demand in the 1990s led to the opening of two tatau parlours in the city. Little has changed in the tattooing process itself, but there has been a transformation in terms of who can receive a tattoo, where and how it is displayed and how it is paid for. Within the new social and geographic contexts that Samoans are increasingly finding themselves in, new ways of thinking about and interpreting the art form have emerged.

The taulima (armband) is probably the most popular form of tattoo among young Samoans in Auckland. The cost of a taulima starts at around $100. As it is both affordable and quickly rendered, it is worn by many young men and young women. Although it has not received much attention in the ethnographic literature, the taulima appears to have been popular from at least the 1890s. A group of 30 Samoan women visiting Berlin at this time were seen by F. von Luschan to be tattooed on the arms with rings and armlets.[21] In recent times taulima have been so popular in Apia among non-Samoans that they were nicknamed 'Peace Corps tatts' by one tufuga[22] because Peace Corps workers were eager customers of this form of tatau as a permanent souvenir of their time in Samoa. Taulima have also found popularity among part-Samoans, some of whom see it as a way of publicly identifying themselves as Samoan.

The tattooing of non-Samoans is not uncommon although it has been a controversial issue among the Samoan community in recent times. We know that Samoan tufuga tattooed Tongans, but there are also records indicating that tufuga tatatau (tatooing experts) tattooed palagi (Europeans) from the earliest days of contact. One such account is from E.J. Wakefield, who, in recounting his adventures travelling through New Zealand in the early 1840s, described two local jail-breakers he met in the countryside:

One of them, an American named McLeod, had assumed the name of Mickey Knight ... He spoke the native language very well, had with him a native wife from Thames, and had been tatued from the knees to the hips at the Navigator Islands [Samoa].[23]

Other foreigners said to have received the pe'a include the 1912 German Governor of Samoa Dr Erich E. Schultz and a number of his officials including the Collector of Customs.[24]

In New Zealand a well-known palagi recipient of the pe'a was painter Tony Fomison. He and a close Samoan friend, Fuimaono Tuiasau, received the pe'a together from Auckland-based tufuga Su'a Sulu'ape Paulo II in 1979-80. Fuimaono Tuiasau has said that Fomison's love of the art of tattooing and the challenge of enduring the painful process itself were key motivations for his seeking of the pe'a.[25]

There is concern among some Samoan elders about the pe'a being worn by non-Samoans, as they feel an ancient custom and art form will be cheapened, misused or lost. Tufuga tatatau Su'a Sulu'ape Paulo II did not share this concern. He saw the tatau as something the wearer cannot exchange or sell, because it is with them for life and in order to receive the pe'a the recipient must have some respect for its history, values and aesthetic. Su'a Sulu'ape Paulo II therefore had no problem taking his art to the world and sharing it with other tattooing enthusiasts.

Whereas in the past the work of the Samoan tufuga tatatau took them to the villages of Samoa and the courts of the Tongan monarchy, today the tufuga has a more international clientele. It is not unusual for tufuga tatatau to be flying to clients and tattoo conventions in cities such as Madrid, Miami and Amsterdam. Overseas clients also come to visit tufuga both in New Zealand and Samoa, and not just for the pe'a. In the 1980s, Lesa Li'o of Siumu tattooed Ioteve Tuhipuha Puhetini from Rurutu of the Austral Islands.[26] After studying drawings of old Marquesan tattoo designs, the tufuga took six weeks to reconstruct a Marquesan tattoo design on Ioteve which started at his neck and shoulders and extended down the length of his body to his ankles. It was a gesture that had a historical precedent and contributed to the renewed interest in East Polynesian tattoo.

Despite the new directions that tatau has taken, the pe'a retains value among the New Zealand-based Samoan community. There is still a role and place for the soga'imiti, and their service and skills remain a central part of the fono.

However, the importance and significance of the malu is constantly being renegotiated. This is in contrast to earlier ethnographic accounts, in which it hardly rated a mention, was not categorised as tatau[27] and was seen almost solely as a learning opportunity for apprentices.[28] Olivia Partsch's study of malu and Samoan women's attitudes to it highlights a number of attitudes to its wearing and its acceptance by the church and the wider community. Her research indicates that the church still exerts some pressure on young Samoans not to be tattooed, as it is seen as 'a spilling of blood' and an attempt to achieve self-glorification. Even so there is strong resistance to this, despite fines and temporary disassociation. The malu was seen by some to be 'a personal sacrifice and an outward symbol and acknowledgement of how they feel about their fa'asamoa and cultural identity'.[29] The study also highlighted a trend for older Samoan women in their late 40s and 50s to acquire the malu.

In an exceptional case from the 1990s not related to Partsch's study, a woman in Auckland received the pe'a. It caused great controversy that is still talked about several years after the event. After much negotiation with the tufuga, she was granted permission to wear the pe'a as a tribute to the memory of her father who had recently passed away.

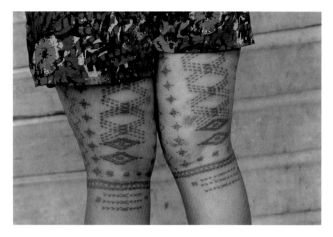

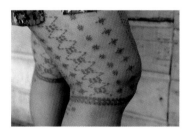

Figs. 8.8 and 8.9 Malu, women's tattoo. (Craig Potton)

For Samoans living in New Zealand there are many ways to negotiate and pay for tatau. The customs and methods vary, as do the income and access to resources possessed by the customer. Many young New Zealand-born Samoans do not have access to the same resources as the older generation in terms of 'ie toga and other exchange items. In many cases cash is the most practical currency and a readily acceptable and disposable substitute. The monetary cost of a pe'a in New Zealand in 1998 started at around $1800-$2000. As with most commercial transactions, one can expect to get what one pays for. The more one pays, the better the quality of the work. In many cases, fa'asamoa prevails when negotiating and paying for the pe'a. Cash payments, the gifting of pigs, 'ie toga and siapo become part of the transaction and are divided and distributed by the tufuga among his helpers.

A very recent development in the history of tatatau is the tatau competition. The inaugural South Pacific Tattoo Show was held in Auckland, New Zealand, in August 1998. Intended to be an annual event, it is sponsored by a number of local business people and is seen as a way to promote the art and the fa'asamoa values associated with it. It is a contest that highlights the aesthetic qualities of pe'a and malu, but also proficiency in the important skills required of the soga'imiti and taupou.

There are twelve judging categories for tatau and seven for malu. These categories examine the lines and appearance of the tattoo, but also the ability of the wearer to perform a range of skills important for the soga'imiti or taupou. The male contestants are required to demonstrate proficiency in the solo 'ava (to wipe the ava bowl), the tautu 'ava (the role of cup bearer), the siva (dance) and manaia (the role of the chiefly son). The women must do the same for the palu 'ava (to mix or make the ava), siva and manaia. In its first year the contest was very well received and the winners of the New Zealand final were to be flown to compete in the grand final held in Apia.

Other artists working in different media are also making a contribution to the survival and reinterpretation of tatatau. Whereas once the motifs of the tatau could be found on the pottery of their ancestors, today Polynesian people are putting these images on garments and clothes, in paintings, on pottery, stationery and internet homepages. While they have moved from the skin to the canvas and beyond, the messages and connections these motifs point to remain the same.

The lines that the tufuga tatatau inscribes upon the skin are lines that connect the wearer to the past, the present and the future. They can indicate where the heart and origins of the wearer lie and can often operate as their passport to work in the service of the matai. Receiving the tatau can be an affirmation of the person and the soul. It can be a public statement of commitment to family, community and culture. It can speak of many things; such as place, values, memories and origins. It is many things, such as an ornament or garment that, once worn, can never be removed.

TUFUGA TATATAU: SU'A SULU'APE PAULO II

Tufuga tatatau Su'a Sulu'ape Paulo II was one of three brothers from a long-established line of tufuga that can be traced back to the beginnings of tatau in Samoa. He was born in Lefaga and his tattooing skills were taught to him by his father, Sulu'ape Paulo I. He played a crucial role in keeping the art alive in Samoa and New Zealand and has passed the skills and knowledge on to his own son. Su'a Sulu'ape Paulo II was one of the foremost exponents of the art, and his skills were widely sought after in Samoa and New Zealand and more recently Europe. He was a popular guest at tattooing conventions and competitions across the world where he won several competitions. As well as preserving and maintaining the art form, Sulu'ape also made room for it to grow and be shared across many different cultures. His attitude and forward thinking ensured that arts of tatau developed yet had a continuity of meaning for Samoans and others in the present. Su'a Sulu'ape Paulo II died suddenly in November 1999, but earlier that year he shared the story of how his life's work in tatatau began; this is an edited extract from that interview:

I was born in a little village, a very remote village in Lefaga called Matafa'a, and my mother is Me'eta'a and my father is Sulu'ape Paulo the first. I remember when I was really young my parents were travelling to Savai'i to Palauli to tattoo some people. We were there for maybe two, three or four months. These are just vague memories. My father would travel for any length of time to tattoo people around the islands. As I was young and was just a baby they would have to take me.

Fig. 8.10 Su'a Sulu'ape Paulo II. (Sean Mallon)

I can't quite remember, but I think I had fancied being a tattooist well before I went to school. When I was growing up my father would walk away and leave his tools in a bowl in the house. And I would just grab the tools and pretend to tattoo someone. Years later I started to tattoo young guys in the village. Eventually when I was in Moamoa at the boarding school I took some of my father's tools with me and tattooed the boys.

I think it was 1967, I was travelling back home on the bus after a football game on a Wednesday before Easter weekend. A cousin of mine who had started tattooing, I think he started around 1963-64, everyone was talking about him because he was coming on real strong. And that was the resurgence of tattooing in Samoa, the exact time. His name was Fa'alavelave Petelo; he had been brought up in my family, but he left to look after his parents in a village called Samatau on the northern side of the island. And he had tattooed this young man standing in the bus. This man and one old man, they were talking and something was said about me and my brothers not having the guts to take the tattooing up. It made me angry, but not against my cousin who is an adopted brother, but mainly I was angry about my older brothers and myself, because I realised that this old man was right. So while I am saying that I was angry, the anger was not directed at my cousin at all. I was happy for him in a big way, but I was angry at myself. For what was said in the bus was quite right, me and none of my own brothers had guts enough to take it up. And I decided then and there that I would take it up when I left school.

I came home at this time and my father was tattooing some people in the other village in Lefaga in Matautu. I made tools the following day – that was Thursday. I made a set of about five tools and I went and saw my father. The young people there that were getting tattooed, they saw me showing the tools to my father and one guy I can remember his name Mutu, he's from the family of Faumui, he asked me if I would like to tattoo his legs. I said yes, I would like to and I just started tattooing and there was no looking back from then on.

I wasn't really overawed by the fact that I was able to tattoo a real person, a real pe'a. I had been tattooing little pictures here and there, but this time I was actually tattooing someone who was getting the pe'a. My father had started the back, but then I did the leg, and there was a gap between the back and the leg but I left it to my father to complete.

When I came to New Zealand in 1973 I brought my tools with me; I knew there were Samoan people because a couple of years earlier a cousin of mine had moved to New Zealand; his name is Pasino Sefo, he lives here in Auckland. He had tattooed two brothers and some other people here in New Zealand, in Auckland before I got here. And so he will take credit for being the first tattooist to tattoo Samoans outside Samoa. So I brought my tools with me, I knew that it was going to happen here because my own cousin was tattooing here.

It didn't take long to get started, as soon as people knew I was here I started working part-time. I took a job at a factory and worked around and then came home and tattooed on the weekends and in the evenings.

What are the trademarks of a good pe'a? It should be straight and neat, and the quality, you'll see the quality…there is a very professional way of applying ink. In some cases you will see that in other areas the tufuga would have been going too far in and has actually minced the skin, and you can tell, it is very visible and you can see it. I think the application is the one important thing, everything has to be consistently even, not with some parts going off, or in some parts going in too deep. That is a mark of inexperience. The knowledge of the designs, the motifs – you have to know that. If you only know a few, then maybe all your work will be just those few. The best, the last, is knowing how to eradicate your mistakes. People don't like to talk about this, but if there was someone in front of me now I could pinpoint the mistakes the tufuga had made. I make mistakes myself, but I am able to hide it.

I think you have to be prepared to do the work, it's very physical, it doesn't look very physical but it is, I tell you it is. If you would like to sit down with me for the whole 24 hours, one day or two, by the second day you would give up. So it is a very very mental kind of work, you want to stretch your legs, you want to stand up, you want to lie down, you want to fall asleep…you can't. You have to sit where you sit from 10 o'clock to 10 o'clock.

UNDERSTANDING THE PE'A AND MALU

The origins of Samoan tatatau motifs can be traced back to around 1500 BC, to the early ancestors of the Polynesian people. At this time the peoples of the Pacific were making the distinctive decorated pottery that archaeologists call Lapita ware. The designs and motifs found on this ancient pottery relate directly to those present in tattoo and barkcloth decoration.[30]

As well as stylistic similarities, archaeological excavations of Lapita pottery-bearing sites in Tongatapu in Tonga have unearthed tattooing chisels. In the Reef Islands in the Santa Cruz group, a Lapita site has produced what appears to be the buttocks of a small baked-clay figurine, bearing images that may represent tattoo. Very recently, a small clay-modelled head with a facial tattoo was discovered at a Lapita site in Papua New Guinea.[31] Furthermore, linguistic reconstruction of the old languages of the Pacific show that the words tatau and uhi (the eastern Polynesian term for tattoo-ing implement) have a very early origin.

Today, a wide range of motifs is available to the tufuga tatatau. There is a common iconography shared by many tufuga tatatau but each also has his own personal set of motifs which he uses from time to time. In general the motifs and designs of the

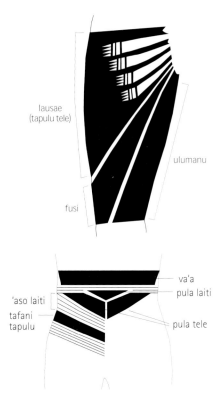

lausae
(tapulu tele)

ulumanu

fusi

va'a
pula laiti

'aso laiti
tafani
tapulu

pula tele

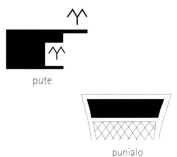

pute

punialo

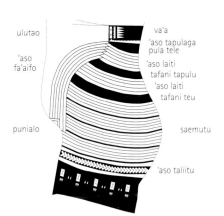

ulutao

va'a
'aso tapulaga
pula tele

'aso
fa'aifo

'aso laiti
tafani tapulu
'aso laiti
tafani teu

punialo

saemutu

'aso taliitu

Fig. 8.11 Main divisions of the pe'a from top: front and inner leg; back; navel; above groin; side view of upper thigh and buttocks. Only main structural divisions are shown (details of motifs omitted).

pe'a refer to the recipient's family history, accomplishments and responsibilities. The underlying structure of the pe'a varies little from artist to artist, but in terms of the finer motifs and design details, each tufuga tatatau interprets and composes the imagery differently.

Several historical sources describe the meanings of the different elements that make up the pe'a. Naturally, and over time, they vary in some details and in some cases are considered by contemporary tufuga tatatau to be incorrect. Te Rangi Hiroa's account, based on his observations of a tufuga tatatau called Faioso in the 1920s, is probably the most detailed, although specific to its time. Like most accounts, it lacks an in-depth exploration of the meaning and significance of the structure of the pe'a and the motifs that decorate it, as they were at that time for that tufuga.

A contemporary explanation/interpretation of the pe'a and the malu follows. These were given by Su'a Sulu'ape Paulo II and are based on two lectures given at Victoria University of Wellington in 1998 and on his essay in *Fomison: what shall we tell them?*[32] The meanings have some semblance to those of the past, but undoubtedly there are some elements and interpretations unique to the artist and to contemporary practice.

In the examples shown here the meanings of the different underlying structural features are described first. Then come interpretations of the smaller motifs that fill and decorate these structures. All descriptions are those related to Su'a Sulu'ape Paulo II and his work. Some details may differ from artist to artist.

THE PE'A

The pe'a is applied starting from the back at waist level and working down to the knees.

va'a - this black strip representing a canoe stretches across the back, with the ulutao (spearhead) on each end extending around and toward the front. The recipient of the pe'a is considered the va'a of his immediate family. The va'a is the family and the ulutao are there to protect them. He who receives the pe'a is the representative of his family and village and must not bring shame upon them.

ulutao - the spearhead that guards the va'a and the recipient's family.

'aso tapulaga - 'aso refers to the narrow rafter lines of the fale (house); tapulaga refers to a ripening. The lines of ripening indicate that the recipient of the pe'a has learnt to see things from a new perspective. Once these three lines are completed the tatau process must be seen through to its conclusion. Failure to continue beyond this point is considered a disgrace to the recipient and his family.

pula laiti - also known as the tama'i pe'a (flying fox) which is known for caring for her young under her wings. In this sense the pula laiti refers to the immediate family surrounded by the three main parts to every village - the matai (chiefs), the tama'ita'i (women) and the aumaga (young men). These are represented by the corners of this small triangle.

pula tele - represents the same principle of caring, but for the extended family. One side of the pula tele refers to the father's side, the other to the mother's side.

'aso laiti - another set of small lines that refers to the genealogy of the father's side. They conclude at the tafani tapulu.

tafani tapulu - this dark borderline is another reference to the father's side of the family, which is considered the stronger side of a person's family.

'aso laiti - this set of small lines refers to the genealogy of the mother's side. Samoan custom decrees that sisters and mothers should be favoured. This set of lines con-

'alu 'alu

'anufe

'aveau

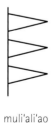

atualoa

muli'ali'ao

Fig. 8.12 Samoan tattooing motifs representing manufactured articles and images from the natural environment.

cludes at the tafani teu.

tafani teu - a dark borderline decorated with respect to the recipient's mother who is always held in high regard.

saemutu - this set of three lines are the lines of adventure and accomplishment. They are the learning lines of the recipient's life and represent the steps undergone from childhood to young adulthood. The third line or step is when the father calls for the tufuga tatatau. It was the custom that if the tufuga was called, no one refused the pe'a, because this signalled they had reached the point of adulthood and had passed the learning lines.

'aso taliitu - tali is to hold up and itu means side. These lines hold up the sides of the body and signify the wearer's childhood accomplishments and their preparations to acquire and wear a pe'a.

'aso fa'aifo - literally, curved lines. They encircle the wearer's being as a person of rank, signifying the wearer's commitment to incorporate his mother's and father's families into his life.

fa'aila tautau - a small window in the dark shaded area of a tatau usually made around a birthmark or spot on the skin. This represents readiness for all circumstances, should anyone in the extended family be in need of help or support.

atigivae - this section behind the knee refers to the firm standing the wearer must take. He must be able to plant both feet firmly on the ground.

muli'ali'ao - literally, muli (end) and aliao (conch). The pointed ends of the conch shell refer to the many duties of the person who wears the pe'a.

lausae (tapulu tele) - this outer area of the leg, darkly filled in, reminds the wearer of his obligations and that there is a dark side to any task. There is a Samoan saying, 'Do not be afraid – the sea is dark but only some parts are dangerous', reminding people that confidence in their ability is more important than any danger.

fusi - literally, a belt, strap or band, it is the sign of a warrior looking for adventure or issuing a challenge to all-comers. It lies next to and complements the ulumanu.

ulumanu - literally, the head of a bird, a cunning and decisive animal, this sign refers to the recipient's ability to solve problems.

punialo - this represents the joining of the paternal and maternal sides of the family; the union finally concluded at the navel, signifying the cutting of the umbilical cord and a departure from dependency.

pute - marks the departure of the baby from the mother's womb and that the recipient of the pe'a has left his childhood behind.

Other motifs are drawn from the natural environment and can also be found in the arts of siapo decoration and in some cases in woodcarving. They are applied at the artist's discretion.

'alu 'alu - jellyfish

'anufe - caterpillar

'aveau - starfish

atualoa - millipede

muli'ali'ao - the pointed end of shellfish

talalaupaongo - the thorned edge of the pandanus leaf

fetu - star, representing wisdom

upenga - net

gogo - tern (seabird) signifying hope

vae 'ali - the legs of a bamboo headrest

talalaupaongo

fetu

upenga

gogo

vae 'ali

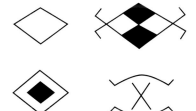

malu

THE MALU

The malu is applied starting from the knees and working up to and finishing at the top of the thighs.

malu - in the context of Samoan tatau this term means shelter/protected. The lines of the malu represent the four areas of the fale (house) where different guests are seated. There is an area for the ali'i (chief) of the host village, the ali'i of the visiting village, the tulafale (orator) and finally the taupou (chiefly young woman). This motif appears behind the knee and if two malu are present it indicates the wearer's link to royalty.

tali malu - the area below the malu motif itself. The wider this area of decoration, the higher ranked the woman is.

fusi - this is the top row of decoration at the top of the thigh. When the fusi is done it is testimony to the patience and endurance of the tattooed woman.

fa'alanuma'aveave - the front of the thigh can be designed in any manner, but the rest of the design always comprises the following parts. Back of the thigh: tasks and obligations inside the house. Outer thigh: tasks and obligations outside the house. Inner thigh: obligations to the women's council, work and tasks such as weaving.

'alu'alu - jellyfish

'anufe - worm or caterpillar

'aveau - starfish

fetu - star, representing wisdom

malu - tattoo worn only by women

gogo - tern

vae'ali - the legs of a bamboo headrest

muli'ali'ao - the pointed end of shellfish

atualoa - millipede

CHAPTER 8

1. T. Tapu, 'Tattoo ritual in Samoa', in Deverell, Bruce and Deverell, Gweneth (eds), *Pacific Rituals: Living or Dying* (Suva: University of the South Pacific, 1987), p. 166

2. A. Gell, *Wrapping in Images: Tattooing in Polynesia* (Oxford: Clarendon Press, 1993), p. 121. This gives the most thorough and detailed comparative analysis of Polynesian tattooing with an extensive interpretation of Samoan tattoo iconography.

3. There are many versions of this story. For further discussion of the Siamese twins and analysis of tattoo origin stories, see Gell, A. *Wrapping in Images*, or Milner, G.B. 'Samoan tattoos and structural analysis', *Mankind* 10: 307-308 (1973)

4. A. Sharp (ed), *The Journal of Jacob Roggeveen* (Oxford: Clarendon Press, 1970), p. 151

5. At one time women not tattooed on the hand were not permitted to prepare 'ava. See Marquardt, C. *Die tatowirung beider Geschlechter in Samoa/The tattooing of both sexes in Samoa*, English translation by Sibyl Ferner, (Papakura, New Zealand: R. McMillan, 1984), p. 21

6. Te Rangi Hiroa (Peter Buck), 'Samoan Material Culture' *Bernice P. Bishop Museum* Bulletin 75 (Hawai'i: 1930), p. 656

7. For a detailed discussion on Samoan matapule, see Kaeppler, A, 'Exchange patterns in goods and spouses: Fiji, Tonga and Samoa', *Mankind*, vol. 11 (1978), pp. 246-52 and Gell. A *Wrapping in Images*, pp. 106-108

8. G. Turner, *Samoa A Hundred years ago and long before* (London: 1884), p. 89

9. Te Rangi Hiroa, 'Samoan Material Culture', p. 639

10. J.W. Hart, *Samoan Culture* (Apia: Ati's Samoan Print Shop, 1996, First published, 1996), pp. 7-8

11. J. Grimwade, 'Tattoo tricks catch on again among Samoans', *Pacific Island Monthly* (September, 1993), p. 43; and T. O'Meara, *Samoan Planters: Tradition and Economic Development in Polynesia* (Fort Worth, Texas: Rinehart & Winston, 1990), p. 74

12. J.B. Stair, *Old Samoa; or flotsam and jetsam from the Pacific Ocean* (Papakura: Southern Reprints, 1983, First published 1897), p. 160

13. T.H. Hood, *Notes of a Cruise in H.M.S. Fawn in the Western Pacific in the year 1862* (Edinburgh:

Edmonston and Douglas, 1863), p. 124

14. A. Kramer, *The Samoan Islands* vol. 2 (Auckland: Polynesian Press, 1995), p. 68

15. Hood, *Notes of a Cruise*, p. 124

16. Te Rangi Hiroa, 'Samoan Material Culture', pp. 641 and 644

17. Te Rangi Hiroa, 'Samoan Material Culture', p. 661; See also Moyle, R.M., *Traditional Samoan Music* (Auckland: Auckland University Press, 1988), p. 146-147 for a review of tattooing songs; Also, A.L. Hunkin, *Gagaga Samoa: A Samoan Language Course Book* (Auckland: Polynesian Press, 1998), pp. 72-73

18. T. O'Meara, *Samoan Planters*, p. 76

19. K. Sua'apa'ia, quoted in Teilhet, J. (ed), *Dimensions of Polynesia* (San Diego: Fine Arts Gallery of San Diego, 1973), p. 86

20. Grimwade, 'Tattoo tricks catch on again among Samoans', p. 42

21. Luschan, F. von, *Beitrag zur Kenntniss der Tattowirung in Samoa*, (Berlin: Verlag von A. Asher & Co., 1897), p. 553

22. Grimwade, 'Tattoo tricks catch on again among Samoans', p. 42

23. E.J. Wakefield, *Adventure in New Zealand from 1839 to 1844 with some account of the beginning of the British Colonisation of the Islands* (Whitcombe & Tombs Ltd, 1908), p. 322

24. N.A. Rowe, *Samoa under the Sailing Gods* (London and New York: Putnam, 1930), p. 85

25. Fuimaono Tuiasau, interviewed by I. Wedde (ed), *Fomison: What Shall We Tell Them?* (Wellington: City Gallery, 1994), p. 84

26. A. Tunumafono, 'Reviving an old art for $35, 000' *Pacific Islands Monthly*, (January 1982), p. 23

27. N. Thomas, 'Pacific Dualities: Bottled Ocean in Wellington and Auckland' *Art New Zealand* vol. 74 (1995), p. 114

28. Te Rangi Hiroa, 'Samoan Material Culture', p. 656

29. O. Partsch, 'Malu: Samoan women's tattoo', unpublished research paper, Diploma of Social Work, (Wellington: Victoria University), p. 54

30. R.C. Green, 'Early Lapita art from Polynesia and Island Melanesia: continuities in ceramic, barkcloth and tattoo decorations', in S. Mead (ed), *Exploring the Visual Art of Oceania* (Honolulu: University of Hawai'i Press, 1979)

31. G.R. Summerhayes, 'The face of Lapita' *Archaeol. Oceania* vol. 33 (1988), p. 100

32. I. Wedde (ed), *Fomison: What Shall We Tell Them?* (Wellington: City Gallery, 1994)

PAINTING AND FOLK-ART

Painting is not recorded as being a strong feature of the Samoan arts, but the area of decorative or folk-art is developing into one of the most accessible and popular forms of visual art in present-day Samoa. Largely decorative in function, painted folk-art is a diverse, colourful and memorable addition to the Samoan village and environment. Neich suggests that several of the decorative arts – including carved and painted decorations and embroidery – might loosely fit under the description of folk-art in that they are internally oriented and not for sale. 'Because of their diversity, very few regularities are apparent, except that perhaps the popularity of flowers as a decorative motif can be noted as the continuation of the Samoan love for flowers and their scent as a body decoration.'[1] While folk-art is a strong element of contemporary Samoan culture, it is seen as distinct from the 'high arts', such as house building, tattooing and siapo manufacture, and considered a result of an individual's creative urge more than any established artistic practice.

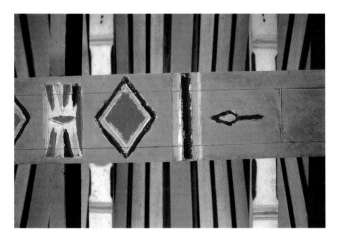

Fig. 9.1 Rafter painting in fale, 1999. (Craig Potton)

In Samoa today, painted decorative art is very common. It appears on pandanus mats, the sides of canoes, inside and outside houses and churches, on buses and on church, school and village banners. Text and images are used to convey village pride, highlight the names of popular sports teams, describe the attributes of certain groups or enhance the appearance of a property or village.

Twenty years ago this was not the case. But although painted figurative art was fairly restricted Neich documented several examples. One of the most interesting was the faleafolau of Leafa Polo at Vaito'omuli[2] which featured painted posts and decorated beams.

All the posts and beams inside are decorated with incised zig-zag lines and triangles picked out in blue and yellow. On the longitudinal main plate beam…which is painted yellow, there are small paintings of flowers, pineapples, trees, leaves and birds in blue, black, red and yellow. All this brightly coloured 'folk art' contrasts strongly with the unpainted posts and beams of the old faletele about 50 m away.[3]

This fale no longer stands, but today many contemporary fale made of imported materials have large areas of painted motifs decorating their interiors. Posts are almost always painted with brightly coloured stripes or bands. Architraves and ceilings feature flowers and leaves, religious imagery and geometric shapes or patterns. Likewise, church interiors are often heavily decorated with biblical images interspersed with passages and words from the scripture.

Religious themes are also prevalent in the painting of banners. At the 1999 Independence celebrations in Apia, school groups, church groups and bands were identified by their distinctive uniforms and banners. Many of these were illustrated with religious imagery or quotes from the scripture. Buses provide another decorative opportunity and are painted with creative signwriting and motifs or specific colour schemes according to their route or destination.[4]

While this type of art may appear very ordinary, in 1980 Neich noted that there was some opportunity for talented individuals to develop a reputation for their skills in this type of work. One such person was Peteli of Vailoa village who was widely known for his work painting decorations onto mats. There was also Timu of Letogo village who carved the exterior posts around the Catholic Old Folks Home (Mapuifagalele) at Vailele[5] and the interior posts at Aggie Greys Hotel in Apia.[6] Twenty years on there is an even greater demand for these skills with painted images and signwriting becoming important features on cars, buses and racing canoes.

Similar practices among New Zealand-based Samoan communities are also apparent, with churches providing the most visible outlet for this type of work. Whether commissioned from people outside the community or from members within it, religious symbolism and imagery is a strong feature. Figurative art appears in Samoan churches throughout New Zealand: on the walls and ceilings, on the cloths of altars and pulpits, on the carpets and also on the uniforms and vestments of the choirs and clergy. These images often 'acknowledge the positive values of the Samoan background of the congregation…' and '…include the incorporation of siapo patterns, the use of cultural artifacts such as the to'oto'o and fue, or simply the colour blue as a reference to the Pacific origin of the people'.[7]

PAINTERS, SCULPTORS, PRINTMAKERS

Beyond the decorative and figurative painting of folk-art, gallery-based art is another area where Samoan painters, printmakers and sculptors are making a strong contribution. The late 20th century has seen increasing numbers of Samoan artists gaining recognition in local and international art markets. This is partly due to a growing interest in the arts of contemporary indigenous peoples worldwide. Developments in contemporary Aboriginal and Maori art have paved the way for other artists from the Pacific region. The market for contemporary Samoan art and Pacific art in general is strongest in New Zealand and Australia, where the majority of exhibiting Samoan artists are based. In these places, painting, sculpture and multimedia work are well represented in public and private collections. Since the late 1990s, however, the market has started to spread to galleries and art dealers in the United States, Germany and France.

There are a number of established Samoan artists in Samoa and American Samoa working as sculptors, painters and printmakers. These include Sau Ueligitone, I'iga Iosua To'afa, Regina Meredith Malala, Sven Ordquist, Momoe Malietoa von Reiche, Vanya Taule'alo and Stefan von Reiche. Their work represents a wide range of styles and approaches that moves beyond the familiar motifs of siapo and tatau. Working in oils, pastels, acrylics, wood and metal, their work extends the visual

Fig. 9.2 Painted post, Savai'i. (Craig Potton)

vocabulary and iconography of the Samoan artist presenting contemporary stories in new media.

A major exhibition held in 1996 at The Seventh Pacific Festival of the Arts in Apia, Samoa showed the work of Samoan painters and sculptors in the context of developments across the wider Pacific. Artists from American and Western Samoa participated alongside artists from Vanuatu, New Caledonia, Fiji, Tokelau, New Zealand and Tahiti. Some were self-taught and others were trained in New Zealand or overseas. Some local artists had been trained at the Leulumoega Fou School of Fine Arts, a school run by Italian artist Ernesto Coter and founded by the Christian Congregational Church in 1987. It was the major art school in Samoa for some time and has been a source of inspiration for students, giving them a strong grounding in a range of artistic techniques and a wider appreciation of Western art history in general. Artists and teachers such as Regina Meredith Malala and Vanya Taule'alo work in other educational institutions in American Samoa and Samoa respectively. Their influence at a tertiary level ensures a practical and intellectual development for artists of the future.

NEW ZEALAND

The work of artists of Pacific island descent in New Zealand has increased in profile dramatically over the last 15 to 20 years. Artists of Samoan descent have been part of this trend and have made the most of the burgeoning opportunities to exhibit with mainstream art galleries and dealers. Their work is part of a diverse art scene that in the year 2001 reflects the multi-cultural nature of New Zealand society.

A leading figure in the development of several Samoan and Pacific island artists during the early 1980s was the painter Tony Fomison. Toward the end of his life he had developed strong bonds and connections with Auckland's Pacific island community. He forged strong friendships with several artists, Niuean painter John Pule, and Samoan painter Fatu Feu'u, nurturing their confidence and encouraging them to bring their art and ideas into the open. Feu'u has described Fomison as his mentor and someone without whose encouragement he would not have been brave enough to exhibit his work. He also considers him a cornerstone in the development and promotion of Samoan artists and their work in Auckland.[8]

In New Zealand the growth in Samoan and Pacific island art in general, in part followed developments in Maori art. In the 1980s government arts policy and funding structures were being geared towards providing a framework for the support of contemporary Maori art. Not long after support for the arts of Pacific island peoples in New Zealand was put in place. Committees were set up to allocate funding to different artists and projects, with community leaders and artists being involved in the decision-making process. Today Pacific arts development policy and funding are administered by the Pacific Island Arts Committee of Creative New Zealand. One of its key aims is to encourage not only the practice and maintenance of Pacific islands' heritage arts in New Zealand but also arts development and promotion across a broad range of art forms.[9]

An early focal point for the interest in Pacific art in New Zealand was the Tautai Art Gallery, which was established on Karangahape Road in Auckland in the late 1980s. The Consul General of Western Samoa, Afamasaga Toleafoa, his wife Phillipa, Graham McGregor, Peter Taouma and publisher Robert Holding were instrumental in setting up this small but important space. Provided rent-free for the first year, the

Tautai Art Gallery was a humble space where several Samoan and other Pacific island artists had their first shows. For many it was the beginning of something unique in the New Zealand art scene.

A number of emerging artists were to benefit from the appearance of this venue and its associated trust. John Ioane, who had graduated from Elam School of Fine Arts three years earlier, had his first solo show at the Tautai Art Gallery in 1988. The Tautai Trust and its fundraising efforts also supported Lily Laita, Lyle Penisula, Michel Tuffery and Utelese Temese, who were all studying or undergoing training at the time.[10] Although open for just over 18 months, the gallery gave these and many other artists a start and raised the profile and awareness of their work within the New Zealand art community.

The legacy of the Tautai Art Gallery today is the Tautai South Pacific Contemporary Arts Trust. With over 100 members and a regular newsletter and website, it is a pioneering initiative intended to take contemporary Pacific art to a wider audience. Through the 1990s the Trust has facilitated a number of exhibitions, symposiums and commissions. These events have helped to support artists and provided opportunities for ideas and networks to grow.[11]

Other exhibitions and organisations have also helped to raise an awareness of Pacific art in New Zealand and nurtured its development. The 1990 exhibition *Te moemoea no Iotefa* at the Sarjeant Gallery, Wanganui broke new ground by highlighting the connections between the work of a contemporary group of artists and older art and images from museums and private collections. Organised by Maori curator Rangihiroa Panoho it featured several Samoan artists, including Lily Laita, Iosefa Leo, Fatu Feu'u, Johnny Penisula, John Ioane and Michel Tuffery. For a long time the catalogue from this exhibition was the only reference to the work of artists of Pacific island descent living in New Zealand.

The touring exhibition *Bottled Ocean* which opened at the City Gallery, Wellington in 1994 featured an even broader range of new and established artists working in a diverse range of media. For several emerging Samoan artists this was their first opportunity to show work in a major institution alongside more established artists. Curated by Cook Islander Jim Vivieaere it was a challenging show that questioned cultural and institutional categories and boundaries in relation to art by Pacific islanders. It examined uneasy issues of identity and ethnicity, and the blurred connections between the artists, New Zealand and the heritage of their island homelands. But perhaps most importantly, it marked and documented what artists of Polynesian descent were doing nationwide at that particular time, and in doing so it also extended the perception of what Pacific island art could be.

Since 1994 there have been many exciting events building on the achievements of these two key exhibitions. A recent example, is *Dolly Mix Wrapper*, an exhibition featuring the art of contemporary Samoan women, curated by Janice Leafa, Jakkie Leota-Ete and Jim Vivieaere. There have been exhibitions in Australia, Germany, the United States and throughout the Pacific. Students of Samoan descent in New Zealand are emerging from art schools in greater numbers and, like the artists of *Bottled Ocean* and *Dolly Mix Wrapper*, they are introducing new ways of thinking about Samoan art. As a result, more private collectors and institutions both locally and overseas are collecting the work of Samoan artists.

However, these developments are also complicating things. For in the art world where there are often overlapping categories of difference, issues of ethnicity can often be problematic. Art by Samoans is often described as Samoan or Pacific, but for those who have grown up in New Zealand, it is equally a product of the unique circumstances in that country. Many young artists of Samoan descent have never been to Samoa, and some probably never will. Painter Lyle Penisula provides an insight into some of these issues, touched upon in the *Bottled Ocean* exhibition and raised in an interview with him in 1997:

I feel comfortable being called a Samoan artist because I have got a Samoan side to me, but I'm not comfortable being labelled just as a Samoan artist. I'd rather be known as a New Zealand artist, because I was born here. I've got a kiwi mum. Everything I am influenced by is from within New Zealand, although I do dig into my father's heritage. There are things there that I want to know and learn because that is part of me as well.…I don't want people to look at my work and pigeonhole it. I am proud of being a Samoan, but I am not just that.[12]

Lily Laita has made similar comments in relation to how she approaches her work, and how her cultural background is part of this:

Being of Samoan descent is part of who I am, it is not the only part … I happen to work in education and visual arts and that's my choice of communication … but the Samoan part is one of various leis – as a woman of Maori and English descent educated in New Zealand, it's integral to what I do, and part of who I am.[13]

In Penisula's and Laita's painting, identity features prominently; it's an important subject for a number of artists of Pacific descent from the same generation. For some the questions arise from their mixed heritage, for others they emerge from immigrating to or being raised in a place where the opportunities and environment are very different from their homeland. Debates about identity are not restricted to artists of Samoan or Pacific descent, but are becoming increasingly significant for these communities as they migrate and spread across the globe.

The ideas and processes of identity have offered a challenge and inspiration to many of these artists as they seek to make sense of who they are and what place they and their heritage have in society. Notions of identity depend on what criteria are set, on what people decide as important contributing factors. But it has already been said that the search for identity is perhaps a journey without an end. Perspectives change and vary, as do environments, geographical locations and personal circumstances. Often the way we think and see things remains unchanged for only a brief moment.

An outcome of this process in terms of art, however, is a changing and diverse range of creative responses. In finding their own voices the painters of Samoan descent working in New Zealand and Samoa have since the early 1970s produced an impressive body of work. The rest of this chapter comprises a selection of images surveying paintings by artists of Samoan descent (some of whom also work in other media) in order to allow the many approaches, subjects and styles to speak for themselves.

SAVEA MALIETOA

Savea Malietoa (1914-1994) was a man with a passion for art and creativity. He was a carver and craftsman who would fashion ukelele from coconut shells or small statues from pieces of wood. It is for his painting, however, that many Samoan residents especially remember him.

For much of his life he painted in oils, but grew to love acrylics after artist/writer

Fig. 9.3 *Untitled*, Savea Malietoa.
(Courtesy Maina Afamasaga)

Momoe von Reiche introduced him to them. Savea's creations were often in demand. His daughter Maina Afamasaga says that locals would refer tourists to Savea saying, "Oh, you want something? Go to Savea, he knows how to paint." They would bring dresses and swimwear to him to decorate with hibiscus and other tropical flowers.

Maina remembers that when she was young the house would be specially decorated with paintings to cater for Aggie's Tours which would bring visitors every two weeks or so. Famous visitors like actors Raymond Burr, Sammy Davis Jr. and Marlon Brando acquired examples of Savea's work, and some of his work is held in a gallery in Scotland. Samoans also sought out his work to use as gifts or to decorate their homes. He was often in demand to travel around Samoa and paint images in churches and occasionally on buses. From the few examples seen of his work and the stories told about him, it seems Savea's careful but untutored hand captured idyllic images of Samoa that would satisfy both local and tourist tastes and provide a small income for his family. But they also reveal the very simple life and pleasures of a man who loved nature and loved to carve, draw and paint.

TEUANE TIBBO

Teuane Tibbo was born in Apia in 1892 and along with the siapo artist Mary Pritchard has been described as a 'matriarch of Samoan art'.[14] Tibbo started painting in 1963 at age 71. She exhibited in Auckland through the 1960s and 70s at the Barry Lett Gallery and is perhaps one of the first painters of Samoan descent to be recognised by the art establishment in New Zealand. Her work is in collections in Australia, Japan and Germany.

Described by art critics as a folk-artist, she was considered one of the best-known painters in this field in New Zealand.[15] Her paintings have been described as … 'colourful, childlike, simple and without fine detail'.[16] Most of her early work is in oils, although she changed to acrylics toward the end of her career. 'She painted pictures from her joyful childhood memories of life in Samoa and Fiji, often arranging them in symmetrical compositions with bold decorative motifs.'[17] In this sense she was influenced by the design work of siapo, her work often reflecting siapo's balance and repetition.

FATU FEU'U

Fatu Feu'u has been working as a full-time artist in New Zealand for many years. Since 1983 he has exhibited in group and solo shows both locally and internationally. Born in the village of Poutasi, Fatu always loved art and had been exposed to it for much of his early life. But it was to be years later before he could realise his aspiration to be an artist. Immigrating to New Zealand in 1966 at age 20, he worked in factories for some time before progressing to the position of colour consultant and designer for an Auckland textile company in the early 1970s. However, it was not until several years later, thanks to the encouragement of New Zealand artists such as Tony Fomison, Pat Hanly and Philip Clairmont, that he developed the confidence to exhibit his own art, which he had worked on in his spare time but had kept hidden away. Since then his distinctive style, based on motifs and decorative art elements from throughout the Pacific, has featured in artworks in a range of media.

Fatu's paintings, sculptures and prints almost always incorporate and explore some aspect of fa'asamoa. This is the common binding element in his entire body of work. Its prominence is a natural expression and extension of his upbringing and the way he endeavours to live and conduct his everyday life. 'To me, fa'asamoa is very much alive. To me, art is not about painting or sculpting. Art is part of everything we do, whether it is building a house, or the way we talk to our family and friends. Something we do

Fig. 9.4 *Tula'i Tamasese*, Fatu Feu'u, 1999, mixed media on canvas. (Photo courtesy of artist)

with respect.'[18] His most recent work has seen him collaborating with Wanganui Museum, to create a series of works in response to an exhibition of the museum's collection of siapo. He describes examining these old textiles and the old designs and compositions as 'fuelling the imagination and good for the soul',[19] but the environment and culture of Samoa provides a stronger calling. Travelling back to Samoa on a regular basis to seek inspiration, Fatu works to maintain the visual and spiritual connection with his roots and home village of Poutasi. 'I have to go, not only to look at the place, but to talk to the people, smell the smells of the food and cooking, the coral on the beach, see the flowers and the bush … visualise the things that I can't always see here.'[20]

LILY LAITA

Lily Laita is of Samoan/Maori (Ngati Raukawa/Rangitane)/English descent and was the first Polynesian woman to graduate from Elam School of Fine Arts at the University of Auckland. Since then she has gone on to make an extensive contribution to the arts, not only through her art but also through her teaching and involvement in arts administration.

Laita's paintings are distinguished by her dynamic and expressive use of colour. Layered thematically in content, as well as in application they link and make statements about different times, people and places. Relationships and the relevance of knowledge are focal points of Laita's work, which often maps or refers to key moments in her life, marking issues that have been particularly relevant for her, or where a discovery or turning point has inspired and moved her forward.

For most of her career Laita has painted on black building paper using her hands and acrylics, but at the same time she has experimented with printmaking, sculpture and ceramic. Lately she has moved to using brushes and oils on canvas. This change in medium and application has only slightly altered her style, but she feels that it has brought a new transparency to her work, different to what she was able to achieve in acrylics.

Fig. 9.5 Painting from the *Nafanua Triptych*, Lily Laita, 2001, oil on canvas.

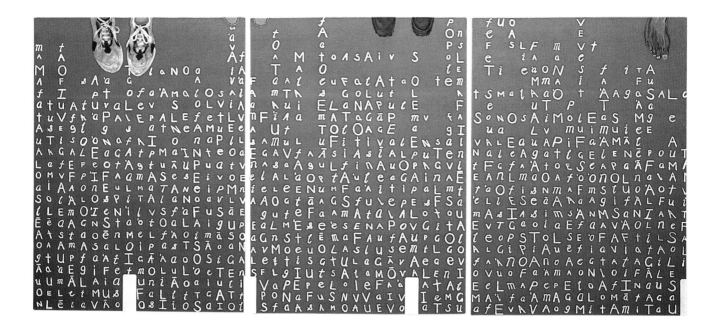

Fig. 9.6 *Letters of different feet*, Andy Leleisi'uao, 2000, triptych, acrylic on wood panels.

One constant in this change of medium and technique is her use of text. Often the only obvious signifiers in her work are the Samoan, Maori and English words. But even these possess some ambiguity or offer a range of interpretations. 'Because my paintings work in layers, there are several meanings, and the words are maybe one of those meanings. Sometimes they may be in sarcasm or relative to one of the layers of the painting, but they are also their own entities in some cases.'

In appearance the work of Lily Laita sits uneasily in a Pacific Art category where visual style is defined by the history and conventions of western art. Her paintings challenge such stereotypes by moving beyond the familiar criteria and iconography that we have come to expect of 'things Pacific'. But masked beneath a canvas of colours and text that invites contemplation, the messages and issues remain.

ANDY LELEISI'UAO

Andy Leleisi'uao is another artist who resists the stereotypes of things 'Pacific'. His art reflects a reality and experience far from the sun-drenched beaches and swaying palms of the tourist brochures. Leleisi'uao sees his challenge and perhaps the challenge for other artists of Samoan descent as being in 'breaking through these stereotypes of Pacific island art and what it is perceived to be. We are so much more. We are a diversity of artists, performers, musicians, poets and writers. So many people try to label us and put us in boxes, trying to tell us what we are, who we are and what they perceive us to be … we are artists.'[21]

In Leleisi'uao's paintings the history and experiences of three generations of urban-based Pacific island communities are explored and commented upon. Leleisi'uao says his art '…features facets of my life, things I have gone through, been through or seen; a lot of it is urban-based, an urban outlook, but there is no one meaning behind my work. We all have our own way of saying things.'

Many of the themes in his painting also relate to experiences common to many Samoan immigrants as well as those born and raised in New Zealand. Immigration, fa'asamoa, unemployment, racism, prejudice and identity are all just as relevant to the present generation as they were two generations ago.

Raised in Auckland Leleisi'uao was a shift worker after leaving Mangere College, 'just enjoying life' and helping to support his family. He would often go to galleries and see the work of other artists. It was here that he realised he had the confidence and passion to make his own art. He has since worked in oils and acrylics and more recently with lithographs. He had his first exhibition in 1995.

NANETTE LELA'ULU

Nanette Lela'ulu is a painter who was born and raised in Auckland, New Zealand. 'Painting is my life, and although it is not always pleasurable, it is definitely challenging. I have always painted and loved art, but the first time I began to paint seriously was when I was 16. It was a way for me to deal with my grandmother's slow pass from this life into the next.'

Lela'ulu, who is largely self-taught, began exhibiting in 1990 with a group show *New Pacific Art in Auckland* held at the Proba Gallery. Her first solo exhibition *Fa'afetai*

Fig. 9.7 *Out of Fa'a Samoa*, Nanette Lela'ulu, 1999, acrylic and oil on canvas. (Courtesy of artist)

came later in 1996. 'It was still closely tied to my grandmother's death. For this first solo exhibition I used siapo which had been given to me by my grandmother in a lot of my paintings.' Since then she has continued to develop her art and exhibits regularly. Her paintings have found a place in the Museum fur Volkerkunde in Frankfurt, Germany, and also in private and corporate collections in the United States, Great Britain and New Zealand.

Many of Lela'ulu's paintings have a photographic quality, as if they have been lifted from a family album, abstracted and given a new life. The environments are familiar, despite haunting shades and facial expressions. In many cases they capture and document the 'afakasi' experience of compromised living between the Samoan and palagi cultures. In her exhibition *Sorrowful Scars Become Us* (2001) she continues this theme:

I have just completed a new group of works based on the union of the Samoan, German and Chinese cultures, using images from all of these that most strongly stir memories of pasts unrelated to each other. Through placing them together on one painting they become entwined and begin to represent a coming together of a new culture of people, namely the 'afakasi.

LYLE PENISULA

Lyle Penisula lives in Invercargill, New Zealand and for many years has been involved with the church and youth in the Southland community. His experiences growing up in urban New Zealand and working and living within the church community are a major focus of his painting. Familiar Samoan motifs and imagery have only a small presence in his work; more common are the buildings, clothes and faces of the urban environment in which he was raised.

Whereas some artists have heavily criticised the role of the church in Pacific island communities, Penisula's work looks at its positive and nurturing influence and the way it has changed his own life. His most recent work looks at the influence of the gospel and the positive changes that can occur as a result of the church's teachings. As a preacher in his community, this is particularly relevant for Penisula. When he looks back over his body of work he says he has often struggled with issues of identity, of being an Afa'kasi (both Samoan and European). But in the church he has found harmony and a common binding thread for both aspects of his heritage.

Fig. 9.8 *Born Again 'afakasi*, Lyle Penisula, 1990s, acrylic on board. (Collection of the artist)

PENEHURO PAPALI'I

Penehuro Papali'i is a popular and well-known artist based in Samoa, and a former student and teacher of the Leulumoega School of Arts. He works in a wide range of media, often on a large scale. His sculptures of animals and themes from nature can be huge and dominating, but he also sculpts on a smaller scale and is a talented painter. Many Samoans will be familiar with his commissioned works in government departments and private businesses and his painting and work in stained glass that decorate churches throughout Samoa.

Papali'i lives and works in his home studio in Lelata village near Apia. His property is a work in progress and beneath the huge, partially-sculptured tree stumps and piles of materials he has put together the beginnings of an art school. With 25 students enrolled in the year 2000, Papali'i is pursuing his dream and personal vision to promote and develop the arts of Samoa.

I first started to realise my talent when I was very little. When I went to primary school in my village at Savai'i I was very interested in doing cartoons and things like that. I didn't realise I was going to enter this school, this college in Apia where a master was waiting for me. So in Savai'i I thought to myself I was the master already, but it was only in 1984 when I came to Apia and was under the Italian maestro Ernesto Coter's teaching that I started to realise what I was doing.

Then he made some exams, some tests to find some artists in order to make a special art class. So I was one of those first picked. I brought for him a small book of all my cartoons and my drawings from Savai'i. He was very interested in that book and he later told me that when he first saw me the he realised that we could develop together, and that's when I started to get more interested in the arts. Every day after that I just wanted to go and see him so he could give me some work to do. That is how I started to get more inspired and started to become more aware that I was going to become an artist.

In 1986 the church decided to make a special school of fine arts at Leulumoega because they saw that there were some students with potential. It still exists now, so I was one of the first in that group. But before I finished that first year of a four year course in fine arts I got a scholarship to go to Japan. I didn't learn many things from the classroom as an artist in Japan, I learnt things from looking and going around the country. Most of the things we did in the classroom there were just like here in Samoa, so nothing was new to me except for some sculpturing techniques – things like that. But most of the time I visited museums and galleries and looked at sculptures on the street. That's how I got interested in the Japanese way of life. When I returned from Japan after two and a half years I went back to the school of fine arts in Leulumoega where I started teaching as an assistant.

In 1995 I put up my first solo exhibition at Feiloa'imauso hall in Apia. It was a successful show and that was the first time that I had put up a show by myself with my own works. It was the first time people here had seen big works and seen me in person. It was really amazing to see my own people there, but most of the people hadn't been in museums and didn't know that you're not allowed to touch a painting or work. But here in Samoa we couldn't stop them touching the balls on the bull sculpture. They asked me 'Why did you do the bull's balls, ah?' and I said there's no bull without balls and they were all laughing. I mean that's the things that inspire me, the

Fig. 9.9 *Landscape*, Penehuro Papali'i. (Craig Potton)

Fig. 9.10 Penehuro Papali'i, 1999.

family life and the animals, very aggressive animals and nature ... things like that. I often work on a large scale because I don't like to destroy the natural shape of the wood. It's already an artwork, so I just want to get it, have a look at it, let it inspire me ... you can't limit your expressions into a small thing, if you feel you want to express yourself, you have to get or use something that's already there.

CHAPTER 9

1. R. Neich, 'Material culture of Western Samoa', *National Museum of New Zealand* Bulletin 23 (1985), p. 58
2. This fale no longer stands and was destroyed in a cyclone in the 1990s.
3. Neich, 'Material culture of Western Samoa', p. 27
4. G. Jowitt and P. Shaw, *Pacific Island Style* (Auckland: David Bateman Ltd, 1999), p. 157
5. Neich, 'Material culture of Western Samoa', p. 59
6. Philip J.C. Dark, 'Tomorrow's heritage is today's art and yesteryear's identity' in Hanson and Hanson (eds), *Art and Identity in Oceania* (Australia: Crawford House Press, 1990), p. 260
7. Betty Duncan, 'A hierarchy of symbols: Samoan religious symbolism in New Zealand' PhD. Thesis (Dunedin: Unviersity of Otago, 1994), p. 353
8. Fatu Feu'u, 'Samoan artists in Samoa and New Zealand', *Art and Asia Pacific* vol. 2:4 (1995), pp. 60-67
9. Creative New Zealand [online], available URL: http://www.creativenz.govt.nz/funding/programmes/piac.html
10. Fatu Feu'u, 'Samoan artists in Samoa and New Zealand', pp. 60-67
11. C. Vercoe, 'A Pacific presence: Tautai at the sixth Australian Art Fair', *Art New Zealand* vol. 90 (1999), p. 40
12. From an interview between S. Mallon and F.P. Pereira, *Speaking in Colour* (Wellington: Te Papa Press, 1997), p. 17
13. Interview with author, (May 2000)
14. Fatu Feu'u, 'Samoan artists in Samoa and New Zealand', pp. 60-67
15. R. McLeod, 'The Innocent Eye, Folk art at the Dowse Art Museum', *Art New Zealand* vol. 48 Spring (1988), pp. 75-79
16. G. Fletcher, 'The Painted Life of Teuane Tibbo' (Manuscript Held at Hector Library, Museum of New Zealand, 1996), p.2
17. Fletcher, 'The Painted Life of Teuane Tibbo', p. 2
18. From an interview between S. Mallon and F.P. Pereira, *Speaking in Colour* (Wellington: Te Papa Press, 1997), p. 17
19. From an interview between S. Mallon and F.P. Pereira, *Speaking in Colour* (Wellington: Te Papa Press, 1997), p. 17
20. Interview with author, (May 2000)
21. Interview with author, (May 2000)

ORATORY

Lauga (oratory) is the strongest and most prestigious of the language arts in Samoa and has produced some of Samoa's great leaders, thinkers and powerbrokers. Performed by a particular class of matai it has a very significant role in fa'asamoa. Through lauga important social and cultural values are maintained, renegotiated and enacted. It presents a protocol for proceedings that acknowledges ancestors and remembers the past, but at the same time dictates and manages the course of events at ceremonial and formal gatherings. It is also where some of the most creative interpretations and representations of Samoan history and culture have been made. It is an ancient art of debate, symbolism, allusion and proverb.

Fig. 10.1 Fue, an orator's whisk, Apia, 1999. (Craig Potton)

There are many variations in the practice of oratory and different schools of thought on correct procedures or protocols. This chapter presents a short overview based on the work of two scholars Tatupu Fa'afetai Mata'afa Tu'i and Alessandro Duranti.[1] Their studies are an excellent starting point for readers interested in a more detailed and expanded discussion of this complex art form.

The arts of lauga are the domain and responsibility of the matai, the holders of specific titles of ali'i (chief) or tulafale (orator).[2] Tatupu Fa'afetai Mata'afa Tu'i notes that, 'Both chief and orator may orate, but untitled women and men cannot. The only slight difference between the speech of a chief and that of an orator is that only the latter may perform the really great and masterful speeches.'[3] There are a few women in Samoa that hold an orator title, but although most oratorical contests are exclusively the domain of men, women do use oratory on a number of occasions, especially in women's committees.[4]

The tulafale are custodians of Samoan culture and history in Samoan society. They are keepers of knowledge and directors of its associated functions and protocols. They play an important role representing the interests of the ali'i in any formal occasions or events, but they are also the mouthpiece and representative of the people of a family, village or district.

The tulafale also have other responsibilities, including the distribution of food and the direction of various ceremonies and presentations. They must accompany their chief wherever he travels and protect his interests in every piece of business or ceremonial function in which he engages. The highest ranking orators are often known as tulafale ali'i. These titles are few in number and indicate that the holders are matai who can either be tulafale or ali'i, depending on the occasion and their own will.[5]

Fig. 10.2 Three tulafale (orator chiefs). (Alexander Turnbull Library, National Library of New Zealand, Te Puna Matauranga o Aotearoa. Ref. No: F116319)

In Samoa oratory is presented in two main settings, either indoors within a fale (house) or outdoors on the malae (village green). In both contexts there are rules governing who speaks and in what order and how this is decided, and there are different conventions of presentation and content for each location. For example, inside the fale the to'oto'o (orator's staff) is not used and the orator delivers his speech sitting with legs crossed. Although not always used, several movements are often made with the fue (whisk) before a speaker commences. This may involve throwing it over the left and right shoulders before placing it on the floor parallel to an imaginary line drawn through the knees. The speech is then delivered with the left wrist on one knee and the right palm on the floor in line with the buttock.

The most significant context for oratory, however, is the malae. T.F.M. Tu'i observes that, 'Oratory on the malae requires an extraordinary performance from the orator'.[6] It is the most public context for speechmaking and therefore everything is under scrutiny. The posture of the orator and his placement of the to'oto'o and the fue are an important part of a performance, but the careful use and delivery of words is paramount.

The orator will generally make full of use of symbolism, allusion, metaphors and proverbial expressions in his speechmaking. Aspects of Samoa's history are often referred to as well as myths, legends and important genealogies. Some of the imagery can be quite abstract in nature and will often associate a person with a thing. In some wedding speeches, for example, the future children of the newlyweds are often referred to as if they were the fruit of the coconut palm and travellers may be referred to as canoes approaching land.[7] Orators may also use other devices in their speeches to make a point or embellish their delivery:

Individual orators have their own bag of tricks for holding attention and highlighting special points. A momentary, sharp increase in volume, the introduction of a bit of humour or sarcasm, or the injection of a familiar proverbial saying may be used to catch the attention or to renew the interest of the assembly. A wise orator plays to his audience and alters his style in response to its moods...[8]

There is a distinction to be made when discussing the different lauga. In the context of a fono (meeting), the term lauga only applies to the speech made at the beginning of the fono, the first speech of the day. The rest of the discussions are a part of what is known as the talanoaga. A lauga in a fono is related to but distinct from lauga made in the context of ceremonies such as a weddings or occasions of welcoming. Duranti makes the following clear distinction:

In ceremonial exchanges, the delivery of the lauga is both presented and received with particular attention to all details that enhance the sacred nature of the occasion and make everyone proud of participating in it. In a fono however both the speaker and the audience are less concerned with performance per se and some of the canons of verbal art are lifted... participants are too worried about what is coming next. The delivery of the lauga in a fono is more like a 'job' that needs to get done than an honor or occasion for the proud display of verbal skills.[9]

The ideal structure of any lauga is composed of several parts (vaega), each of which fulfils a different function in the course of events. The structure works as a guide or framework that the orator will work with to suit the requirements of the occasion. The following outline is based on that developed by Tu'i and Duranti.[10]

Fig. 10.3 A fue made from horse hair. (Museum of New Zealand, Te Papa Tongarewa)

1. Folasaga (also called tuvaoga or paepae-ulufanua) - the introduction or opening address, which includes the fa'alupega, the ceremonial style and the address of an individual, village or district.
2. 'Ava - the kava presentation.
3. Fa'afetai i le alofa o le atua – the references to ancestors and the expressions of gratitude and thanks to God.
4. Taeao – literally, mornings. The recounting of important events in Samoa's history.
5. Pa'ia – greeting of the sacred titles. A reminder of the power of mythical historical figures and their descendants.
6. Faia or mataupu – the agenda.
7. Fa'amatafiga o lagi – literally, the clearing of skies. The wishing of good luck, peace and prosperity to the visitors and then to the orator's own party.

Fig. 10.4 A fue made from 'afa (coconut fibre cord). (Craig Potton)

Oratory can be intensely competitive, and a good or bad performance affects the prestige of not only the orator but also those he represents. Competition is usually strongest for the right to address or speak to an assembly first. The debate over who has this privilege can last a few minutes or more than an hour. Important considerations in these discussions include an individual's rank, but also their knowledge and eloquence. Engaging in this type of activity is called fa'atau, which literally means 'to provoke contention'.[11] It is in this competitive aspect of oratory that the skills, character and knowledge of an orator first reveal themselves.

Anthropologist Derek Freeman has noted some incidents he witnessed which capture the intensity and competitive spirit of Samoan oratory. In his discussion he describes how oratory can be very emotional, with angry responses exchanged when one speaker interrupts another during the fa'atau process. Sometimes these exchanges could end up in physical violence. Any opportunity for a tulafale to shame a rival into submission would be quickly exploited.[12] In one case he mentions how a tulafale who had interjected on another, questioning his knowledge of genealogy, was promptly put in his place with the words: 'You talk like a Fijian! Don't speak to me of that which lies beyond your understanding!' Needless to say the humiliated tulafale at once withdrew from the proceedings. The frustration and elation experienced in oratory is also made clear in these observations:

Because of the unsurpassed rank of the Tui Manu'a and his attendant talking chiefs, no tulafale from elsewhere in Samoa is able to win a fa'atau contest on the ceremonial ground of Ta'u. I have seen talking chiefs of high rank from Western Samoa reduced to tears when faced with this overwhelming situation. Equally strong emotion is sometimes displayed by those who triumph in a fa'atau contest. On occasion even a seasoned talking chief will be so overcome as to weep in the elation of victory.[13]

Fig. 10.5 Lauaki Namulau'ulu Mamoe (18??-1915), a leading tulafale from Safotulafai, Savai'i. (Alexander Turnbull Library, National Library of New Zealand, Te Puna Matauranga o Aotearoa. Ref. No: PAcoll 3060-008)

In Samoa oratory is an art where relationships and hierarchies are honoured and reputations made. Some of Samoa's most skilled teachers and leaders have emerged from the ranks of the tulafale. Many of them are natural leaders and have intense ambition. One man who epitomised the potential influence and achievements of the tulafale was Lauaki Namulau'ulu Mamoe (18??-1915), a leading tulafale from Safotulafai, the political centre of the Fa'asaleleaga district on Savai'i. [In the late 19th century Namulau'ulu and Tuilagi were two of the most important orator titles, the holders of which could on occasion speak for the whole of Savai'i.[14]]

Lauaki was known throughout Samoa for 'his mastery of history and legend, for his talents as a speaker and political negotiator, and for his prowess in war'.[15] He went on to lead an important political movement called the Mau (Opinion) of Pule. The term Pule was the collective name given to a number of influential orator groups on Savai'i. The tulafale and tulafale ali'i of the Pule spoke for the principal nu'u and district of Savai'i as a whole and served its ranking ali'i.[16]

The aim of the Mau of Pule was to challenge German rule and try to secure more Samoan involvement in the affairs of government. Under Lauaki's leadership the movement was initially successful, but struggled due to factionalism. In 1909 the German Governor at the time took Lauaki into custody because of his resistance to the colonial authority. Later Lauaki and nine other chiefs and their families were exiled to Saipan in the Mariana Islands as punishment for refusing to give up their opposition. Six years later in 1915 the New Zealand government sent a ship to bring Lauaki and his supporters home. But Lauaki died from dysentery during the return voyage. He had, however, made his mark and initiated an important process that would see the eventual independence of Western Samoa.

Writing in 1970, J.W. Davidson noted that Lauaki Namulau'ulu Mamoe was still remembered with affection and respect: 'In Saipan, where the exiles maintained the conventions of their homeland in a village they built near Tanapag, the commanding figure of their leader has not yet been forgotten. In Samoa, old men recall the splendours of his oratory'.

Today the Namulau'ulu title is held by tulafale ali'i Namulau'ulu Tofa Fa'amau Pusa Fonoti. After many years of living and working in Samoa he now lives in Levin, New Zealand. He continues to play an important role in Samoan community affairs, especially in the church where he is a minister. Here he tells us how he came to receive the Namulau'ulu title, what it means to him and some of the skills and responsibilities of the Samoan orator:

NAMULAU'ULU TOFA FA'AMAU PUSA FONOTI

I was born on March 12th 1932 at Sale'imoa. I am from the Aleipata, my father was from Amaile and my mother is from Levi, Sale'imoa. We stayed in Aleipata and that is where I was brought up for most of my life. I came to Apia and went to school at Mulivai, the Marist Brothers' School. I was brought up in the Catholic Church and that is where I was educated.

Namulau'ulu Lauaki was a chief among the family of my wife. That is how I got a title from their family; because my wife's father is part of the Namulau'ulu family. The title is a very high-talking chief title not only of the village, but also the district as well as the whole of Samoa. Namulau'ulu Lauaki was a well-known man in the past, because of his attitude and the fact that he was strong for the Mau of Pule movement at the time as well as for the country.

Fig. 10.6 Tulafale ali'i Namulau'ulu Tofa Fa'amau Pusa Fonoti, 2001. (Theresa Mallon)

Before I received the Namulau'ulu title, I had received another title – Tofa. It's a chief's name from Saipipi; it is a very special chief title of Saipipi and when you come to my wife's village her family is the highest of that village. I have a title also from my own father as well, Fonoti from Amaile, and then I got another title from my mother, that's Fa'amauiapi from Vailu'utai. So I had experience before I received the title of Namulau'ulu. I was very grateful because, not only the title of Namulau'ulu, but all the other titles, they are high chief titles as well. I'm 68 years of age now and I got the title of Namulau'ulu when I was about 50 years of age.

When I was young my father was the first man to pass on the knowledge of the matai. My father was a high chief of Amaile and whenever he went to a meeting he would take me there with him. This was because it was the only school house for the young. When it was time for people to come to our home he would appoint me to go and prepare the 'ava ceremony. That is how I started my life.

I have always been a friend to lots of orators especially in Savai'i. What I did was make sure to always go and be in company with those orators. In my town there was no special education or subjects to learn in school like now, no, what we learnt in that time was at the matai's house. So whatever happened, say like a village meeting, I would have to be there. I'd like to listen and catch up with the ideas of speech and the ways of matai life. There was one chief I would go and see every evening and talk about things because he was a talented man. Leilua Pilia'e Kose is another man in my village who gave me a lot of experience. Tuilagi is another man I would discuss things with. We would talk about the past and present of the Samoan way of life. They have both gone on to be members of Samoa's parliament.

Fig. 10.7 Tulafale, Independence Day celebrations, Apia, Upolu, 1999. (Craig Potton)

The failauga has to understand what they are saying and they have to understand what the purpose is of what they're saying. This is because there are different types of problems that can come up and different ways of lauga. There is different lauga when we meet visitors, and it's different when you are going to speak on behalf of a family at a funeral ceremony or at a marriage ceremony and so on. An important skill is to understand the different ways of saying what needs to be said and according to the right purpose. And being able to anticipate any problems that may come up. You also have to understand relationships between or among the other chiefs and relate this to the other village relationships. You have to know every way of addressing other villages as well as their history. Because if you don't know these things the other villages will criticise you severely. Sometimes some of the orators will treat you as if you don't know anything, so you have to prepare for those occasions. So the skills of the failauga are to understand and be prepared for everything. Not only at times when they are appointed to do something, but also to just be prepared for now, tomorrow, whenever.

CHAPTER 10

1. See Duranti, A., *From Grammar to Politics: Linguistic Anthropology in a Samoan Village* (Berkeley: California University Press, 1994); and Tu'i, T.F.M., *Launga: Samoan Oratory* (Suva: Institute of Pacific Studies, University of the South Pacific, Apia USP Western Samoan Extension Centre National University of Western Samoa, 1987), p. 1. See the Bibliography for further writing by Dr Duranti on the Samoan oratory.

2. Meleisea notes that tulafale literally means 'house foundation', but the term is usually translated as 'talking chiefs' or 'orators' in recognition of the role played by the tulafale in speaking on behalf of the chiefs. Meleisea, M., 'To whom gods and men crowded': chieftainship and hierarchy in ancient Samoa', in Huntsman, Judith (ed), *Tonga and Samoa, Images of Gender and Polity* (Christchurch: Macmillan Brown Centre for Pacific Studies, University of Canterbury, 1995), pp. 19-35

3. Tu'i, *Launga: Samoan Oratory* (Suva: Institute of Pacific Studies, University of the South Pacific Apia USP Western Samoa Extension Centre National University of Western Samoa, 1987), p. 1

4. Duranti, *From Grammar to Politics*, p. 174

5. A. Duranti, personal comment, (2000)

6. Tu'i, *Launga: Samoan Oratory*, p. 17

7. Tu'i, *Launga: Samoan Oratory*, p. 20

8. Holmes, cited in Tu'i, M., *Launga: Samoan Oratory*, p. 17

9. A. Duranti, 'Heteroglossia in Samoan oratory', in *Pacific Studies Special Issue: The Arts and Politics* vol. 15:4 (Hawai'i: Institute of Pacific Studies, Brigham Young University, 1992), p. 167

10. Tu'i, *Launga: Samoan Oratory*, pp. 22-26

11. D. Freeman, *Margaret Mead and Samoa: The making and unmaking of an Anthropological Myth* (Canberra: Australian National University Press, 1983), pp. 148-149

12. Freeman, *Margaret Mead and Samoa*, pp. 148-149

13. Freeman, *Margaret Mead and Samoa*, pp. 148-149

14. J.W. Davidson, 'Lauaki Namaulau'ulu Mamoe, a traditionalist in Samoan Politics', p. 268, in Davidson, J.W., and Scarr, D.A. (eds), *Pacific Island Portraits* (Canberra: Australian National University Press, 1970), pp. 267-299

15. Davidson, 'Lauaki Namaulau'ulu Mamoe', p. 267

16. M. Meleisea, *The Making of Modern Samoa* (Suva: Institute for Pacific Studies of the University of the South Pacific, 1987), p. 15

CHAPTER 11

THEATRE

FALEAITU: SAMOAN COMIC THEATRE

In Samoa there is a form of comic theatre known as faleaitu, which literally translates as 'house of spirits'. Faleaitu has long been a part of Samoan culture and retains an important presence in Samoan communities abroad. It is recognised as the most formalised of Samoa's humorous performance genres[1] and is an important way of dealing with tensions and conflicts in a community by providing a mirror in which the audience can see aspects of themselves.

There are several scholars whose excellent research should be consulted for a full and authoritative account and commentary on faleaitu.[2] Here the customary role and characteristics of faleaitu are briefly outlined as a prelude to some contemporary developments in theatre generally.

Early accounts of faleaitu generally describe performers in the familiar terms of clowns, buffoons or jesters. One such description comes from the missionary George Turner who in the 19th century wrote:

Court Buffoons furnish some amusement at dancing and other festivals, and also at public meetings. If a chief of importance goes to any of these assemblies, he has in his train one or two Merry-Andrews, who, by oddity in dress, gait, or gesture, or by lascivious jokes, try to excite laughter.[3]

These Merry-Andrews or clowns continue to play an important role at many Samoan gatherings. In her research Caroline Sinavaiana identifies two forms of public clowning that are practised commonly: spontaneous clowning, which is usually associated with dance and choral singing; and scripted clowning, which is a more formalised expression based on rehearsed songs and comic sketches.

It is the comic sketches that are known as faleaitu.[4] Samoan playwright John Kneubuhl describes what appears to be a 19th century historical and customary context for faleaitu in the following terms:

… in the Samoan village, there was a fale, or house, set aside for the aitu, or spirit… In the villages, the aitu could be a rock, a piece of tapa, anything uniquely different, but perhaps a coconut shaped in a funny way. The aitu for each village would be kept in a hut. So if you have a fale and you're doing theatricals – dancing or singing perhaps – and you release that spirit into that house, that house becomes a fale aitu or house of that spirit… A fale aitu is therefore a spirit house that is used for performing comedic sketches.[5]

Fig. 11.1 Poster for *Tatau: Rites of Passage*. Pacific Underground, 1996.

Today faleaitu sketches are performed as part of larger concerts or fundraising events and take place between or after sets of songs or dances. The sketches themselves provide a medium where conflicts can be addressed, commentary made and the routine and order of everyday life forgotten. Popular targets for the faleaitu practitioner are 'those authority figures normally commanding deference and respect, like political leaders, pastors, parents and teachers'.[6] This is highly significant in a society where respect to those in authority is very important. In the satire and comedy of these performances gentle and humorous suggestion is a potential political tool. More often than not, those being made fun of are present in the audience and it requires great skill to address important and serious issues in a humorous way. But the scope of the

Fig. 11.2 Poster for *Tusitala and the House of Spirits*, Pacific Theatre, 1996.

faleaitu also goes beyond the immediate community and culture and can just as easily make fun of foreigners, and the attitudes and mannerisms of Western culture.[7]

It is young untitled men who have customarily taken on the role of performers in faleaitu. The role of the leading comedian can be likened to that of a ghost or spirit in that the messages and criticism of the comic sketch will be performed and projected through him. As Caroline Sinavaiana comments, 'it is the ghost who delivers the punch lines that carry the social or political criticism home to the particular authority figure being lampooned'.[8] In this way almost anything goes and almost everything is forgiven in the context of faleaitu because it is generally accepted that it is not the performer who is doing the talking or making the criticism, but the voice of the spirits.

A common purpose of faleaitu performances today is to raise funds for different projects or activities, such as church buildings or village events. Some faleaitu groups travel to other villages, islands or even overseas for this reason. Faleaitu are also regularly performed as part of Independence celebrations in Samoa and in American Samoa they are often seen on television.[9]

Faleaitu also maintains a strong presence and popularity in Samoan communities overseas. Longtime contemporary practitioner Petelo has performed for Samoan audiences in Los Angeles (but has on occasion reappeared for shows in Samoa). Likewise in New Zealand faleaitu retains a presence among the large Samoan community: a New Zealand version of faleaitu regularly appears at major national comedy festivals and occasionally on television.

One of the differences between Samoan-based and New Zealand-based faleaitu performances seems to lie in the way the Samoan language is used. In Samoa the humorous subtleties and innuendo, and the clever and sophisticated use of language are often hidden within the oratory. In New Zealand the humour and performances are a more physical type of theatre, where body language and actions are more important in conveying the message or idea.[10]

This type of performance can be seen at the Auckland Secondary Schools' Maori and Pacific Island Arts Festival in New Zealand where the art of faleaitu is encouraged and promoted in competition. Skits have included hilarious and very physical re-enactments of television lottery draws and all-star professional wrestling bouts. There is a special category for faleaitu and the judging criteria is interesting in that it reflects the current New Zealand Samoan community's perceptions of what constitutes a good performance. Marking criteria from the official 2000 event score sheets included scores for performers' enthusiasm; stance and posture; ensuring there were no sarcasms or put-downs; the effective use of polite expressions; originality; and audience response. Another category was cultural appropriateness – which covered a troupe's awareness of fa'asamoa and their respectful use of humour and the Samoan language.

Sinavaiana touched on the criteria of a good performance mentioning that 'One's degree of skill or accomplishment is measured by how many different characters and voices can be convincingly projected in a single performance'.[11] So in a genre of theatre where the unpredictability of the 'spirits' is supposed to reign there are some interesting differences between the New Zealand and Samoan contexts as to what constitutes a successful performance.

Two people who have been studying faleaitu in New Zealand and Samoa for over ten years are Justine and Paul Simei-Barton. In 1987 they established a theatre company – Pacific Theatre – founded on the concepts and principles of faleaitu to see if what was a very old theatrical practice could offer a theory and technique for a new type of contemporary theatre. In all their productions since 1987 they have used aspects of faleaitu, be it in stage performances, training for actors and actresses, script development and workshops.

One of their plays, *Tusitala and the House of Spirits* (1996), is a story about Scottish writer Robert Louis Stevenson and his experiences in Samoa in the late 19th century when he met a faleaitu troupe during the civil war. It's notable for its use of faleaitu, and because it also introduced the art to a new generation of young Samoans and Pacific islanders. In 1996 Pacific Theatre was also instrumental in initiating a week-long faleaitu workshop involving two faleaitu experts, Caroline Sinavaiana and performer Siaki. It was the first time a workshop of this nature had been conducted and the idea was to get elders with expertise in faleaitu to teach aspects of it to a younger generation of people, so they could use its concepts in their own theatrical work. Out of this workshop came a faleaitu troupe called The Brownies.

The Brownies perform a contemporary style of faleaitu founded on Samoan ideas but in many respects unique to the experience of New Zealand-based Pacific island communities. Vela Manusaute and Canada Alofa are a trained actor and a stand-up comedian respectively, and since 1997 have worked together to bring a different humour and view of society to New Zealand audiences. Vela was born in Niue and is of Samoan and Niuean descent, Canada was born in Samoa where his father was a faleaitu practitioner; he came to New Zealand when he was eight years old. Their faleaitu production *F.O.B. - Fools of the Bacific* (1997) won the 1997 Chapman Tripp Theatre award for Best Male Comedy. In the true nature of faleaitu, The Brownies have brought some memorable scenes and humorous but hard-hitting commentary to the stage. Much of it is slapstick and tends to play on stereotypes and political incorrectness, but there is often a serious and sometimes alarming undertone. One controversial scene involved the drunken brandishing of a

Fig. 11.3 Faleaitu performers Vela Manusaute and Canada Alofa, 2000. (Sean Mallon)

machete during a Samoan wedding, but the more light-hearted moments include re-enactments of Samoan rugby games and mock nightly news presentations. The Brownies make no apology for their indiscretions and honesty, and say they try to use the comedy of faleaitu '... to make people just slightly uncomfortable and have a good look at their culture'.[12]

FALEAITU PERFORMER: VELA MANUSAUTE

The idea for The Brownies started in a workshop, a faleaitu workshop held by this master from Samoa called Siaki. From there that's where Canada and I hooked up. Canada was a strict stand-up comedian and I had just come out of New Zealand Drama School. With my drama background and Canada as a stand-up comic we decided to do faleaitu as there was no regular faleaitu performances for Samoans in New Zealand.

You have to understand the Samoan ways before you do faleaitu. I was lucky because I was brought up in the islands, so was Canada, we are both island born and we were brought up in the islands and brought up here. So the material we use is from both these points of view.

Our faleaitu has got no rules and has a lot of audience participation. If you see faleaitu in Samoa you'll freak out, to the palagi it's like 'that's not theatre!' but to we Samoans that's faleaitu, you have been possessed by the spirit. Of course, we are poking fun at society but we are able to get away with it because people are saying, oh that's faleaitu, that's the spirits talking through them. We believe in the spirit and when we perform in public the laws of drama school are not on. Depending on how good the spirit is, the show will be good or bad, and if you start swearing then you have got an evil spirit...

I'll tell you, faleaitu in Samoa is different, faleaitu in Samoa is ... well, if the audience are not laughing then you have got a problem, man. Or if you insult someone, make sure people are laughing, because when people are laughing, what happens is that it just goes through them, but when people have stopped laughing they are thinking. That's what I got from Petelo and Sumeu, masters of faleaitu. In Samoa if you are not funny they let you know you are not funny.

SAMOANS AND PACIFIC ISLAND THEATRE IN NEW ZEALAND

Sinavaiana has noted that the earliest 19th century accounts associate theatrical performances in Samoa within the context of dances: 'With Christian suppression of licentious contexts, entertainment began to include skits, as separate dramatic inter-ludes between songs'.[13] Aspects of Western theatre were to further influence Samoan performances; later in the colonial era travelling theatre troupes would use props, set up stages lit by torchlight and perform plays influenced by European stories. 'Plots might come from sources like Shakespeare, but troupes localised the material,'[14] observes Sinavaiana. The imitating or lampooning of foreigners was and to some extent still is popular.

Plays based on legends and biblical stories are the most common type of theatri-cal performance in Samoan communities. These short plays feature strongly, especially on religious occasions such as White Sunday, Easter and Christmas. Since the early 1980s, however, Pacific island theatre in New Zealand has seen Samoan stories come to the stage in a more formal and professional way. But the work of Samoan actors, directors and playwrights is still very much a pioneering endeavour.

Pacific island theatre in New Zealand has a relatively short history and is little more than 20 years old. The beginnings of a Samoan contribution can be traced to Pacific islanders' involvement in Maori theatre, which was particularly strong in the early 1980s. A small but significant group at this time was Taotahi ma Uo based in

Wellington. Comprised mainly of young Maori and Polynesians, most ex-pupils of Wellington High School, they had initially got together with the encouragement of a very creative English teacher as part of their English class activities. Afterward they ended up at the Wellington Arts' Centre as part of the Wellington Summer City programme. Taotahi ma Uo was formed just after the controversial Springbok rugby tour in 1981 and was quite political in its focus. Then out of this environment of cultural and ethnic issues came the enthusiasm to produce the first professional full length Samoan play written and performed in New Zealand. Called *Le Matau* (The Fish Hook) it was developed by Stephen Sinclair and Samson Samasoni and premiered in 1984 at the New Depot Theatre.[15]

Le Matau is the story of a young man, Ioane who comes to New Zealand from Samoa and becomes a successful real estate agent. The story follows how he turns his back on his fa'asamoa, changing his name and eventually becoming regarded by his family as someone who has sold out. The themes it explores were relevant to many young Samoans at the time. Taotahi actor Eteuati Ete recalls the issues involved:

It was about the conflict that a lot of first and second generation Samoans were facing in New Zealand at the time. They were living in a palagi world, where they had to almost think like a palagi, but at the same time also as a Samoan. So it was the dilemma that many Samoans living in New Zealand ultimately have to face, taking on New Zealand values and culture but also finding a way to hold onto some fa'asamoa.[16]

This focus on the process of immigration and the clash of cultural values was to remain central in the work of writers and directors to come. *Le Matau* is perhaps significant as it was one of the first of several productions to give confidence and experience to a new Pacific voice in the New Zealand theatre scene. But this was also the objective of another initiative running successfully in South Auckland around the same time. Known as Statement Theatre, the project was organised by Samoan actor Nathaniel Lees who had been involved in theatre since the early 1970s.

Fig. 11.4 Poster for *A Frigate Bird Sings*, Pacific Underground, 1996.

I started my own theatre group out there in South Auckland called Statement Theatre. We used to go out to the primary schools, secondary schools, intermediate schools there and get them to tell us any problems they were having at school, what it was like living out there. There were three of us and it went great. We did our own little scenes and plays out there.

In terms of writing the stories it was basically their stories and the richness of what they were telling me... what they were telling us that kept pulling us together. At one of the schools we went to there was Jay Laga'aia and he watched us when we came and performed there. He and I have since done two-man shows together. We were talking one day and he said when you guys came over to our school it was the first time I realised that we could do theatre, that brown faces on the stage were as acceptable as anything else. Actually doing and performing theatre was a possibility, was an option...[17]

Fig. 11.5 Poster for *Fresh Off the Boat*, Pacific Underground, 1994.

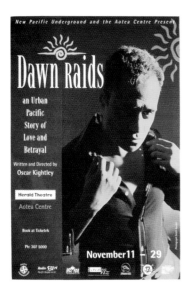

Fig. 11.6 Poster for *Dawn Raids*, Pacific Underground, 1997.

Jay Laga'aia went on to establish himself as a theatre actor and is now known for his roles in New Zealand and Australian film and television. It was with people of Jay's generation that the future of Pacific theatre now rested.

Lani Tupu and Eteuati Ete were the first and second Samoans respectively to successfully audition and go through the New Zealand Drama School. This experience was crucial in the young actors' development. Eteuati comments:

It gave me great confidence knowing that you were one of 12 to be selected to go there. It certainly gave me the skills and tools to work in theatre and I think the two years were really invaluable, it just gave you an insight into how powerful theatre could be as a medium.

One of the most difficult things I found when I left drama school was trying to find Samoan theatre. I was asked to do a lot of Maori roles, and I love Maori theatre, it's given me a lot and I hope I have given it as much as it has given me, but at the end of the day I wasn't Maori and there weren't the roles for Samoans. When Taotahi was disbanded I really had nowhere to go. When I made a return to theatre it was 1991 and I wrote and performed The Johnny Smith Myth. *It was about a Samoan rock star that became world famous. If no one was going to write the roles for me I was going to have to write the roles myself.*

Since this time there have been many other initiatives and people whose work has breathed life into the development of Pacific island theatre in the 1990s.

One of these was a Christchurch-based group of young Polynesians who got together in 1991. They formed a collective that produced, wrote and acted their own plays and eventually became known as Pacific Underground. Since then they have been the trail-blazers for a Pacific island voice in New Zealand theatre. The group's aim as outlined in its initial brochure was 'to develop professional theatre that explored current issues for people living in the Pacific'.[18] Their first efforts took the form of a play called *Gifted and Fresh*. It toured to local schools and received a positive response. Co-written by Simon Small and Oscar Kightley, it told a story about young people struggling with their parents' expectations and having to juggle the values of two cultures in one society. Although the theme wasn't new, it was probably the first time that Pacific Underground's young audience had seen Polynesian stories on stage. Anton Carter, Pacific Underground's manager comments:

We were one of the few Pacific island theatre groups that was touring, so for schools it was probably the only exposure that they would ever get of brown people on stage being brown people and being positive and good. So our school and community performances were really an effort to say to the parents of the kids, 'hey look these young kids have skills and it's about a job and if they want to act they can act. Don't force them into factories, don't force them into things that you know about'.[19]

Far from being a contrived effort to do something culturally different, Pacific Underground's motive was more a natural urge to tell stories that were part of their own experience.

half-caste
half-brothers
same father
different mothers

Sons

By Victor Rodger

HERALD THEATRE
SEPT 18 - OCT 9 1999

BOOK AT TICKETEK
09 307 5000

Fig. 11.7 Poster for *Sons*, Pacific Underground, 1995.

We never tried to compete with palagi playwrights or other theatre companies. It wasn't a conscious thing of 'this is our market and this is what we're going to do', it was more of a 'who are we, where are we from, and what are our stories about?' This was the start of Pacific Underground, it was where the company started.[20]

Pacific Underground went on to produce plays that toured nationally. All were Samoan stories that incorporated the themes of immigration, culture clash and the growing generation gap, but they all seemed to translate well and were understood by the largely multicultural audience. In many ways the themes and issues were not unique to the Samoan experience, just presented from a Samoan perspective.

Fresh Off the Boat (1994) written by Simon Small and Oscar Kightley and directed by Nathaniel Lees, describes the struggles of a Samoan man (played by David Fane) trying to adjust to life in New Zealand. It was a major hit and had extended seasons in Wellington and Auckland. It later toured to Australia and Samoa.

Tatau: Rites of Passage (1996) was also a critical success and played in Auckland and Australia. It follows the story of a troubled man and how receiving the pe'a is his homecoming and his return to his roots. A highlight of the show was the actual tattooing of a man on stage by renowned tufuga tatatau Su'a Sulu'ape Paulo II. In the play the tatau is used as a metaphor for the journey undertaken by the protagonist.

A Frigate Bird Sings (1996) is the story of Vili, a fa'afafine (Samoan transvestite) in search of identity and a sense of integrity after immigrating to New Zealand. It brought writers Oscar Kightley and David Fane together again with seasoned actor Nathaniel Lees, who took a directorial role.

The following year Kightley went on to write *Dawn Raids* (1997) a work based on the infamous New Zealand government crackdown on Pacific island overstayers in the 1970s. It brought a dark period in New Zealand's recent history to the stage for the first time and presented it through the eyes of a Samoan family.

In 1998 a play penned by New Zealand Drama School graduate Victor Rodgers called *Sons* (1995) scooped several prizes at the Chapman Tripp Theatre Awards. Originally premiered in Christchurch 1995, it is a semi-autobiographical story of what happens when an 'afakasi (part Samoan or half-caste), who has been raised by his palagi mother, contacts his estranged Samoan father for the first time in a decade.

The 1990s were a period of learning, gaining experience, making theatre and developing talent. The amount of work produced by such a small group of actors and writers and the fact that they also toured so extensively is testimony not only to their success but their enthusiasm for the craft. Overall the reaction to this new voice in New Zealand theatre was positive, although certain issues and the way they were confronted still posed a challenge to some members of the island community. Anton Carter remembers the reaction to some of the shows:

The initial response from the island community was 'What is this? What right do you have to be doing this? And who gives you that right?' We had a far bigger reputation in Auckland than we did in Christchurch. People knew us, we had an audience and one that was growing. In Christchurch it was more difficult because of the demographics and also because the Pacific island community was and still is really conservative.

We challenged a lot of people, a lot of the elders, a lot of the younger people, mainstream theatre and everyone. Some still look down their noses at us. It's like, 'you haven't been to drama school so you can't be an actor. You are brown people and brown people don't act, they just sing songs' so we are still challenging the perception and saying 'Hang on … We can actually write very clever and very serious plays, as well as very humorous plays. We can really do whatever we want to do and we should be allowed to do that.[21]

Fig. 11.8 Still from Makerita Urale's play *Frangipani Perfume*. Diana Fuemana as 'Naiki'. Bats Theatre, 1997. (Sarah Hunter)

Out of Pacific Underground came a group of people with experience in many aspects of theatre. The lack of funding made it necessary for everyone to be a jack-of-all-trades and able to contribute in a range of capacities so Pacific Underground not only produced many fine actors, actresses and directors, but also a strong group of administrators and technicians.

Independent from Pacific Underground, several other Samoan writers, actors, directors and producers also made their mark in the 1990s. Established in 1987 by Paul and Justine Simei-Barton, Auckland-based Pacific Theatre produced several productions in the early to mid-1990s founded on concepts of faleaitu. Their productions included a Polynesian retelling of Shakespeare's *Romeo and Juliet* (1992), *The Contest* (1994) and *Tusitala and the House of Spirits* (1996). For several years they also toured a popular children's pantomime called *Lupe and Sina*. Several actors, including David Fane, Shimpal Lelisi, Canada Alofa and Vela Manusaute, started their careers with Pacific Theatre, but as its members have moved on to other work the company has changed its focus. A current project is a documentary on the art of faleaitu.

Based in Wellington, director, producer and playwright Makerita Urale has also made a contribution to theatre in recent years. Her effort brought a perspective not seen so often in Pacific theatre to that point. Urale had produced *A Frigate Bird Sings* for The International Festival of the Arts in 1996 and she quickly followed this up by writing and producing her own play *Frangipani Perfume* the following year. Directed initially by Pacific Underground's Erolia Ifopo, it was a black comedy about three unruly Samoan sisters and their opinions on 'Makelika Mead', 'Einstein's theory of relative-ty' and the stereotypes of Pacific island women. The show premiered in Wellington in 1997 and toured to Auckland in 1998 and at the time Makerita commented that: 'Most of the women characters in Samoan theatre to date have been written by men … there hasn't been a show like this focusing on women. It's a story that hasn't been told yet…'[22]

But the play considered by some to be a landmark in Pacific island theatre in

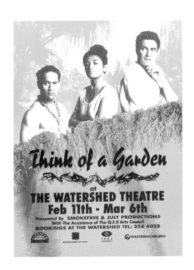

Fig. 11.9 Poster for *Think of a Garden*, Auckland production, 1993.

Fig. 11.10 Poster for *Naked Samoans Talk About Their Knives*, 1998.

New Zealand is *Think of a Garden* by John Kneubuhl. *Think of a Garden* premiered at Auckland's Watershed Theatre in 1993 and the cast included Lani Tupu, Jay Laga'aia and New Zealander Martin Sanderson. In 1995 the play was taken to Wellington's Taki Rua Theatre and recast with Sima Urale and Eteuati Ete. In that year it went on to win New Zealand Theatre awards for Best Director, Best Production, Best Female Supporting Actor and Best Set Design.[23] John Kneubuhl is one of Samoa's accomplished playwrights; he worked for many years in Hollywood as a writer for television and has episodes of *The Fugitive*, *Hawai'i Five-O* and *Perry Mason* to his credit. While he was also influential in the Hawai'ian theatre community, he is best known in New Zealand for *Think of a Garden*. It was considered by many to be an important play because it showed the way that Samoan stories could be written and developed for stage. Fittingly, pioneering actors Eteuati Ete, Lani Tupu, Nathaniel Lees and Sima Urale were there. Eteuati Ete comments that:

The major one for me was Think of a Garden. *I think for me that was the peak in terms of Samoan theatre in New Zealand. Because there you had a writer who was a brilliant writer and I was working with Nathaniel Lees, someone I admired as a director, and with someone like Lani Tupu as well, and we had a great cast. That for me was a highlight of my career.*[24]

A trilogy of plays by the Naked Samoans has been one of the latest theatrical explorations of Samoan and Pacific islanders' lives in New Zealand. Beginning with *Naked Samoans Talk about their Knives* (1998) the approach and humour were a welcome break for a group of actors who had been involved for several years in serious issue-driven theatre. Oscar Kightley:

When we first set up, all our plays were all so bloody serious and filled with issues. We just wanted to break from that, we just wanted to do a play that was stupid. Not stupid, but filled with stuff that we wanted to do, stuff that we laughed about. So Naked Samoans Talk about their Knives was almost like a release… To release and to do stuff that made us laugh, but which was generally really risky and rude.[25]

Much of the material in the Naked Samoans' series drew upon the common upbringing of the actors and writers involved. The familiar issues and dialogue formed a real point of connection for the audiences. Oscar Kightley again:

We drew a lot upon our upbringing for raw material for our shows. Particularly with the Naked Samoans style of comedy, we rely on that familiarity and recognition for a lot of our humour. The reactions we get are people recognising an aspect of what they themselves lived with and grew up with. I do think it's fairly typical and relevant to most people because the material works.[26]

In some respects the Naked Samoan productions are like faleaitu in that the brash, cutting humour and sarcasm is forgiven by the typically conservative Pacific audience, just for that moment. Like faleaitu, the spirits are talking, and things that usually remain unsaid are presented in an artificial context where they are masked by humour and parody. So while the Naked Samoans themselves see their shows as a release or as stupid, risky and rude, what they produce is perhaps more serious, relevant and issue-driven than they care to acknowledge.

Samoan theatre in New Zealand is still at an early stage. There is only a small group of actors and even fewer writers and directors. But they are part of wider developments in Pacific theatre where the future looks promising. Talents such as Toa Fraser are bringing other stories from different cultural perspectives to the mix. As part of a wider effort by those of Pacific island descent to bring their own experiences to the stage, Samoans have made, perhaps through weight of numbers, a strong contribution. Samoan stories have contributed to a changing local theatre scene which is increasingly capturing the diversity of the society of which it is a part. Maori theatre has long been part of this process as have plays such as the critically acclaimed Indian immigrant story *Krishnan's Dairy* (1998). They add to a multicultural list of New Zealand theatre productions that grows longer each year. In assessing the Samoan contribution to Pacific and New Zealand theatre, Anton Carter, former manager of Pacific Underground, and now Pacific Island Arts Advisor at Creative New Zealand perhaps sums it up best:

The contribution has been one of just being pioneers, being the first to do a lot of things. The first Pacific islands play, the first Pacific island director… The way theatre is produced here is still very family orientated. Everybody knows everyone. Everyone works together on productions and supports everybody else. The real strength and legacy of the work to date lies in how together we have built a foundation and put a stake in the ground for future generations.[27]

PLAYWRIGHT: JOHN ALEXANDER KNEUBUHL

As mentioned above, a landmark play in the development of Pacific island theatre in New Zealand was *Think of a Garden* by Samoan playwright John Kneubuhl, yet his contribution to theatre and drama in general extends well beyond the Samoan community. This short account of John Kneubuhl's life and work was written by his niece and Hawai'i based playwright Victoria Nalani Kneubuhl:

Fig. 11.11 Playwright John Kneubuhl. (Photo F. Sutter, courtesy of University of Hawai'i Press)

John Alexander Kneubuhl was born in 1920 in Pago Pago, American Samoa of a Samoan mother and American father. Growing up bilingual, he naturally learned to form cultural bridges during his childhood. John attended Punahou School and subsequently was accepted to Yale University. At Yale, his writing talents were nurtured in the prestigious 'Workshop 47' which accepted only the most promising writing students. It was during these years that John studied with Thorton Wilder, one of America's most important playwrights.

After graduation, the World War and a tour of duty with naval intelligence, John returned to Honolulu. He wrote several plays and became the assistant artistic director for the Honolulu Community Theatre. His historical play, The Harp in the Willows, *was a landmark event in establishing a genuinely local theatre movement. John promulgated the slogan 'Pacific plays for Pacific playwrights'. His vision of Hawai'i's artistic and cultural value far exceeded that of Honolulu society in the 1940s. Toward an island theatre he said, 'We want to have a far greater representation of the various groups that make up island society, and we hope for the day when they can appear solely in plays for and by them'. In 1949 John left for Hollywood and local theatre was robbed of an articulate and passionate spokesperson. John had a successful career as a Hollywood screenwriter and wrote for nearly every major television network in the 1950s and 1960s.*

In 1968, John left what he called the 'essential hollowness' of his work in Hollywood and returned home to Samoa. He once again took up writing for the stage and generated some of his finest work, which is now being produced and published throughout the Pacific. John became a moving force in education and was essential in establishing the Community College of American Samoa. He also embarked on a new career of classroom teaching which he pursued with passion and dedication. John was a formidable advocate for establishing bi-lingual and bi-cultural education in the schools of Samoa. The remainder of John's life represents an unfailing concern for the Pacific, its people, history, culture, arts and environment. He died in 1992 and is buried on his family land in Leone, Samoa.

PLAYWRIGHT AND ACTOR: OSCAR KIGHTLEY

Samoan playwright Oscar Kightley has been a leading figure in the development of Pacific island theatre in New Zealand. He was a founding member of the theatre company Pacific Underground and in 1998 he was awarded the Sunday Star Times Bruce Mason playwriting award. He has also acted and written for television.

Fig. 11.12 Oscar Kightley. (Jeff Evans)

I was born in Samoa and came to New Zealand when I was four after my dad died. I grew up with my auntie and uncle in West Auckland. I left school at the end of my sixth-form year and my journalism teacher saw this advertisement for journalists – on the job training. He applied for me … I didn't apply because I have always been fairly … not lazy, just kind of laid back. I was lucky to get that position, so I was a journalist for four years and that's where my first kind of formal writing began. Writing articles and feature pieces was good because that taught me how to write and to communicate. The thing about writing as a reporter is you write to be understood, you're trying to impart to people things that have happened, or explain issues, so what you write down on the page is very important in terms of it being clear.

On April 1st 1991 I arrived in the South Island for the first time having never been there ever. I drove down in my Valiant and it was a real culture shock. It was while I was there that me and some other friends with no jobs, who shared this love of performing and showing off, all started to hang out at this place called the Polynesian Performing Arts Trust.

When we started there we thought, well, we wanted to perform, but there weren't really any parts for Polynesian actors, especially in Christchurch – where it's so white it's not funny. So the easiest thing was just to write material for us to do and that's basically how we started. So it's ironic that it started in Christchurch because there's not that big a Polynesian population down there and of that population there's not that many involved in the arts compared to a place like Auckland.

At the end of that year we applied for and got funding to write a main bill, which was called Fresh Off the Boat. That toured to Wellington and Auckland and that's when our support grew. Fresh Off the Boat was just amazing in Auckland, we did a six-week season which was only originally going to be three weeks. The response that it got and the people that came … it was just eye opening. Here was this young moe pi not really taking art that seriously and doing it as a muck around kind of thing. I think that's when I really came to realise the importance and responsibility … the need to be accountable.

I believe Pacific island theatre has to be accountable to the community that it serves. It's really weird because no other theatre does that, you never get the Circa Theatre people saying we have to do stuff that serves our audience, and that creates an awareness of things. But for some reason because we are islanders we get the oldies saying you have to do this, you can't swear – blah, blah, blah. So a lot of Pacific Underground's work, was all very serious … but there was always a very humorous undercurrent.

On one hand I'm a Samoan playwright, but on the other I'm also a playwright in theatre, I *serve theatre and my community. I had a bad review once that came from a theatre perspective and that was disappointing for me as a practitioner because I like to be good at what I do, because it's a craft. However, the community's response was the Dettol on this gag, it kind of stung at first but it was soothing. It's hard sometimes as a writer, as you are owned by the community, but you're also a theatre person. You can say 'nah ... stuff that review, my cousin came and he loved it. I'd rather listen to what my mum says about my play than a newspaper critic, because she's coming from a different level'. At the same time, however, you do serve your craft.*

When I first met Simon Small, whom I co-wrote Fresh Off the Boat *with, he had done a course and he said the structure should be this, this and this. It should have two turning points, a climax and a resolution and that was kind of the loose structure that I followed. As I've gone to see theatre and as I've gone to see how other people do it, – like the way Nathaniel Lees played with* Frigate Bird *and chopped it up – it makes you realise what's possible and how you can break the rules. A great book that I read is called* The Art of Creative Writing[28] *by Lajos Egri. It's the art of creative writing and was written about 60 years ago and that's the book that I've kind of used as my bible. Everyone says a story should have a beginning, middle and an end, but he says a story should start in the middle and just get more and more interesting. I've learnt my craft just by doing and making mistakes; it hasn't all been fun, there's been lessons learnt in bad reviews, but it's been a learning process. It's the whole cliché – make characters that the audience cares about – and then throw all these things at them and see how they deal with it.*

ACTOR AND DIRECTOR: NATHANIEL LEES

Nathaniel Lees is one of the most experienced Samoan actors in New Zealand. He began his involvement with theatre in the 1970s and has acted and directed in many productions for stage, television and film. His most recent film credits include the role of Ugluk in *Lord of the Rings: The Two Towers* and *The Return of the King; Matrix: Reloaded* and *The Matrix: Revolutions.*

I started in theatre 24 years ago. At that time you could have counted the number of brown people, let alone Samoans, involved in theatre on one hand. I've always loved theatre, I've always loved language from when I was about 11. I met this teacher who was this Shakespeare fanatic and we used to read tracts of Shakespeare and analyse it ... and I loved it. For me theatre was a medium that was so under-utilised by our people. The community I lived in was totally Samoan and the problems that used to go on, although they were quite violent, I always thought they were much more important than what was going on out in the palagi world.

After working at the Mercury Theatre in Auckland being a door opener, standing on the side while the other people did all the talking, I started to see the theatre as an opportunity for Samoans and Pacific islanders to be able to tell their stories. Tell their stories to other people, rather than to just each other in their own groups, where they would usually perform or get together. One of the first plays I did at the Mercury Theatre was a play called The Naval Officer. *It was about the killing of Captain Cook in Hawai'i and the language that they wrote for us to say on stage, it was made up ... you know ... it was bullshit. They made no effort to make authenticity any part of it. That was the regard they had for Pacific island integrity in theatre at that time. For me the turning point came with the work we did with Statement Theatre in South Auckland. Those young people out there came and talked to us about what was happening to them and then watched us as we put together the piece. They then came and watched the piece. It gave them a sense of identity and a medium that wasn't what they initially thought. That for me was the start of a movement. A lot of those people – and I'm not taking credit for saying so – have actually gone on now and are musicians, acting on TV and doing all*

Fig. 11.13 Nathaniel Lees. (Courtesy of artist)

kinds of things. That increased awareness when they were young, gave them the insight to go on and be a performer.

The play Think of a Garden *was a high point for me. It came after I'd directed* Fresh Off the Boat *and a couple of other things, working with groups such as Pacific Underground. I was asked to go over to Australia to a Pacific island writers' workshop, but I said I couldn't because I was working. They said we've got this new play by this chap called John Kneubuhl, a Samoan playwright. Immediately I said OK, send me a script and I'll have a look. So I had a look at that script and it was one of those times where I thought … this is a play I've been waiting for all these years, and I knew it as soon as I'd read his opening breakdown of the scene.*

The opening talks about his parents dying in a boat, what it's like at his house. His use of imagery and language did the same thing for me that it does when I read Shakespeare. I went over to Australia managing to get Lani Tupu and Eteuati Ete to go over with me and we worked on that play there. Maori actress Rena Owen went over as well. Even just sitting down and reading the play, it affected us – the three Samoans – so much that tears were shed nearly every time we read it. It was such a joy to read about ourselves and our language that we knew it would reach whosoever came to see it.

Out of respect to John we did it exactly as he wrote it. I didn't change anything, we didn't cut out anything, we did everything exactly as he wrote it. Up here the response to the show was extraordinary, people were moved to tears. All the Samoan people who came to the Auckland show got up at the end, sang for us and talked to us. At the end of the play we had to sit there and listen to these people saying how happy they were that they were actually alive to see their young people on stage doing these things. It was extraordinary.

Then we went down to Wellington and did it differently. A lot of the images in there, including the set design, everything about it, the feel about it, became mine. I talked it over with the others, with Lani and Eteuati, and they gave me the licence to go for it basically and so I did. In the script John puts down everything, the way the set looks, what sound effects happen, everything. He saw it in its entirety, that play, and so that's what we did up in Auckland. In Wellington there was a feeling about it that I wanted to change – more of a spiritual aspect that I wanted to bring out. The set design, the women who designed the sets down there … it was perfect. That's the high point so far of any Pacific writing I've seen. Afterward we talked a lot about the influence John's play had had on us and where we actually were in terms of the quality of our work in theatre. We came down to saying we have to work harder, just let ourselves go and aim higher.

In terms of influences when I first started, I watched George Henare[29] work and clearly from a technical point of view that man's skill in taking on a character and transforming words into a living thing was something that I admired intensely and I still admire about him. I have also worked with a lot of directors, some good and some not so good, and in terms of watching them work and seeing how they go about realising their idea of something, the concept of a play, that's been helpful....

As for my family, the very first time I had my picture in the paper it was 'fine, do what you want Nathaniel' and that was it. As long as there's recognition for what you do … 'it must be a good thing that the boy's doing because he's in the paper and now we've seen him on TV and on the films'. My daughter and a lot of the children of my generation have no problem going to theatre, going to see a play. This is the generation that's really going to change things … the ones that are coming through now. It was a big problem earlier, you know, … then it was like 'let's go see a play' and the response would be... 'eh?'

CHAPTER 11

1. Caroline Sinavaiana, 'Comic theatre in Samoa as indigenous media', *Pacific Studies* vol. 15:4, (December 1992), pp. 199-210

2. See Vilsoni Hereniko, 'Clowning as Political commentary: Polynesia Then and Now', in *The Contemporary Pacific, A Journal of Pacific Island Affairs* vol. 6:1, Spring (University of Hawai'i Press, 1994), pp. 1-29; Caroline Sinavaiana, 'Where the spirits laugh last: comic theatre in Samoa', in Mitchell, William E. (ed), *Clowning as Critical Practice: Performance Humour in the South Pacific* (Pittsburgh: University of Pittsburgh Press, 1992); See also Kneubuhl, V. 'Traditional performance in Samoan Culture: two forms' *Asian Theatre Journal* vol. 4 (1987), pp. 166-176

3. G. Turner, *Nineteen years in Polynesia: missionary life, travels and researches in the islands of the Pacific* (London: John Snow, 1861), p. 211

4. Sinavaiana, 'Where the spirits laugh last', p. 192

5. V. Hereniko, 'Comic theatre of Samoa: an interview with John A. Kneubuhl', *Manoa: A Pacific Journal of International Writing* vol. 5:1, p. 101

6. Sinavaiana, 'Comic theatre in Samoa as indigenous media', p. 211

7. Sinavaiana, 'Comic theatre in Samoa as indigenous media', p. 193

8. Sinavaiana, 'Comic theatre in Samoa as indigenous media', p. 196

9. Hereniko, 'Clowning as Political commentary', p. 20

10. Justine Simei-Barton, interview with author (2000)

11. Sinavaiana, 'Comic Theatre in Samoa as Indigenous Media', p. 197

12. 'Interview with The Brownies', *Pacific People Magazine* no. 6 (Auckland: April 1999)

13. C. Sinavaiana, 'Music and Theatre: Samoa', in Kaeppler, A.L. and Love, J.W. (eds), *Garland Encyclopaedia of World Music Vol. 9, Australia and the Pacific Islands* (New York: Garland Publishing, Inc. 1998), p. 236

14. Sinavaiana, 'Music and Theatre: Samoa', p. 237

15. H. McNaughton, in Sturm, Terry (ed) *The Oxford History of New Zealand Literature in English, 2nd edition* (Auckland: Auckland University Press, 1998), p. 380

16. Eteuati Ete, in an interview with author, (2000)

17. Nathaniel Lees, in an interview with author, (2000)

18. Nathaniel Lees, in an interview with author, (2000)

19. Anton Carter, Pacific Underground Manager 1995-1998, in an interview with author, (2000)

20. Oscar Kightley, in an interview with author, 2000

21. Anton Carter, interview with author, (2000)

22. M. Amery, 'Flower Power', *Pavement* issue 30 (Auckland: 1998)

23. M. Urale, 'Telling it how it is: Pacific Island Theatre in Aotearoa New Zealand', *Artlink* vol.16:4 (1997), p. 29

24. Eteuati Ete, in an interview with author, (2000)

25. Oscar Kightley, in an interview with author, (2000)

26. Oscar Kightley, in an interview with author, (2000)

27. Anton Carter, interview with author, (2000)

28. Lajos Egri, *The Art of Creative Writing* (New York: Carol Publishing Group, 1995 [first published 1965])

29. George Henare is a distinguished Maori actor of stage and screen.

CHAPTER 12

PHOTOGRAPHY AND FILMMAKING

Samoa has long captured the attention of photographers and filmmakers. Over the last hundred years images of its people and landscapes have appeared in postcards, tourist brochures, magazines, books and films. European photographers were active in Samoa since the late 19th century with the earliest photographs being made for military and documentary purposes from at least the 1860s.[1] Later, at least three photographers were to reside and work for extended periods in Apia. The work of resident photographers John Davis, Alfred John Tattersall and Thomas Andrew[2] can be seen throughout this book. Much of their photography was made for turn-of-the-century postcard markets in Europe and North America.

Throughout the 19th century and well into the 20th century, Samoa and many other Pacific islands were seen in the west as an exotic paradise, with lush vegetation, fertile land, strange peoples and even stranger customs. Photography, art and literature of the period were important in the effort to sell the promise of opportunity to European settlers and businessmen. They promoted trade, and other economic and commercial interests but also contributed to the opening up of the Pacific and the growth and patronage of trade and shipping lines.

Apart from these interests, the popular taste for exotic Pacific postcards and photographs at the turn of the century provided an important market for photography of Samoa and 'surrogate gratification' for those that could not afford the luxury of a Pacific island cruise.[3] The picture postcard craze began around 1880 and was internationally widespread by 1900.[4] Postcards from Samoa and many other foreign places, were so popular that they were reproduced, sold and distributed in their thousands throughout America and Europe. Alison Devine Nordstrom, who has written extensively on photography of Samoa, notes that a survey of fifty photographic collections in the United States uncovered more than fifteen thousand photographs made in Samoa between 1870 and 1925. Thousands more are located in museums in Europe, Great Britain, New Zealand and Australia.[5]

This interest in tourist and exotic images extended into the mid and late 20th century and up into the present day. From the 1960s through to the 1980s photographers such as James Siers[6] and Frederick Koehler Sutter[7] toured and lived in the Pacific islands. The photography of James Siers had covered Polynesia generally and Fiji specifically up until 1970, when he wrote and produced the successful photography

Fig. 12.1 *Crucifixion of Christ with Tatau, a Classical Study*, 1999, Greg Semu. (Courtesy of artist)

153

book *Samoa in Colour*. This book was the third in a series of photographic books he made on the Pacific islands. The majority of his work at this time perpetuated the now long established images and stereotypes of the island paradise, with beautiful women and children, plummeting waterfalls and sweeping beach vistas. This reflected the ongoing market for Pacific photography at the time, when there was increasing access to air travel and a corresponding development of tourism. The cover dust-jacket of *Samoa in Colour* perhaps gives the intentions of Siers' work away, extolling the notion that 'Both Western Samoa and American Samoa have much to offer the tourist, as the delightful photographs and instructive text of *Samoa in Colour* will show'. The same paragraph later describes the people of Samoa as 'the warm, laughing, hospitable Polynesians, who speak truthfully when they say they live in Paradise'.[8]

In contrast, Frederick Koehler Sutter took a different approach, and his three extensive photographic studies of Samoan people and culture reflect this. A professional anthropologist, his involvement in photographic anthropology began in 1962. He lived and worked in Samoa and his images show that he had a very different relationship and sensitivity to his subjects. He was genuinely interested in the people and the culture. His photographs in many cases move well beyond the standard conventions of the tourist image and attempt to show Samoa as a more complex society, one that had migrated to all the corners of the earth, and one whose people were engaged in a wide range of occupations and lifestyles. It's a striking body of work in both its approach and accompanying narratives. In these books Samoans play gridiron, tend horses, go fishing, they are doctors, scientists, artists, writers, politicians and businessmen. They are people with a past and a present.

In film there have been similar markets and motivations that have influenced the image making process. Most films about Samoa to date have been made by non-Samoans and are generally documentary in style. *Moana: Romance of a Golden Age* (1926) made by Frances and Robert Flaherty was an early film financed by the Paramount Picture Studio in Hollywood. Based on the romance of a young Samoan couple, Moana and Fa'angase, it follows Moana as he goes through the process of being tattooed and completing the rite of passage into manhood and eventually winning the hand of his lover. Originally conceived as an ethnographic documentary, the 'set up' scenes and contrived performances conspire to make these films compelling examples of 'Hollywood mythmaking' albeit from today's perspective.[9]

Fig. 12.2 Stills from *Sons for the Return Home*, 1979. (Stills Collection, Nga Kaitiaki O Nga Taonga Whitiahua The New Zealand Film Archive)

Two other films significant for the Samoan stories they brought to the screen are *Sons for the Return Home* (1979) and *Flying Fox in a Freedom Tree* (1990). Both were made by New Zealand filmmakers but adapted from novels written by New Zealand based Samoan author Albert Wendt. *Sons for the Return Home* is a love story set in

New Zealand and follows the relationship between Sione, a young Samoan man, and Sarah, a palagi woman. Through their experiences the film touches on issues of racism, immigration and the difficulties of negotiating relationships and understanding between two very different cultures.

Flying Fox in a Freedom Tree (1990) also focuses on this negotiation of culture difference. Set in Samoa it is based on the second part of Wendt's novel, *Leaves of the Banyan Tree*. It tells the tragic story of a young man called Pepe and how palagi customs and values conflict with those of fa'asamoa, destroying his life and his relationships with those closest to him.

Throughout the 1990s, Samoan stories and experiences continue to appear on the screen, with initiatives such as New Zealand's Tala Pasifika short film series being particularly important. In these films aspiring Samoan writers and directors have joined other Pacific people in learning how to write, produce and direct their own screenplays. The films tell New Zealand based stories dealing with contemporary themes and issues affecting the lives of urban-based Pacific peoples. As pioneering efforts to bring Pacific stories to a wider audience, they are a significant beginning.

Filmmaking and photography are now two fields where young Samoans are making a contribution to recording and documenting their people and culture. Embarking on similar explorations to the European photographers of the past, they are capturing landscapes, people and stories that reflect the attitudes and experiences of their own time and environment; their work offers new insights but usually within familiar conventions and photographic styles. It is interesting that they have an affinity yet at the same time a distanced curiosity toward the many familiar subjects they choose to focus the lens upon. Their ways of seeing offer an insight into what they value, who they are, and the community and the environment in which they live. But in a sense they are tourists of their own culture, involved and living within it, but also documenting and looking in from the margins.

It has been over 100 years since the first photographic images were made in the Samoan Islands. This chapter looks at what two contemporary Samoan photographers and one filmmaker are adding to these fields. It tells their story in their own words and provides a small insight into a visual art form where the possibilities are vast and are still being explored.

GREG SEMU

Greg Semu is an Auckland-based photographer whose images have attracted the attention of galleries and curators in New Zealand, Germany, France and Australia. He exhibited at the 5th Biennale d'Art Contemporain de Lyon 2000 and was voted best new photographer at Paris Photo 2000. Working primarily in black and white, Greg's studio is the street and the environment and space of his subjects. A major part of his work has been to capture the lives and people of the growing Polynesian community in New Zealand, but his explorations have been much broader and taken him to communities and photographic opportunities in New York, Germany and Samoa. He has also worked in film, directing and co-directing, and contributed to a number of music videos including the memorable 1995 Sister's Underground clip *In Your Neighbourhood* with Kerry Brown. He is currently working and living in Paris where he is a freelance photographer.

As a young child there was always cameras around the house. My brothers and sisters were

Fig. 12.3 Greg Semu. (Jeff Evans)

all like sort of home photographers and so I always had and always enjoyed going through photo albums and I got to play with the cameras and things, so that was pretty much my first introduction. But also through modelling … as a teenager. I found I didn't quite like the experience of it and preferred the other side of the camera.

I studied photography for one year at Carrington Polytechnic in Auckland. I learnt a few technical skills there, but I think the year I started it was a new course and there wasn't a strong structure to it. But apart from that there were facilities available, a darkroom, camera gear and there were also some really good tutors. But my attendance was quite poor…

That was around 1990; that was my formal training in photography and then after that I kind of like went to magazines like Planet and Stamp and I did lots of work for them. So I guess you could say I am pretty much self-taught. Planet magazine was a big, influential magazine, I think it was one of the first magazines that actually took notice of the Polynesian influence in New Zealand. Through working with Planet I published a lot of my photography and learned a lot about the technical and the theoretical side of producing a magazine … it gave me a grounding in professionalism I would say, through finding out things through experience … also through the magazine we were able to promote Polynesian people, fashion and music.

These days I'm classified as a street photographer: documentary and portraiture photography is what I do. I am always interested in real life and portraits of real people as opposed to the contrived sort of world of magazines and media. What interests me the most is other people, basically … and the way people live and dress, their whole idealism … I'm not interested in still life and cars or rugby.

I have really old camera gear, it may be even classified as antique, but I have a Rolleiflex twin lens which is a medium format 2 1/4 and very much older than I am. And I have got a Polaroid, which is also older than I am. I just use whatever tools I can get my hands on, if I have to draw it, I'll draw it, I'll draw you a real good picture. But my camera gear is really basic, I have a manual camera, I have a 35 mm camera which I don't like to use … it's more out of necessity, I guess, and not really my preference, but at the end of the day you make do with what you have. Most people's reaction to my camera gear is that it's antique, it doesn't go … but I think it keeps me humble too you know, it's not about my camera gear, it's about the experience and at the end of the day you make whatever format that you have on hand work for you. I do believe that taking photographs is about an experience, it's a contact, or it's a moment, it's all about a feeling…

Working as a street photographer, as a portrait maker, often you are taken in the wrong way. There will be moments when you see photographs that are like just really magical moments and you know you have to take a photograph … and there have been times when I have invited people or requested to take their photograph and they've denied me. And you take it personally for the moment, but … fair enough.

I think basically as soon as I came out of polytech I kind of attracted attention from the art field. I think one of my first exhibitions where I was invited was Bottled Ocean curated by Jim Vivieaere. That was a significant exhibition because it showcased Pacific island vision within New Zealand and it showcased a lot of young artists with a whole lot of senior established artists. For Pacific consciousness I think it was a very important show.

The art community has been generally very receptive to my work, but what reflects my work is my community and what is going on, what I am photographing. I think art in general can be self-indulgent, whereas my photography is more about the people I meet and who I have photographed, and I really feel like they are the heroes of the photograph. Sure I press the button, but it's about the people who are in it. Being a people photographer, its more about them than about me. I always try and uplift the people I photograph, make them feel good. Not pump them up though with flattery and stuff…

The response from the Pacific island community is kind of positive, but at the same time it means I get classified as a Pacific island photographer and I can't photograph caucasians. But that's a kind of negative aspect on a commercial level, on a positive level I'd like to think that young people can see that there are things, other occupations, we can pursue other than lawyers and doctors. I think that me being a visual artist is not your normal occupation for Samoan people, the kind that our parents like us kids to aspire to…

You know, it's not your normal occupation, but every day I am quite grateful that I can operate at this level, but I don't know how long I can sustain it for. I intend to put a lifetime into it. Like many jobs they are a dime a dozen – photographers … it's challenging and you have to apply yourself, but I think that's with any job though. No one is guaranteed security anymore these days. You just have to persevere and be self-motivated. I am pleased that I have been able to photograph a consciousness that has been growing, that is still growing, of our Polynesian aware-ness of our own specific identity within our New Zealand community.

EVOTIA TAMUA

Evotia Tamua has been involved in photography since 1988. From work in photo-graphic labs and as a fashion photographer's assistant she developed a firm foundation and technical grounding before eventually deciding to pursue her own career as a photojournalist. Since 1994 much of her work has documented or featured the Pacific island community both in New Zealand and overseas. Her images have been pub-lished in major magazines, periodicals and books.

Her first solo exhibition *Islanders* was at Archill Gallery, Auckland in 1996. Her photographs have also appeared in overseas exhibitions, including the Pitt Rivers Museum, Oxford 1999 and the Australian Centre for Photography, Sydney 1997, but her current energies and interests lie much closer to home.

Evotia, like her cousin Greg Semu, is one of the few Samoans working in photog-raphy. As Greg has already pointed out 'visual artist is not your normal occupation for Samoan people', but for a medium that is so accessible and well-used by Pacific island people, the possibilities of photography as an art form are perhaps as yet under-appreciated and not fully understood.

Fig. 12.4 Evotia Tamua. (Jeff Evans)

I am the eldest of my brother and sister. My mother raised us from when I was about 10 years old after my father passed away in Samoa while he was there on a family matter. I am from Salelesi, which is my father's village in Upolu. It's between Solosolo and Lufilufi, and is one of those small villages that you could easily miss as you whiz by on a bus.

I had always loved art at school, but my best friends were always better painters and better drawers than I was. When I was first interested in photography, I felt that it was something that was instant and took less time than painting and I was good at it. I liked the technical side mixed with the creative aspect, so if you can compose a picture and know how to expose it, then you are pretty much on your way to having a good photograph. I work with 35 mm format camera and I shoot in both colour and black and white.

I have a wide range of lenses from a 17 mm to a 500 mm. I quite often shoot with the 300 or 500 mm lenses for sports photography, which requires bigger lenses, but I'll also use a wide-angle lens to get close and capture all the surrounding action of the game because it gives the photograph a sense of time and place..

I am interested in photographing people in all different kinds of situations: whether it is a set-up shot in a studio, as in formal portraiture, or somebody sitting in a crowd or getting an action shot on a rugby field. I used to cover a lot of Pacific island festivals, and I still do that every year, and that's what I use to market myself. When I first started freelancing I had to put myself out there in one area so people could see that my strongest point was photographing Pacific island people. I feel that I have moved on from there but I'm still known for that work. When I show people sports pictures they don't believe that I can do that type of work.

I think what the art world has been interested in, in terms of my work, is the Pacific island perspective of Pacific island people. At first I saw it as, I was just a photographer, and so I thought, 'so what? I am just a photographer anyone else can do this'. But what I take for granted, which is what I see as everyday normal kind of living in the islands or in New Zealand among the Pacific island community, another viewer can look at it and have a completely different response. What I might find as everyday the other person might think 'Oh my gosh, what is that

Fig. 12.5 *A break from gardening*, 1996, Evotia Tamua. (Courtesy of artist)

and why are they doing that?'. I have had some interesting exhibitions out of this kind of work.

I had my first solo show at Archill Gallery in Grey Lynn in 1996. The opening night was really fun as it was full of people who don't ever get to go to these kinds of functions. They were my uncles, aunties and my little cousins. I had to organise my relatives to pick up the others or else they would not have turned up. One of my aunties got the invitation in the mail and thought it was just a flyer-advertising-type thing in the mail. And she just biffed it … and I said 'didn't you read it, it was addressed to you?'. And she said, 'Oh, I thought it was just something like a KFC voucher'. It was a really good night though, as I just wanted all the little kids as well as all the older generation to be there and have a look. I don't know what effect it had on them – long term – but I just wanted them there and it was good to be exposed to something different like my pictures … artworks.

There was a shot of a Cook Island family in their home, and they had just fed me dinner and I thought this was good because there is the grandmother on one side of the room and the grandfather on the other side. It's a really nice shot, and a lot of people thought why did you photograph them like that for, they didn't even dress properly for it? For them a photographer should make sure the people look really nice and they couldn't believe I took photographs of people in a singlet and just a mu'umu'u in their home.

The advertising shot that I used for the show was a picture of my mother after she had been gardening, having a break. She is wearing gumboots, a flowery dress and sun hat and she was really mad at me for taking photographs of her. I had to really beg her to let me use that picture. She didn't like it because she wasn't presented in the way that she wanted people to see her. It was too real I suppose. She wanted to be in her Sunday best. She got over it … eventually, especially with everybody commenting that it was such a cool photo. She would just roll her eyes and pull my hair at the same time.

I am currently studying photography at Elam at the University of Auckland. This is my first year there. Due to all the experience that I have had, I am in year three which will enable me to do a Bachelor of Fine Arts in two years instead of the standard four years. I feel that I have got the technical skills, but I have to brush up on darkroom work, and learn about digital media. The library at Elam is really good, having access to those books, to the photography equipment, learning about different equipment and looking at videos and movies about photographers and their works. Being forced to go to galleries to see photographers' works - (I am one of those people that if it's somebody I know I will turn up, otherwise I don't bother going).

I guess I was a bit of a cowboy before and what I mean by that is that, if I saw something good I shot it and that's what I did. I didn't think about it and I didn't think of how it could be used later on for something, and I didn't think of it as in a photo essay and have some other pictures that corresponded to that one shot. Being around people that talk about ideas and reading photography books and learning about other photographers, how they approach their work, I am actually looking at and approaching my work differently now. I have found photographers that I can relate to as far as my work is concerned. I have always liked the Magnum photographers because of their photojournalism and I have found some women photographers whose work is very strong and similar to what I do. Photographers such as Henri Cartier-Bresson and Margaret Bourke-White, are who I look at and think – if they could do it back in the 1940s or 50s with limited equipment and film speeds, then I shouldn't have any excuses for not achieving the same results now.

SIMA URALE

Filmmaker Sima Urale has a different relationship with the camera lens in that her work captures moving images, edited, arranged and manipulated to create a mood, relate a story, a feeling or an interpretation of events. Sima's films to date challenge the images and perceptions of the Pacific.

Her most acclaimed work to date is the black and white short film 'O Tamaiti. This 1996 production won eight international awards, including the prestigious Silver Lion at the Venice Film Festival. Urale went on to make *Velvet Dreams*, and this too has toured the world to widespread acclaim. *Velvet Dreams* is almost a mock documentary and follows the search for a painter of Pacific island 'Venuses' – bare-breasted Pacific island women – painted in glowing colour on velvet. Sima comments: 'It's about … the clichéd image … [those] very sensual paintings… But I think the film goes a bit deeper than that, and it's really about the subjects, those women, and about the white painters who, in a way, colonised the Pacific by painting these women…'[10]

Fig. 12.6 Sima Urale. (Jeff Evans)

I was born and raised in Fagamalo in Savai'i. That's our dad's village. We immigrated to New Zealand in 1974 and I was only six years old then. There are six children in our family I am the fourth oldest.

I got involved in film through theatre. I did this Access course in theatre and then the New Zealand Drama School course; I graduated, then did two years of acting. By the end of the two years I wanted to get involved in something that was more accessible as a medium, something other than theatre. Something that appealed to a broader audience, because I discovered after two years in theatre that it was the same theatre crowd coming. Lots of them weren't Pacific islanders, it was mainly a palagi audience, a certain age group … then we were doing re-hash plays, some really good plays, but I did not find them all that relevant to society or even relevant to myself either … Then I started looking to film schools in Australia.

I looked around New Zealand for a film course and there was basically nothing … not with the sort of intensity I was looking for. Filmmaking is a lot more practical, it is about movement and doing things, it's not about writing a heap of theories and papers. So I looked to Australia because their courses were full-on practical – it was actually hands-on filmmaking. You were actually filming – making them, directing them, cutting them – the works.

I was accepted into Swinburne Film and Television School and in my third year it amalgamated with the Victoria School of the Arts Film and Television School. While I was at film school I experimented a lot. I was probably one of the more experimental students. I was quite surprised that not many of the other students were really interested in playing around with sound and imagery, cutting styles and stuff like that. I saw it as playtime because I knew that in the professional world you would never get to experiment or play around that much. So I basically went for gold and played as much as I could. So I was quite broad in my approach. It was basically just finding out what film could do for me. It was not about exploring issues or anything like that, it was more about just what the actual medium could do for me, you know, imagery-wise, pace, how emotive dialogue can be or images without dialogue, so I was fairly experimental. What I came away with was a lot more confidence in the area, just knowing what a sound person does, what a cinematographer is all about, knowing what all those crewing roles are all about, it just boosted my confidence tenfold.

After I graduated I came straight back to New Zealand and did a play called Think of a Garden. *But in that same year, 1995, I started writing and we shot* 'O Tamaiti *which is a 15 minute short film funded by The New Zealand Film Commission. It was a black and white film and it's been screened all over the world and done pretty well. It's all in Samoan and subtitled in English. It surprised me it did so well because it's spoken in Samoan and it's about Samoan kids.*

'O Tamaiti *was really inspired by experiences of having to look after the younger siblings, which we all have to do. And it's a really good thing to learn, but at the same time it's so easy to*

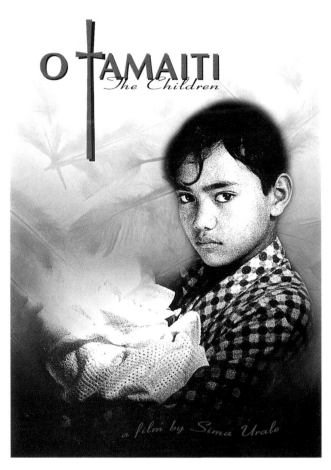

Fig. 12.7 Brochure from 'O Tamaiti, The Children. (Courtesy of the New Zealand Film Commission)

misuse kids, to use them as adults rather than seeing them for what they are. A really strong image for me comes from the times when I have gone to a Samoan wedding or funeral and I have seen toddlers looking after other little toddlers while their parents are busy running around. They are just babies themselves and they are given so much responsibility.

I shot the film in black and white to take away a lot of the stereotype images of Pacific islanders. Up until then a lot of Pacific island images were fairly bright, kitsch, with quite crass colourings. Clothing was always outrageous, people were always wearing lavalava. There is not one lavalava in 'O Tamaiti. I guess I did this just to make a point that we all don't go around in jandals and have plastic flowers in our houses. That we are changing as a culture.

I guess I really don't try and push the issue of my cultural background that much; only if it comes natural and feels strong and feels good, then I will go for it. And I guess that's how I feel about any project. If I feel strongly about it enough I'll do it, because in the end it's not about whether it's the cultural thing, it's about whether the film-maker feels strongly about it. You know, so it sort of crosses the barriers of whether you are Samoan or not.

I just love directing; writing is amazing, writing is a really awesome skill to have but a really hard one. I think it's the toughest, because it is really hard to come up with good writing. Directors need a good sense of organisation – like really good. It's like running an army sometimes and trying to keep cool, for me it is also about trying not to stress out. A director needs a passion for telling a story, but also must have good ideas. You have to be able to get along with people and be able to express yourself really well. You have to be able to express the look and the feel about a film.

For me film is a really good way of expressing myself and what I feel strongly about. These

Fig. 12.8 Still from 'O Tamaiti, The Children. (Courtesy of the New Zealand Film Commission)

days things are going more visual and film is a good medium because it is so accessible, so it's a good way of telling stories. There is so many different processes and ways of working, there is no right way … I like to plan ahead, I like to think things over again and again, I like to think why I am thinking of this shot, why this look or style? I am really plodding and I think a lot before I actually get to shoot. I like working to a plan.

CHAPTER 12

1. A.D. Nordstrom, 'Popular photography of Samoa: production, dissemination and use', in Blanton, Casey (ed), *Picturing Paradise: Colonial Photography of Samoa 1875 to 1925* (Southeast Museum of Photography: Daytona Beach Community College, 1995), p. 22

2. Nordstrom, 'Popular photography of Samoa, p. 26

3. Ann Stephen, Introduction in *Pirating the Pacific: Images of Travel, Trade and Tourism* (Australia: Powerhouse Publishing, 1993), pp. 15-16

4. Nordstrom, 'Popular photography of Samoa, p. 20

5. Nordstrom, 'Popular photography of Samoa, p. 11

6. James Siers, *Samoa in Colour* (Wellington: A.H. and A.W. Reed Ltd, 1970)

7. Frederick K. Sutter, *Amerika Samoa: An Anthropological Photo Essay* (Honolulu: University of Hawai'i Press, 1984); and *Samoa: A Photographic Essay* (Honolulu: University of Hawai'i Press, 1971); and *The Samoans: A Global Family* (Honolulu: University of Hawai'i Press, 1989)

8. James Siers, *Samoa in Colour*

9. Caroline Vercoe, 'Fantasy Islands: Hollywood's Samoa' in Smith, A. and Leonard, A. (eds) *Bright Paradise: Exotic History and Sublime Artifice* (Auckland: Auckland Art Gallery Toi O Tamaki, 2001) pp. 101-106; also note: Later in the 1970s Flaherty's daughter went to Samoa to record a sound track for the film and it was re-released as *Moana of The South Seas* (1980).

10. Ed Rampell, *Velvet Venuses*, Director Sima Urale (1999). http://www.geocities.com/Wellesley/3321/win16c.htm

CHAPTER 13

FAGOGO AND LITERATURE

Samoan culture is rich in stories. And there are many ways in which these stories are communicated, performed and passed on, for example poetry, song and storytelling. Oratory is the strongest language art, but it is through Samoan literature written in English that a broad audience is now reading about Samoan society and culture.

Samoan creative writing first emerged in the 1960s, and had a great boost in the 1970s with the publication of several novels and poetry collections. So when we talk about Samoan literature and Pacific literature in general we are talking about developments that are still fairly recent. Today, with better access to education, other literatures and ideas, and new technologies and media the opportunities to write and be published have greatly improved.

Samoa has always had a strong oral literature, one characterised by genealogies, mythologies, songs and stories (although arts like tattooing and siapo could also be described as a written literature of sorts). Samoa's oral literature had its reservoir and wellspring in the art of fagogo.

Fagogo is a form of Samoan storytelling which can be described as a performing art, almost a type of theatre, where people, events and stories are brought to life through the skills, voice and actions of a narrator. It takes place mostly at night among small groups of people, usually in a private individual's home.[1] The stories always include one or more songs known as tagi, which are sung by the storyteller at certain points during the narration. They also have an element of rhyme giving them a musical quality and making them easier to remember, and entertaining and interesting to listen to. The telling of fagogo is like a performance where a storyteller's personality, timing and style of delivery must keep the audience enthralled. For some established writers fagogo was a formative influence in their love of the arts and history and their own efforts and achievements in storytelling. It has been argued that Samoan creative writing has been a search for the written fagogo,[2] a literature that captures a Samoan view of the world and a Samoan way of saying things and relating a story. (To some extent Samoan writing for theatre captures aspects of this unique character – an ingredient that is difficult to pinpoint, but also recognisable and familiar.)

Poet and artist Momoe Malietoa von Reiche recalls the fagogo of her childhood:

I was brought up on The Arabian Nights *apart from the fagogo. These were the stories they would tell us at night-time when we went to sleep. We used to have these old ladies that were brought in especially. My father's aunt, who was blind, she was a storyteller and the whole family surrounded this lady. It was like going to the movies. We would sit there listening in the dark to this lady telling stories. It was so much more fascinating because your mind would work overtime creating fantastic images and places.*[3]

Fagogo are full of supernatural characters and often feature speaking and singing animals who can change form into sau'ai (ogre-like creatures).[4] These characters interact with heroes and heroines, such as the famous Tigilau and Sina. In the course of the stories all kinds of adventures and dramas take place and, through the narratives, important messages are related to the audience. Richard Moyle who recorded and analysed over 200 fagogo in the 1960s wrote that fagogo often highlight the contrast and conflict between culturally acceptable and unacceptable behaviour:

Fig. 13.1 Book jacket for *Sons for the Return Home*, 1973.

In most cases, the stories deal directly with the repercussions arising from such behaviour, the events building up to the climaxes, often identified by the singing of the tagi, and followed where necessary, by a positive reassertion of acceptable values in the form of punishment. The fagogo end as they begin, in a climate of acceptable social conditions, but having had those conditions and values tried, tested and vindicated and therefore restored. To this extent fagogo depict behavioural principles…

The appeal of the fagogo is universal; for children the attraction centres on humour, and the unfolding of perilous episodes; for adults, such elements are of interest, but recognition of the underlying seriousness of theme or plot adds a new dimension to their listening.[5]

Today many Samoan storytellers explore familiar themes and use similar mechanisms in order to tell their stories through the written word. The developments in Samoan written literature have been well documented in an essay by Peggy Fairbairn-Dunlop. In a detailed account she suggests that 'the search for Samoan writers has been to capture on paper the elusive essence of the fagogo art they remembered from their youth'.[6] This statement is probably true for the majority of Samoan writers, particularly those who were raised in Samoa, but the present generation includes writers who have had little access or exposure to fagogo. The challenge for them is to find their own way of telling stories, one inevitably shaped by the many different locations, lifestyles and environments where they are producing their work.

From the early 1800s until the 1950s literacy in Samoa was the preserve of and entry to the worlds of the church, government and business. It enabled business to be conducted, improved communication and opened the way for people to learn new things. Creative literature as we know it today was slow to emerge, the only writings by Samoans being family papers and a few historical documents. It wasn't until the 1950s and 1960s that writers such as Fanaafi Ma'ia'i and Apelu Aiavao made pioneering efforts to translate popular English literature into Samoan and also produce Samoan literature resources for schools. This made different stories, such as English

Classics, available to Samoan readers and took their eyes and thoughts beyond the bible page, newspapers and the forms and documents of government. An interesting aspect of these translation initiatives was the desire to retell the stories and give the texts a Samoan tone and style reminiscent of fagogo.

Fairbairn-Dunlop attributes the beginnings of a broader effort in Samoan creative writing to the early 1960s and a new political awareness among the many Samoans who were being educated overseas. Changes in thinking and in Samoan creative writing grew as writers started reflecting and writing on issues of nationhood, colonisation, identity and their own life experiences. Students who had studied or worked overseas started to ask new questions and formulate new ideas and, as Fairbairn-Dunlop puts it, 'explore more positively the possibilities and boundaries of writing in both English and Samoan'.[7]

A young Samoan exploring these possibilities in the 1960s was Albert Wendt whose work was just starting to appear in magazines and journals. Like several other writers he had been educated and attended university in New Zealand. His contribution at this time broke new ground because – Fairbairn-Dunlop again – '… he was a Samoan, and writing about topics, emotions and feelings Samoans could identify with, using imagery that had instant appeal'.[8]

Wendt's writing and teaching has been important in the development not only of Samoan literature but literature in the Pacific. From the 1960s through to the 1970s literary magazines and journals provided other Samoan writers with opportunities to publish their work. The Mana pages in the *Pacific Islands Monthly* were initially an important outlet and later it developed into a respected literary journal of the same name. Produced by the South Pacific Creative Arts Society based in Suva, Fiji it was certainly the most widely circulated. It gave the reading public access to a variety of prose and poetry and was a forerunner to the growing confidence and opportunities that were to come.

In 1973 Albert Wendt achieved a significant first with the publication of his novel *Sons for the Return Home*, the first written by a Samoan and later made into a motion picture. It was the story about the relationship between a Samoan man and palagi woman in 1960s New Zealand. It highlighted the racism, the clash of cultures and the experiences and relationships within New Zealand communities undergoing social and cultural change.

The publication of creative writing by Samoans steadily increased from the mid 1970s to the early 1980s. This writing included several collections of poetry and two more novels from Wendt – *Pouliuli* (1977) and the award winning *Leaves of the Banyan Tree* (1979) – and volumes from four poets of whom three are still making strong contributions to Samoan literature today.

Sano Malifa published his first collection of poetry *Looking Down at Waves* in 1975. Malifa is from Afega and was educated in Samoa, although he has also travelled widely and lived and worked abroad. Aspects of these experiences are reflected in his poetry, as are the conflicts and tensions between the individual and a communal ethic of his homeland.[9] In 1992 he produced another collection of poetry, *Song and Return*, part of which is strongly political and critical of the abuses and hypocrisy of the post-colonial government. His first novel, *Alms for Oblivion*, was published in 1993 and tackles similar themes from an introspective and semi-autobiographical standpoint.

Ruperake Petaia's first collection of poetry was *Blue Rain* published in 1980. His second, *Patches of the Rainbow*, was published in 1992. He has also written and published short stories. Much of Petaia's poetry critically evaluates the impact of moderni-

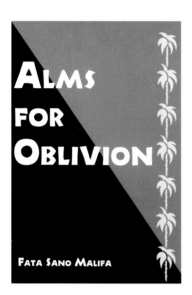

Fig. 13.2 Book jackets for *Alms for Oblivion* and *where we once belonged*.

Fig. 13.3 Momoe Malietoa von Reiche. (Craig Potton)

Fig. 13.4 Ruperake Petaia. (Sean Mallon)

sation on Samoan society and culture. Western education, church and religion, the alienation between generations and corruption in politics are all major themes in Petaia's work. But he has also made room for personal reflections on family values, relationships and ancestors. Petaia works in both Samoan and English, and his work is widely studied in classrooms throughout the Pacific. It has been translated into several languages including French, German and Russian.

Momoe Malietoa von Reiche also published collections of poetry in the 1970s: *Paa Alimago on wet days* (1979) and *Solaua: a secret embryo* (1979). Von Reiche was educated in Nelson, New Zealand and is well known as an artist. Like Sano Malifa, her travels have inspired some of her work, but it is intensely personal. However, for the most part von Reiche's poetry retains a familiarity and relevance in that it explores themes and issues affecting many families and women. As Sina Va'ai comments in *Literacy Representations in Western Polynesia*, 'The bulk of her poems focus on betrayal, infidelity and the personal turmoil caused by this within the institution of the family'.[10] Despite its often traumatic subject matter, von Reiche's poetry is lightened a little by her sense of humour. Momoe Malietoa von Reiche retains a strong connection to writing and the arts and runs a small gallery near Apia which provides art and dance workshops, exhibits paintings and sculpture, and holds poetry readings.

A recent and popular success story has been performance poet and writer Sia Figiel. Her poetry won her the 1994 Polynesian Literary Competition and she has published four books, the latest being *They Who Do Not Grieve* (1999). In 1997 she was winner of the Commonwealth Writers Prize for the Best First Book in the South East Asian and South Pacific Region for her novel *Where We Once Belonged*. The story focuses on an adolescent Samoan girl named Alofa and her view, experiences and discovery of life in Samoa. An interesting aspect of her work and creative life is that Figiel is a storyteller and performer as well as a successful writer. Her live poetry and performance is perhaps one of the most contemporary manifestations of fagogo, shared with only a few at a time within the context of a performance or reading. In 2000, Figiel released some of her poetry on compact disc, with Kiribati poet Teresia Teaiwa. Titled *Terenesia*, it preserves the performance aspect of Figiel's work and allows new audiences to experience it in its telling. This is one example of how the art of fagogo lives on in the new generation albeit in a modified form. In contrast her writing is more widely accessible and has introduced a written voice of the younger generation of Samoans to the English-speaking world.

Apart from these widely-known writers, many other Samoan writers have continued to be published in magazines, journals and anthologies. Two important Pacific anthologies in English that featured Samoan writers were *Lali* (1980) and *Nuanua* (1995), both edited by Albert Wendt. These anthologies brought Pacific island writing in English to a wider audience in a format and volume that was widely available. They also showcased the depth and diversity of writing talent across the Pacific region. In the introduction to *Nuanua*, Wendt suggested that '… the urgent need is to publish national anthologies in our indigenous languages … If our indigenous languages are to remain strong and inventive their literatures should be taught and read widely'.[11]

Efforts in this direction were made with *Tatou Tusi Tala – Let's Write Stories: An Anthology of Samoan Writings* (1999) published by the Samoan Language and Culture Programme and the Fealofani O Samoa club at the University of Hawai'i at Manoa. With contributions in both Samoan and English, the editors stated that their selection reflected 'the complexity and duality of being Samoan, the struggles and accomplishments that occur in trying to keep one foot in the Western and one in the Samoan world'. It is a pertinent point to make in an era when the Samoan community is so widespread, for it is in the interplay of cultural values that the future forms and character of Samoan literature lie. How future Samoan writers manage this balancing act is crucial. What they experience, what they choose to read and write, and how they connect these to their upbringing and heritage will help them shape and create their own fagogo. It is a process that will produce a literature with as much meaning, relevance and authenticity as that of the past.

Fig. 13.5 Sano Malifa. (Sean Mallon)

ALBERT WENDT

Albert Wendt is Professor of English at Auckland University. As already mentioned he is a key influence for many current writers in Samoa and a leading figure in the development of literature in the wider Pacific as well as New Zealand. He has published in most of the literary genres and is currently developing his first full-length play *The Songmaker's Chair*. It's a play that looks at three generations of a Samoan family that has been in New Zealand for over 40 years, and is a fitting development in a career that has seen stories and commentary about many aspects of Samoan life experience, both native and migrant.

I have always had an interest in telling stories because I came from a family very rich in oral storytelling and traditions. My grandmother was a great storyteller and was an authority on fa'asamoa, history, genealogy and so on. She handed a lot of this to us in the form of stories. The Christian church, in which I was brought up, is also very rich in stories, with the oral traditions of the bible as well as hymns and music. I used to spend a lot of my childhood with my relatives in the villages and that's also where I acquired some of my interest in the arts and storytelling.

Fig. 13.6 Albert Wendt. (Jeff Evans)

I was born and bred in Samoa and came to New Zealand in 1953 at the age of 13. I had most of my education here. That explains the reason why I write in English, but of course I've been in and out of Samoa over the years. When I came to New Zealand I went to boarding school and I was very lucky to have been in English classes run by teachers who were very inspiring. They encouraged us to read lots of books and write, and that's when I started writing.

The compulsion to write is a compulsion you cannot really explain. Like people who want to draw every day and those who want to read books every day. I've always had this passion for writing poems and stories. It's been explained in some cultures as a 'disease', but I don't look at it as a disease. I think it is a gift. People have tried to explain where the gift comes from, but it doesn't really matter to me where it comes from. Once you have it and you pursue that compulsion, it becomes a part of your life. There have been times when I've stopped writing and said that's it, but the drive and urge to do it returns and won't leave me alone.

I write poetry, short stories, essays, articles and novels. The challenge is always how do you use this talent? How do you use it to write short stories? Can I write a novel? The challenge is also how do I keep developing this talent? After I write a short story, can I write a novel? Then there are choices in subject matter, what do I write about? For instance you finish writing a novel, a family saga, and then you think, well, can I write a science fiction novel? The challenge is whether you can do it. I could spend the rest of my life repeating the novels that I've written in the past and make more money. However, I want to experiment ... see whether I can write a science fiction novel, or whether I can mix novel and poetry ... to see if it works.

In many ways the language itself takes you there. Once you sit down and start using language it takes you, without you knowing it, where it's going to go. I'm sure that's what happens to painters. I never plan a poem or novel. I've discovered as I've gone along that if I know what I'm going to write in a novel, I don't write that novel because the mystery has gone. I think it's the process of discovering, and it's the process itself that takes you to discover these things.

All my reading over the years has influenced my work and I don't mind the influences. As a matter of fact I acknowledge it in my books by imitating these writers' styles. In modern literature they say you've got to be original ... absolute rubbish. No one can be original in writing a novel, no one can be original in making a painting. The view that I've always held, and it's a view that's prevalent in Samoa, is that you learn from other song-makers and it's a tribute to them if you take their styles and use it in your work. It doesn't diminish you as a song-maker because people say you're copying or imitating, no ... as long as you know what you're doing. I tell my students most of the poems you read are a recycling of other poems. The only thing the writer brings in that is unique is a different way of looking at the thing and writing about it. Nothing is new. But we can renew it by the way we write about it or paint it or whatever.

I sometimes get annoyed when critics look at the work and misinterpret it. They don't understand our culture and don't know how to read it completely. I don't mind the analysing, the analysis of my work, which is founded on the knowledge of fa'asamoa and the knowledge of Samoan people, but when it's written by critics who don't have that knowledge and don't really care if they have it, I get really annoyed. There has been a really mixed reaction to my work, ranging from very high praise to condemnation. A lot of people in Samoa who have never read my work condemn it because I attack the church, the establishment and the middle classes. I don't mind their criticism. They also forget, that my work is only my version of Samoa, Samoans and other people. We all have our own versions and representations.

CHAPTER 13

1. R. Moyle, *Fagogo: Fables from Samoa in Samoan and English* (Auckland: Auckland University Press, 1981), p. 7
2. P. Fairbairn-Dunlop, 'Samoan Writing: searching for the written fagogo', in Sharrad, P. (ed), *Readings in Pacific Literature* (New South Wales, Wollongong: New Literatures Research Centre, University of Wollongong, 1993), p. 139
3. Momoe Malietoa von Reiche, interview with author, (1999)
4. Moyle, *Fagogo: Fables from Samoa in Samoan and English*, p. 23
5. Moyle, *Fagogo: Fables from Samoa in Samoan and English*, p. 47
6. Fairbairn-Dunlop, 'Samoan Writing: searching for the written fagogo', p. 136
7. Fairbairn-Dunlop, 'Samoan Writing: searching for the written fagogo', p. 140
8. Fairbairn Dunlop, 'Samoan Writing: searching for the written fagogo', p. 141
9. Sina Va'ai, *Literary Representations in Western Polynesia: Colonialism and Indigeneity* (Apia: National University of Samoa, 1999), p. 111
10. Sina Va'ai, *Literary Representations in Western Polynesia*, p. 129
11. Albert Wendt (ed), *Nuanua: Pacific Writing in English Since 1980* (Auckland: Auckland University Press, 1995)

FURTHER READING

Malifa, Sano *Looking down at waves* (Suva, Fiji: Mana Publications, 1975)
Malifa, Sano *Song and return: poems and a satirical play* (Apia, Western Samoa: Samoa Observer, 1992)
Petaia, Ruperake *Patches of the rainbow* (Apia: Samoa Observer, c1992)
Petaia, Ruperake *Blue rain* (Western Samoa: University of the South Pacific Centre and MANA Publications, c1980)

von Reiche, Momoe Malietoa *Paa Alimago on wet days* (Apia, Samoa: Samoa Printing & Publ. Co., 1979)

von Reiche, Momoe Malietoa *Alaoa: above the gully of your childhood* (Apia, Western Samoa: Western Samoa Historical and Cultural Trust, 1986)

von Reiche, Momoe Malietoa *Solaua: a secret embryo* (Suva: Mana Publications, 1979)

von Reiche, Momoe Malietoa *Tai: heart of a tree: a collection of poems* (Auckland: New Zealand New Women's Press, c1988)

Wendt, Albert *Sons for the return home* (Auckland, New Zealand: Longman Paul, 1973)

Wendt, Albert *Flying fox in a freedom tree* (Auckland, New Zealand: Longman Paul, 1974)

Wendt, Albert *Leaves of the banyan tree* (Auckland, New Zealand: Longman Paul, 1979)

CHAPTER 14

ADORNMENTS

Personal adornments and decorations in Samoa have taken many forms. People have dressed, coloured and cut their hair, tattooed and oiled their bodies and worn garments fashioned from different plants, fibres and materials for centuries. But it was from abroad, from the islands of Fiji and Tonga, that some of Samoa's most treasured materials and articles of adornment were sought. These items were traded and brought to Samoa to dress the finely woven 'ie toga (fine mats) and decorate the headdresses, necks and bodies of matai (chiefs), manaia (chiefs' sons) and taupou (ceremonial village maidens).

Adornments can be markers of status or office, or purely items of decoration. Some are very significant in Samoan life and have protocols pertaining as to who can wear them and on what occasions. They can embody histories and memories of individuals and families, highlight relationships and are sometimes the focus of stories. Many of the adornments used over the last 200 years continue to have an important place in Samoan society today.

Like their ancestors before them, Samoan artists and craftspeople today make adornments using diverse materials acquired from a range of places. Their work speaks of many relationships, between people and places and also people and things. As well as being items of decoration, their work is a medium through which old and new relationships are explored, stories told, commentary made and history examined.

COMBS

Up until the early 20th century, combs were worn in the hair as an item of adornment. They were made from coconut leaflet midrib or pau wood, the former consisting of a row of long coconut midribs that had been cleaned, smoothed and fastened together to form the 'teeth' of the comb. The toothed end fanned out and was generally wider than the other end where the midribs were fastened together with strands of hair or coconut fibre. The lashing was often very decorative.

Three types of combs are recorded as having been made in Samoa since European contact.[1] One was the selu tuaniu, which was made from green leaflet midrib and undecorated. In contrast to this was the selu tuiga made from dry coconut leaf midribs and elaborately decorated with small coloured beads and strands of hair. As its name suggests, it was once used as part of the tuiga (headdress) before the lave frame and decorative mirrors were introduced.[2] The third type of comb was the selu pau, the wafer-thin frames of which were carefully cut from wood in the same manner as

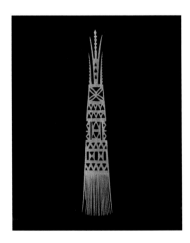

Fig. 14.1 (Opposite) 'Ula lei (necklace) made from ground whale tooth. Collected by Dr Augustin Kramer, late 1800s. (Photograph Anatol Dreyer. Courtesy of Linden Museum, Stuttgart, Germany. Ref. No: 89.157b)

Fig. 14.2 Selu pau – a decorative wooden comb cut from one piece of pau wood. Collected by Alexander H. Turnbull late 1800s. (Museum of New Zealand, Te Papa Tongarewa, Ref. No: FE000887)

Fig. 14.3 Selu tuiga – a comb made from dried coconut midrib that has been scraped, rounded and fastened together with coconut fibre bindings. Collected by Alexander H. Turnbull late 1800s. (Museum of New Zealand, Te Papa Tongarewa, Ref. No: FE000888)

Fig. 14.4 Pale fuiono (headband) made by Ianete Vainu'u, 1999. A long strip of black cloth acts as a foundation for the rectangular sewn-on arrangement of coloured sequins, stars and beads. Savalalo market, Apia, Upolu. (Museum of New Zealand, Te Papa Tongarewa, Ref. No: FE011296)

wooden fans.

Today the midrib and wooden combs have disappeared and been replaced with a huge range of imported and locally made substitutes. Coconuts are the favoured local product for making combs, and all manner of brand names, family names, national greetings and patterns are cut from the highly polished shells. These sit alongside imported plastic turtle shell combs decorated with limitless combinations of words, flowers and embossed colours.

HEADDRESSES

Headdresses in Samoa range from the very simple to the very elaborate. They often consist of a leaf or flower worn in the hair, a piece of siapo wrapped around the head, or an elaborate assemblage of feathers, shell and dyed hair called a tuiga. The ad hoc and often one-use nature of headdresses (and personal adornment in general) allows for a great deal of innovation and invention.

The most elaborate and certainly the most important headdress is the tuiga. As one of the most recognisable symbols of Samoan status, it was customarily worn by manaia and taupou. The tuiga today still retains an important place in Samoan communities, although aspects of its appearance have been greatly modified.

The tuiga as it was at the turn of the 19th century is described in detail by Kramer in *The Samoan Islands* and Te Rangi Hiroa in *Samoan Material Culture*. At this time it was typically a composite headdress made of several parts that were put together when required for wear. These were built up around a pou (post-like foundation) made from wrapping cloth around the head. The ends of this cloth were tied and twisted into position so a post-like form projected from the top of the head. This became the foundation and support for the other headdress elements that were tied onto it.

The first elements tied to the pou were several strings to which were attached many long tassels of hair. These strings formed what was called the lau ulu. Each tassel was looped and fastened into an eyelet shape at one end, through which they were threaded onto a long string. Some of these strings were made long enough to hold up to thirty tassels of preferably thick frizzy hair. The more tassels and strings of hair, the thicker the tuiga would appear. The preferred colour of the hair was a very light brown. So the very dark hair of most Samoans was lightened by one of two bleaching processes.[3] The first was achieved by rubbing the hair with coral lime and then exposing it to the sun and rain for up to several months. After this time the liming process was repeated until the correct hair colour was acquired. The second method involved soaking the hair daily in salt water and exposing it to the sun until the hair bleached to satisfaction. The juice of wild oranges is also said to have assisted the hair in developing the preferred light-brown colour.[4] Today, in the absence of suitably processed hair, light-brown coloured synthetic wigs are known to have been used, although in most cases the hair is replaced with feathers.[5]

The lave is the decorated framework of wooden sticks worn at the front of the headdress. This framework was either tied together or fixed to a plate of material such as turtle shell. The individual sticks of the lave had strips of barkcloth tightly wrapped around them. Te Rangi Hiroa suggests that the lave was formerly composed of the selu tuiga, a decorated comb made from coconut midrib. This, he says, was superseded by the wider open framework that we know today, its greater surface area allowing for small glass mirrors to be incorporated into the design.

The pale fuiono (forehead band) is tied across the front and base of the lave helping to hold it in place. The pale fuiono was once made of a braided strip of coconut fibre decorated with two rows of cut nautilus shell pieces. Imported especially from Tonga, these nautilus shells were very rare and valuable.[6] Occasionally two pale fuiono were worn at the same time to create a more prominent band of decoration. The use of the pale in this way can be seen in many turn of the century photographs. Today pale fuiono are made from all kinds of applied decorations such as beads and

Fig. 14.5 Samoan chiefs wearing tuiga. The large shells in the headbands are nautilus shells. (Auckland War Memorial Museum, Neg. No: B8856)

sequins. Nautilus shells once used in the past, remain especially rare.

Once all these pieces were fitted together on the head the tuiga was complete. The finishing touch was often a set of red parakeet feathers attached on top as added decoration. In the absence of a lau ulu (tassels of hair on a string), these red feathers alone could be worn on the head. Depending on which material dominated the tuiga, the headdress was called a tuiga'ula (red feathers) or a tuiga lauulu (human hair).[7]

In fact there is a fair amount of artistic licence involved in the creation of tuiga, particularly in the present day. The scope for innovation is demonstrated at events such as the annual Teuila Festival in Apia and the Auckland Secondary Schools' Maori and Pacific Island Cultural Festival in Auckland. At these events are many manifestations of the tuiga, all recognisable in basic form, but made from a great range of materials with many additional colours besides the mandatory red. While mirrors retain a prominent place on the lave, they are often replaced with large imported shells, and the framework of the lave itself is often tightly wrapped in red material or wool.

This inventiveness is not new and is certainly evident in this account from the late 1950s, where the girls of St Mary's School in Apia made tuiga for a one-off dance performance, using the most common of materials in place of hair – coconut husk:

At boarding school the nuns got together about ten girls, and we made tuiga, about ten tuiga for a dance, for a group of tourists on a ship from America. They had asked us to give them a performance. So we all dressed up as taupou and we made our own tuiga from the coconuts. We used mirrors and we used sticks going up, feathers … but to make the hair we had to clean out the pulu mai le popo [fibre husks of the coconut] to make sure they came out like strings, then we tied them up the way you do on the tuiga. We had heaps of rolls, and we made ten tuiga for ten girls. For the pale we used the tree fa'apapa, and some of the seeds we call saga, they have got seeds like beads, like rosary beads, they are shaped like that, and we picked them and mixed them up with other beads to make the pale. That's how we did it back home at boarding school, because we could not afford to buy the right things, that's how we made the hair from the popo.[8]

In the possession of one Samoan family in New Zealand is a tuiga with close to 100 years of associations and memories. As such it is a very important treasure and family heirloom, one that has been maintained and passed on through several generations and of great value and significance to the family who own it. Mrs Epi Setefano:

The tuiga was in our family a long, long time ago before I was born. In our family there was always someone to do the tuiga. These are the very special things in every family.

The first old lady, she is still alive now, she is over 80 years old, she was one who wore the tuiga of our family when she was young. In those days, well I often helped my mother in preparing the tuiga for my cousin who was a taupou. She used to ask me to watch or hold onto something while she did something else, you know supervise things like that, that's what I carried on when she passed away, I carried on myself.

The tuiga is the responsibility of all the girls, the ladies, the daughters of the family and they pass it on to the next one. All the daughters of the family are entitled to wear it. My daughter has worn it here in New Zealand many times. Once at the opening of the college when she presented the ava, she was wearing the full tuiga, and again at another presentation she wore the full tuiga.

In the tuiga I see now they use anything. They do it like a cap or a hat and you just put it on the head and that's it, anybody can just put it on. But what I have got is human hair, the hair of our old ladies. I still hold onto what I have for the sake of our ancestors.

It has often happened that people come to me and ask to borrow the tuiga, but these are the things that you don't have to look for because you should own it, it's something you own, you don't have to look for it, you always have it.[9]

When Te Rangi Hiroa wrote his description of the tuiga in the 1920s he said that the drawback was that it was not put together in a structurally permanent combination.[10] Today the most common type of tuiga is exactly that, with tuiga in Samoa and New Zealand being made as one-piece structures with all the appendages and decorations attached to the outside. It is a very rare thing to see the old style of composite tuiga. But despite these material and cosmetic changes the tuiga still holds its place as the headpiece of the chiefly family and is still used in much the same way for the same dances and ceremonial occasions. In considering the delicate and fragile construction of the tuiga, it is worth remembering that it is an item to be worn with grace and dignity. For example, in the important standing dance known as the taualuga, the tuiga encourages the central dancer, usually a taupou or other high-ranking person, to stand straight, hold their head still and dance with good posture.

NECKLACES

'Ula (necklaces) were made from a variety of natural products that included fresh leaves, scented flowers, fruit, seeds, shells and whales' teeth. With the exception of whales' teeth, all are still commonly used today. Threaded together in various combinations, 'ula are worn for festive occasions and given as gifts to arriving or departing guests. They are common in many Samoan homes and not only adorn the occupants, but hang upon pictures, statues and walls.

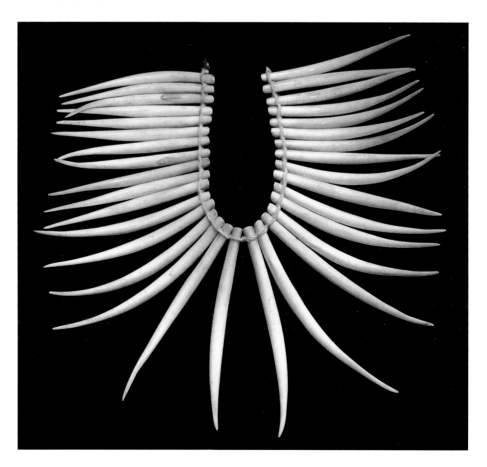

Fig. 14.6 'Ula lei (necklace) made from ground whale tooth. (Photograph Krzysztof Pfeiffer, Auckland War Memorial Museum, Neg. No: 54756.3)

Increasingly, synthetic objects such as bottle tops, plastics, coloured beads, sequins and even wrapped confectionery are becoming part of the accepted range of materials used in 'ula. 'Ula today are often made from coloured plastic curled and cut in the shape of flowers and leaves. But they can also be made of perfectly fabricated silk flowers, strings of which can be bought at the markets for a few dollars.

The whale-tooth necklace is the most valued of Samoan necklaces and is generally worn only by chiefs and their sons and daughters. Known in Samoa as 'ula lei they were formerly a distinct marker of status and to some extent an individual's wealth or influence. They were also items that were generally imported into Samoa. Like so many of Samoa's arts they highlight wider relationships with nearby Tonga and Fiji.

The 'ula lei is made from teeth of the sperm whale that have been split and ground down into curved and pointed pendants. These are smoothed and polished, then a hole is drilled through them and they are threaded onto a cord and worn around the neck.

'Ula lei are rare and valued perhaps because of the difficulty in acquiring them. Many originated in Fiji. There they were made for Fijian chiefs by Tongan and Samoan canoe builders and later their descendants who began settling in Fiji in the late 1700s. It was not long before they were also made for wear in Tonga and Samoa.[11]

Initially, the Tongans themselves may have supplied most of the whales' teeth for the craftsmen. The Ha'apai group of islands, where many of Tonga's beautiful whale ivory carvings originate from, lie on the path of a sperm whale migration route. Many whales pass this point during August and September en route to the Antarctic where they spend the summer months.[12] Inevitably some were washed up or stranded and so were harvested for their teeth and bone. The coral reefs off Vava'u are also documented as being a source of whale ivory.[13]

In fact in Fiji whales' teeth were so highly prized that concealment of a tooth could result in death for the offender:

In the Fiji islands, whales' teeth are held, if possible, in still greater estimation, for it would be dangerous there for a man, unless he be a great chief, and even then, if he were a foreigner, to be known to have a whale's tooth about him; the personal possession of such a valuable property would endanger his life: the axe, or the club, on some unlucky occasion, would deprive him of it forever, and of his life too.[14]

Fig. 14.7 (top) 'Ula lei – whale tooth necklace,1996. A replica made from white plastic and bone pieces threaded onto a nylon line. (Museum of New Zealand, Te Papa Tongarewa, Ref. No: FE010594)

Fig. 14.8 (bottom) 'Ula fala –pandanus key necklace, painted red. (Museum of New Zealand, Te Papa Tongarewa, Ref. No: FE010595)

But in the early 19th century the arrival of American and English whalers and traders saw an increase in the supply of teeth and also introduced metal tools to local craftsmen. This possibly led to the development of the slim sabre-tooth shape of many sperm whale tooth necklaces, which went on to replace the stubbier whale tooth necklaces made from pilot whale and false killer whale teeth.[15]

There is one characteristic of some Samoan 'ula lei that seems to distinguish them from those more common in Fiji and Tonga. Whether it was a matter of taste or merely to conserve materials, Samoan 'ula lei were typically half the length and cut much thinner than those of Fiji.[16] It is difficult to determine whether this was typical practice without sighting a range of well-documented examples, but in many photographs we see manaia and taupou wearing shortened versions of 'ula lei. Another accessory often seen in photographs was the use of a row of pearl-like beads to decorate the 'ula lei neckline.

A popular substitute for the short style of 'ula lei are imitations made using the closed blossoms of the pualulu tree.[17] These are still commonly seen around the necks of performers in the islands, although increasingly popular and more durable are imitations made from long slivers of bone separated by small white plastic reels.

If an 'ula lei necklace was not available for an important occasion, an 'ula nifo was often worn in its place.[18] This was a necklace made from a single boar's tusk that was curled and almost circular in shape. The tight curl of the tusk was achieved by taking out the opposing canines from the upper jaw of a tame boar. From the lower jaw the tusk would grow upward, and instead of grinding against the upper canines, it would continue to grow through the space left behind when they were removed. Over time the tusk would naturally curl around the back down over the lower jaw forming an almost closed ring,[19] making it both a rare thing and highly prized. Once removed it was usually worn tightly around the neck and tied with cord or barkcloth.

Another necklace, less rare but which still indicates status, is the 'ula fala. Most often worn by tulafale, they are made from pandanus fruit and being often painted red they are difficult to miss at any ceremony or function. They are important markers of status, but like many aspects of Samoan culture, the etiquette and customs concerning their use are always changing and thus a point of debate.

An incident that illustrates this occurred in 1999 when the Prime Minister of New Zealand, Jenny Shipley, attended the funeral of former Samoan Prime Minister Tofilau Eti, wearing an 'ulu fala given to her by a Samoan colleague. At the time she was criticised by Samoan commentators in New Zealand for wearing it at such an occasion, with one stating that 'the 'ula fala was worn only at festive, celebratory occasions and was inappropriate for more sombre events, such as funerals'.[20] This prompted a letter to the editor of *The Dominion* newspaper from a New Zealand-based matai, who argued that Samoan culture had evolved in all directions and there were no guidelines for the 'ula fala's use.[21] The debate soon dropped out of the headlines, but it highlighted the important issue of the contentious and changing nature of fa'asamoa.

Fig. 14.9 'Ula nifo (boar's tusk) worn on neck or as an armlet. Collected by Dr Augustin Kramer late 1800s. (Photograph Anatol Dreyer, courtesy of Linden Museum, Stuttgart. Ref. No: 89.159)

TAULIMA AND TAUVAE

Taulima (armlets) were usually made from leaves, seeds or shells. Taulima made from banana leaf and ti leaf were the most common and can still be seen today. Quickly made and disposable, they are twisted and tied around the arm and are usually worn for special dances or for serving special foods.[22]

A more durable and permanent armlet was the boar's tusk. The 'ula nifo as described above was usually worn around the neck to decorate the chest. But on occasion a single boar's tusk was worn on the upper arm tied in place with a cord.

Fig. 14.10 Tauvae (anklet) made from cotton material and bottle tops. Purchased from the Aavalalo market, Apia, 1994. (Museum of New Zealand, Te Papa Tongarewa, Ref. No:FE010416)

White cowrie shells were also worn on the arm in this way.[23]

Like taulima, tauvae (anklets) are often made from leaves and worn for the same special occasions. Common in many male dance troupes today, particularly in New Zealand, are long white raffia tassels worn tied around and below the knee and extending almost down to the ankle. There are many variations along these lines, but as substitutes for leaves these bright tassels shake and rustle with every step and effectively highlight the leg movements during a dance.

Another type of tauvae also used in dance but less common today is made from large brown and flat elliptical seeds known as tupe. These seeds come from the pods of a climbing plant called fue'afa[24] and are also used in games and to hang on 'ula. To make the tauvae the seeds were cut in half and attached to short strips of barkcloth. These were then fixed to a separate strip that was tied around the ankle. The dangling hollow seeds rattled as the dancer moved around. In the late 1920s the style was for males to wear a single seed on each hanging strip whereas women would wear two.[25] Occasionally this type of tauvae can still be found, but is tied together with 'afa (cord plaited from coconut fibre) or strips of imported cloth. In another contemporary version bottle tops are strung together, because they also produce a distinctive rattling sound which is what is required in a dance.

TO'OTO'O AND FUE

To'oto'o are long wooden staffs used by tulafale (orators). Along with fue and 'ula fala they are important symbols of office. The to'oto'o is generally very plain and undecorated in form but smoothed and polished in finish. It is usually made to stand not taller than the tulafale himself and there are a number of conventions about how it should be used and handled.

The fue, as mentioned, is the other item of regalia important for a tulafale. High chiefs would also carry them but only when appearing as orators. Said to resemble fly switches in appearance, fue are made from lengths of braided coconut fibre attached to a short wooden handle. In the 1920s, however, it became the custom to use horses' hair exclusively for high chiefs. Fue with short tassels were made for use inside the fale while those with long tassels were for use outside.[26] Fue are curious items of regalia in that while they could probably be used to shoo away flies, they were more likely to be cleverly swished to and fro over the shoulder to stall for time. This impressive and dignified looking action would give the orator an opportunity to gather his thoughts and decide what to say next.

Figs. 14.11-14 Ili (fans). (Photographs Krzysztof Pfeiffer, Auckland War Memorial Museum, Neg. Nos: 50813, 4094, 23541.2, 41215)

FANS

Fans are another accessory widely used in Samoa. The most common fan is made primarily from dried coconut leaf. Used mainly around the home to create a breeze and chase flies, they are known as ili aupolapola. (Te Rangi Hiroa recorded the term ili aulamalama, but this seems to have now disappeared from use.[27]) A second more significant type of fan is the ili tea. Made exclusively for the use of chiefs, taupou and honoured guests, they are said to have been made from young unfolded coconut leaves that had been bleached in the sun. When they were last described in the literature by anthropologist Roger Neich, there was real pride in owning an ili tea. They were kept in a special place and only brought out on particular occasions.[28]

There were also special wooden fans known as ili pau after the wood of the pau or manapau that they were fashioned from. Geometric shapes and patterns were cut out from the thin body, making the ili pau a light and delicate accessory. The quality of the openwork varies greatly, and among the examples sighted in museums it ranges from extensive and delicately cut to very minimally decorated with the body of the fan quite thick. Due to the thinness to which the pau is cut, most examples of ili pau are small in size with narrower proportions than fans woven from leaves. These characteristics make them fragile and prone to damage – (refer Chapter 7, Woodwork and Sculpture).

RINGS, BRACELETS AND BROOCHES

Rings, bracelets and brooches are other forms of adornment made in Samoa. Popular from at least the 1920s to the present day, they were originally typically made of turtle and coconut shell. A small collection of jewellery of this type is in the Museum of New Zealand. It is characterised by brooches, pins and rings made from turtle shell and coloured glass. Many of them feature a silver inset of words and/or motifs. A few other examples of bracelets collected in the 1960s show the pan-Pacific appropriation of ideas and motifs. Made with the same inset elements, they feature motifs such as swordfish, turtles and Fijian bure (houses) alongside the words Apia and Samoa. But as well as borrowing other cultural motifs or symbols, new and handy materials were also utilised. In 1964 brooches and pins were commonly made from toothbrush handles and the rims of sunglasses.[29] These techniques of manufacture and style of item are still commonly found in the Apia markets.

Today body adornments are made by almost anyone who requires them for a dance, event, or special occasion. They can be strings of shells or of sequins, the possibilities and manifestations are many, and more and more artists are starting to specialise in the design and manufacture of body adornments. Their productions explore aspects of life, history, custom and culture, and although they echo the same craftsmanship and styles of 'ula lei, 'ula nifo and tuiga, they incorporate new materials and allude to different stories and concerns.

Contemporary jewellery makers in New Zealand make many references in their work to their heritage and things that affect their lives, yet they also work cross-culturally, drawing on new ideas and technologies to better extend and express the messages and meanings in their work. Two jewellery makers of Samoan descent working in this way are New Zealand-based Ela To'omaga and Niki Hastings-McFall.

To'omaga often makes use of natural materials, a popular choice for generations of Samoan adornment makers, demonstrating exquisite detail in her plaiting of fibre and her choice and placement of shells and feathers. Her work with adornments

Fig. 14.15 *Taefu, Muaulu, Latu, To'omaga*. 'Ula (necklace) made by Ela To'omaga, 1996. The title of the work refers to the artist's father's matai names and is dedicated to his memory. The artist says that it is a fa'aula – 'like an acknowledgement of my father, his matai status and his role in the wider aiga'. (Museum of New Zealand, Te Papa Tongarewa, Ref. No: FE010574)

complements work she has previously done in costume and garments.

Hastings-McFall works with a wide range of natural and synthetic materials and, from legends of Samoa to the missionary experience, her themes reflect the personal explorations she is making into her Samoan heritage.

NIKI HASTINGS-MCFALL

I had always made things, but I never really thought that art or making or creating would develop into making me a living. I was sort of brought up thinking that art was something you do if you can't do something else. At school there was an academic stream and then there were the art students, and so art was always treated as something that was never an option for me. I just did stuff in my spare time, but never really took it seriously. I had just got back from a couple of years overseas and decided that I didn't want to bum around. So I went down to the local Labour Department to see what courses were available and one of them was jewellery and I thought, well, I like jewellery, I'll try that. So I went to Manukau Institute of Technology.

In the second year at Manukau, an art curator named Jim Vivieaere came round and was looking for people for his Bottled Ocean show. I was doing a whole lot of work with shells and

stuff like that because I used to live by the beach. He came in and my tutor said, 'Oh, there's this guy here and he's looking for a Pacific islander', and I had just met my father that year and said I couldn't really qualify as a Pacific islander. I was really pissed off because I had to stop work and go and talk to him and I said, 'Look, you won't like my stuff because it's not Pacific island and I'm not really what you're after'. I was quite grumpy because I didn't want to stop working. He ended up using it because it was from the ocean so it was quite relevant though not necessarily Pacific. That was sort of the beginning of things and then I thought oh gosh people are actually interested in it and that really … well I was pretty hooked on it by then. That show was really good for me.

My mother's parents, who are palagi, brought me up; my father was Samoan-German, born in Samoa, and that family moved out here about 30 odd years ago. I didn't meet that side of the family until roughly seven or eight years ago now. Once I sort of met them, my interest in Samoa came about, wanting to explore that side of the family.

My heritage is a lot more overt in my work now because when I first met my father I thought, there's been this huge Pacific renaissance and it's going on for quite a while. I actually remember a woman I met at school who was Samoan and Chinese; she did a lot of very Pacific-influenced work using tapa designs and things like that. I thought that me doing something like that was really jumping on the

Fig. 14.16 (top) Niki Hastings-McFall. (Jeff Evans)
Fig. 14.17 (bottom) *Sina's Eel*, Niki Hastings-McFall, 1996. The title refers to the Samoan story of the origin of the coconut tree. The piece comprises a coconut-shaped amulet attached to a string of several plaited synthetic cords. (Museum of New Zealand, Te Papa Tongarewa, Ref. No: FE010609)

bandwagon. I thought that because it's really popular and people buy it, I thought it really wasn't my place to do that. In the end I just started reading about Samoa, looking for anything I could get my hands on, and the more I read about it the more interested I got in it and the more my work got to being all about the Pacific.

The work that I've been doing over the last year has got, well I did this show in Melbourne and the work for that was based on the lei necklace and stuff like that, but it was all made out of, based on suburban materials. I seem to be getting away from the jewellery thing really and starting to turn to more object-based work rather than specifically body ornaments. I guess you can call it mixed media work rather than installation.

The things that make it all worthwhile and valid are the opportunities you get. To be in a good show or make a piece that you know is really good. It's also just about having the freedom. I work seven days a week, but it's not like work for me, I make a living doing what I enjoy. I think it's really good if you can get to that stage. You can be quite successful even if you are not wealthy.

CHAPTER 14

1. Te Rangi Hiroa (Peter Buck), 'Samoan Material Culture', *Bernice P. Bishop Museum* Bulletin 75 (Hawai'i, Honolulu: 1930), pp. 622-628

2. Te Rangi Hiroa, 'Samoan Material Culture', p. 627

3. Te Rangi Hiroa, 'Samoan Material Culture', p. 627

4. A. Kramer, *The Samoan Islands* vol. 2 (Auckland: Polynesian Press, 1995), p. 333

5. A tuiga made by Paula Chan Cheuk incorporates synthetic hair.

6. Kramer, *The Samoan Islands* vol. 2, p. 335

7. Pratt cited in Kramer, *The Samoan Islands* vol 2, p. 332

8. Iutita Mallon, interview with author (December 1999)

9. Epi Setefano, interview with author (February 2000)

10. Te Rangi Hiroa, 'Samoan Material Culture', p. 169

11. F. Clunie, *Yalo I Viti* [a Fiji Museum Catalogue], (Suva: Fiji Museum, 1986), p. 49

12. J. Hjarno, 'Social Reproduction: towards an understanding of aboriginal Samoa', *Folk* vol. 21-22 (1979), p. 106

13. K. St Cartmail, *The Art of Tonga* (Nelson: Craig Potton Publishing, 1997), p. 97

14. J. Martin, (Mariner, William), *An Account of the Natives of the Tongan Islands* (London: John Murray, 1818)

15. Clunie, *Yalo I Viti*, p. 49

16. Kramer, *The Samoan Islands* vol. 2, p. 336

17. Kramer, *The Samoan Islands* vol. 2, p. 331

18. F.J.H. Gratton, *An Introduction to Samoan Custom* (Papakura: McMillan 1985, first published 1948), p. 116

19. Clunie, *Yalo I Viti*, p. 157

20. *The Dominion* (March 29, 1999)

21. *The Dominion* (April 7, 1999)

22. Te Rangi Hiroa, 'Samoan Material Culture', p. 630

23. J.B. Stair, *Old Samoa; or flotsam and jetsam from the Pacific Ocean* (Papakura: Southern Reprints, 1983, first published 1897), p. 116; an illustration depicts a woman wearing two armlets made from shell as well as a tight-fitting necklace.

24. Te Rangi Hiroa incorrectly describes these seeds as coming from the ifilele, they are actually tupe, which come from a vine-like climbing plant Kramer calls fue'afa. See A. Kramer, *The Samoan Islands vol. 2*, p. 455. Another reference refers to the vine as fue'vai (*Entada phaseoloides*). See Parnham, B.E.V., 'Plants of Samoa', *New Zealand Department of Scientific and Industrial Research Information Series* no. 85: pp. 1-162

25. Te Rangi Hiroa, 'Samoan Material Culture', p. 630

26. A. McKenzie, *Samoan Customs* (Apia, Samoa: no date), pp. 2-3

27. Te Rangi Hiroa, 'Samoan Material Culture', p. 633

28. R. Neich, 'Material culture of Western Samoa', *National Museum of New Zealand*, Bulletin 23 (1985), p. 28

29. D. Pitt, *Tradition and Economic Progress in Samoa* (Oxford: Clarendon Press, 1970), p. 240

CHAPTER 15

COSTUME
AND GARMENTS

Fig. 15.1 Studio photograph of Suega and her sisters taken by Thomas Andrew in the 1890s. (Alexander Turnbull Library, National Library of New Zealand, Te Puna Matauranga o Aotearoa. Ref. No: PA7-01-14)

Samoan costume has long been a medium of artistic expression and creativity. Descriptions of Samoan costume over the last 200 years started with the simple leaf skirt and a small selection of fibre textiles. But over this period items of Samoan clothing and costume have ranged from the very simple to the very elaborate. In combination with personal adornments, skilfully-made garments and textiles remain an inspiration in the present day. Like many aspects of Pacific art and culture, clothing and garments are being reinterpreted and re-presented as new generations look back to their ancestors and origins, and assign new values to old ways of doing things or new ways of doing things to old values.

Today there are dressmakers and designers on every island in the Pacific and Samoa is no exception. Here the skills of embroidery, sewing and weaving are fostered and nurtured among the women of the aualuma (women's association). The ways in which available materials are used, adapted and transformed capture (for often the shortest time) the creative spirit of those who want to dress up and look good for the occasion. From the making of flower wreaths and necklets to the sewing of a two-piece puletasi (two-piece dress), the making of garments for work or leisure requires great dexterity, imagination and skill.

As well as covering and decorating the body, garments worn in Samoa can signal a person's social status, wealth, the occasion they are attending or place they are travelling to. They can indicate membership of a certain group or organisation, and even a person's occupation. Some of these uses and purposes have changed over time and some of the textiles and garments of last century have now disappeared from use. But Samoan dress, and its design and use, remains laden with innovation, significance and value.

WAIST GARMENTS

Probably one of the oldest and most simply made of Samoan waist garments is the titi. Worn on the waist either on its own or as an overskirt, its style and appearance have persisted through many influences and changes. To the present day its simple but functional form is still finding a place at important occasions, dances and festivals, and also on fashion catwalks.

Te Rangi Hiroa provides the most complete description of Samoan waist garments as they were in the late 1920s. In terms of manufacture, he identified two types of titi. In one, strips were attached to the braid or cord that formed the waist attachment, some types of which were plaited afterwards. The other was the 'ie, which commenced with a weaving technique and finished with the waist attachment.

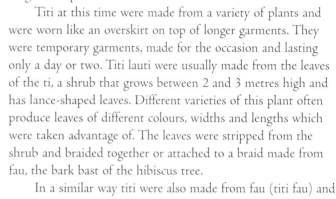

Titi at this time were made from a variety of plants and were worn like an overskirt on top of longer garments. They were temporary garments, made for the occasion and lasting only a day or two. Titi lauti were usually made from the leaves of the ti, a shrub that grows between 2 and 3 metres high and has lance-shaped leaves. Different varieties of this plant often produce leaves of different colours, widths and lengths which were taken advantage of. The leaves were stripped from the shrub and braided together or attached to a braid made from fau, the bark bast of the hibiscus tree.

In a similar way titi were also made from fau (titi fau) and fagai'o bast (titi fagai'o) as well as pandanus (titi fala) and feathers (titi'ula). The difference being that in these examples the leaf and feather elements were hung from cords.

Titi fala were made from stripped pandanus leaf undersides discarded in the weaving of certain types of mat. They were sometimes dyed with turmeric or imported dyes and the hanging elements were sometimes decorated with pieces of pandanus sewn on in an appliqued effect.

Fig. 15.2 Titi (dance skirt) made in 1920 from hibiscus fibre, seeds, shell and cloth. Made for use in performances when the Prince of Wales visited Samoa in that year. (Museum of New Zealand, Te Papa Tongarewa, Ref. No: FE003418)

Titi'ula were, as the name suggests, made from the red feathers of the Fijian parakeet. Being the same feathers used in making the fringe for the 'ie toga they were often scarce and much sought after. Because of the rarity of the feathers, titi'ula were most often worn by taupou. In this sense it signified rank or status. In 1927 Te Rangi Hiroa noted that in the absence of the preferred red feathers, titi'ula were often made from the green feathers of the Samoan parakeet. Today titi 'ula are made from chicken feathers that are usually dyed red or green, although sometimes purples, yellows and whites are used.

Fau and fagai'o were also used to make a woven form of waist garment characterised by a wide waistband woven in a check pattern with individual fibres hanging down forming the length of the skirt. A variation on this style saw the waistband woven in a twill pattern with rosettes and other applied ornamentation attached. An appliqued waistband featuring the Union Jack can be seen in an example of a titi fau made for the visit of the Prince of Wales to Samoa in 1920.

The 'ie tutu pu'upu'u was a short woven waist garment with braided tails and hanging fringes.[1] When the garment was worn, it hung over itself with the braids and fringes forming what is essentially a one-piece skirt and overskirt. Te Rangi Hiroa recorded three varieties of this type of garment. They varied in their technique of

Fig. 15.3 Women of the Socialite Club, Apia, Western Samoa, 1920s. Note the use of 'ie toga as dresses. (Photograph Alfred John Tattersall, Alexander Turnbull Library, National Library of New Zealand, Te Puna Matauranga o Aotearoa. Ref. No: PA series 7:A)

Fig. 15.4 Three unidentified women, two wearing 'ie toga and the third a siapo with a titi over the top of it. Two of the women are wearing selu tuiga in their hair. (Photograph Malcolm Ross circa 1910. Alexander Turnbull Library, National Library of New Zealand, Te Puna Matauranga o Aotearoa. Ref. No: 1/1-006643)

manufacture, the colour they were dyed and the material they were made from. The examples he described were bleached white, but they could also be dyed black in a mixture of black candlenut dye and brown o'o.

'IE TOGA

'Ie toga (fine mats) were also worn as a skirt and held in place around the waist with a belt of barkcloth called fusi. Two fringes of feathers – one on the front and one on the back – were often incorporated into the design so that when the mats were folded over two rows of feathers were visible at the same time. Sometimes open-weave edges were used as a further enhancement. 'Ie toga would be worn in this way only by taupou, manaia or high-ranking matai.

'IE FAU AND 'IE SINA

'Ie fau and 'ie sina were shaggy mat-like waist garments worn on important occasions by women of status. The term shaggy mat is an appropriate description as the entire outer surface of the mat is covered in thin strings or tags attached by a special technique. This made them heavy to handle compared to other similar sized textiles.

'Ie fau were brown shaggy garments made of the bast of the fau tu, a variety of hibiscus. Their natural colouring was a yellowish brown and their characteristic thick shaggy covering was achieved by attaching the long fibre tags very close together during the weaving process. In general 'ie fau were considered coarse in texture.

By contrast 'ie sina were finely made and softer in texture. Their distinguishing quality was their white colour, from which their name derives. They were made from the bast of the fau pata. The fine and delicate appearance was achieved by splitting the fibre into very narrow wefts with a shell. Again, fibre tags attached during weaving

Figs. 15.5 and 15.6 'Ie sina. Presented in 1977 to the Manawatu Science Centre and Museum in Palmerston North, New Zealand, by Alice Hunt. It once belonged to her mother who was born in Samoa in 1869. It is believed to have been given as payment for a debt sometime in the late 1800s and passed on through the family. (David Lupton)

created the shaggy appearance. On completion the whole garment would be bleached by soaking it in sea water and drying it in the sun. Later it would be repeatedly washed in fresh water and treated with the leaf of the fisoa, which assisted the garment in developing its white colour.[2]

Shaggy garments were also stained a dark red, using a mixture of earth in a wooden bowl, or black, by submerging the garment in the mud of a swamp. The dark red garment was called 'ie ta'ele after the soil used to colour it, and the black garment 'ie fuipani after the pani bark stain used to ensure that the swamp mud adhered.[3] John Williams writing in the early 1830s gives a description of how an 'ie ta'ele was worn, and what accessories could be worn with it:

The dress of the Chief woman…consisted of a red shaggy mat round the loins hanging down about half way to the knee with a corner tucked up to expose the whole left thigh nearly up to the hip. Her body was oiled with scented oil…She was then tinged off with an orange coloured rouge prepared from the turmeric…A row of large blue beads decorated her neck while a pair of bracelets of the same coloured beads were strung around her arms.[4]

'Ie sina and 'ie fau are no longer made today and seem to have almost disappeared from living memory. Very few Samoans spoken to were familiar with the names of these garments or recalled ever seeing one in their lifetime. But good examples still survive in museum collections and some families. A beautiful 'ie sina can be seen in the Manawatu Science Centre and Museum in Palmerston North, New Zealand. Presented to the Museum in 1977, it once belonged to the donor's mother who was born in Samoa in 1869. It is believed to have been given as payment for a debt sometime in the late 1800s. A prestigious garment, it has been passed on in the same family since that time and is a reminder of the family's strong connection to Samoa.

INTRODUCED STYLES AND INFLUENCES

Early accounts give the impression that Samoans were very adaptable in their attitudes to dress and made the most of any new materials or creative opportunities that came their way. The arrival of missionaries, and the traders and merchants who followed, saw the introduction of new materials and styles, as well as new ideas of modesty and appropriate attire. Among the first garments the missionaries introduced were the tiputa (barkcloth ponchos). As described in Chapter 5, Siapo, tiputa had significance as a type of uniform for those people who had converted to the Christian faith. They signified the wearer's association with the new religion, and their membership of a new group in the community. But the missionaries also introduced items of clothing more a hindrance than an asset in the tropical climate, including straw bonnets, the long all-covering Mother Hubbard-type dress, trousers and white shirts.

Interestingly, these new items were quickly taken up by new converts and were much coveted and sought after. The skills of a few creative individuals soon saw local substitutes being made in place of the real thing. Writing in 1861, missionary George Turner said that Samoan women were rarely seen without a tiputa, and that straw bonnets and shawls were in so great a demand that 'In the lack of the former some of the women showed great ingenuity in manufacturing a novel and very durable article from tortoise-shell (sic).'[5] This fascinating example of local craftsmanship is in the British Museum and is made from pieces of turtle shell carefully stitched together creating a very robust and solid bonnet. Its edges have been covered and finished in what appears to be a patterned cotton cloth, thus preventing cuts or abrasions from the sharp edges. Tiputa were also elaborated upon with siapo inspired designs and patterns, and two examples have been seen made from finely woven pandanus.[6] The smaller of the pandanus tiputa from the Museum of New Zealand has red cloth sewn around the edges, with tufts of red wool thread forming small feather-like decorations.

For men in the colonial period, the white shirt and wraparound of calico cloth became very popular and widely used. There are many old photographs from Samoa of chiefs and others wearing various combinations of local and introduced dress, including hats, blazers and naval jackets. Turner said that 'clothing in such a climate is a burden' but the demand for these types of cotton goods increased with every year that he was in the islands.[7]

The calico lavalava that became very popular could be plain, as in a straight blue colour, or patterned in a wide range and variety of designs. For a short time in the mid-1880s an interesting and popular choice in Apia were the colours of old England. As British Consul at the time William Churchward wrote, 'A favourite pattern not long since was the Union Jack *pur et simple*, which suddenly made its appearance in the form of big handkerchiefs, which were used either as lava-lavas or shawls'. According to Churchward, one British patriot, outraged at the use of the British colours in this way, tried to seize upon and confiscate every Union Jack he saw worn by a Samoan, either 'paying him for it or giving him something of less pronounced individuality in exchange'. This did nothing but increase the trade in the fashionable article, so by the time this man had given up his 'Jehad''… he had become the happy possessor of some hundreds of yards of Union Jacks, and a goodly collection of Royal Standards'.[8]

As more imported cloth became available, other styles and types of garment were made and incorporated with local dress. It is possible that at this time printed patterned cloth influenced siapo patterns and compositions as it did with similar textiles in other Pacific islands.[9] Certainly the conventions of freehand siapo mamanu provided ample scope for this to occur.

Other garments that have become part of the Samoan wardrobe include the 'ie fai taga and the puletasi. The 'ie fai taga is a specially cut lavalava that has been machine stitched along its waist edge and fitted with pockets and in some cases a belt fitting. It is believed that this style was introduced by Native Medical Practitioners returning from Suva,[10] where the form of the lavalava had in some instances acquired a distinc-

Fig. 15.7 Turtle shell bonnet made in the mid 1800s. (British Museum, Ref. No: K120861)

Fig. 15.8 Illustration of turtle shell bonnet from *Nineteen years in Polynesia* by George Turner. (See endnote No. 5)

Fig. 15.9 The well-known matai of Apia, Seumanutafa Pogai in black, with Charles Taylor, Fa'atoaga, Fa'apito (soldier). (Photograph Winkelmann, Auckland War Memorial Museum, Neg. No: 2651)

tive cut and appearance with an often jagged lower edge.

The puletasi is the most popular of Samoan women's formal garments. It is a two piece outfit consisting of a long skirt and a short or long sleeved blouse. Seen almost everywhere Samoans are found, it has been used and decorated in many ways to suit many different occasions. It is believed to have been modelled on Edwardian-style garments from the turn of the century, with their often billowed sleeves, long skirts and modestly cut neckline. The tidy and formal appearance of the puletasi is a popular choice of uniform with choirs and school dance groups, and is often decorated with printed bands of siapo motifs and patterns.

Siapo motifs and patterns also find a place on many other forms of garment either entirely covering the garment or as a fringe or detailing. Priests' vestments made from imported material by the Carmelite Sisters at Vailima also use tapa motifs.

Barkcloth or siapo was used to make garments, most notably the tiputa, but they were also worn as a turban for fishing or as a protection against club blows during war. In times of peace, however, only chiefs were permitted to wear such turbans. Finished siapo was also made into full-length garments and bodices. An example of a siapo bodice in the Museum of New Zealand is dyed dark brown and decorated on the outside with strings of red lopa seeds sewn to the cloth. It is very small and was probably made for a child. Other turn of the century photographs show longer dresses made from siapo.

COSTUME TODAY

In recent times the undecorated barkcloth itself is becoming a sought-after material by Pacific island dressmakers and designers. Its raw qualities capture an understated natural-fibre look that seems to have become quite appealing and is finding a place on catwalks and at special occasions such as weddings. In 1997 Jakkie Leota-Ete commissioned a plain barkcloth dress from Auckland-based Samoan designer Paula Chan Cheuk. She remembers that:

I first saw the work of Paula Chan at the 1994 Pasifika Fashion show [an Auckland-based show featuring fashion, culture, contemporary dance and music] in Auckland. In the traditionally inspired section, she presented a puletasi or two-piece outfit, made of tapa with sennit braiding. This was the first time such a contemporary garment using traditional materials had been used/seen and it was truly spectacular. I vowed then that, if I ever got married, she would be the woman to make my dress.[11]

In discussing her work Cheuk says the inspiration for the design was classical European but the materials were very much Samoan. The dress consists of a full-length gown decorated with coconut fibre and shells, a long tapa train and tapa headpiece, both similarly decorated, and a bouquet of coconut fibre and tapa. The dress is decorated with hand-tacked cords made from 'afa (plaited coconut fibres). Cheuk says that she first used 'afa as an applied decoration in 1995 for a dress she designed for the Pasifika Fashion show in Auckland, New Zealand:

I thought, 'afa is always used in building fales back home. And I thought surely it can be done, because I have used cords in the European way of using cords and so I thought why can't I use 'afa. It's the same technique but only the difference is in the materials, totally different materials.[12]

The tapa cloth also presented its own set of challenges, being a fibrous and fragile material to work with:

Well, tapa is a delicate fabric and because it is made from paper mulberry bark, it needed to be handled with care. What I did with this dress was to back the tapa with ordinary cotton cloth just to give it more reinforcement. Because being a delicate fabric I did not want it to part. It worked well, it came out really well.

When people saw the dress they were so amazed to see how a tapa cloth could be made up into a dress and not really an ordinary dress, a really different dress. When I went to the wedding and people saw the dress when Jackie first walked in, they thought it was silk because it had the look of raw silk. It wasn't until they came close and felt the fabric, that's when they were sure ... they said they never thought it was tapa because from a distance it looked like raw silk.[13]

Designers of Samoan descent in New Zealand are making strong statements and innovations in terms of Pacific-inspired fashion. Their work, and that of other designers of Pacific island descent, is featured at shows such as Fashion Pasifika and competitions such as the Miss South Pacific Pageant. For the island-based communities these pageants are big annual events and they provide a creative focus for designers and an opportunity to display their work. The inclusion of categories for Oceanic and Pacific wear in other high profile fashion pageants has built upon the enthusiasm and success of a thriving design community.

Another Samoan designer also based in Auckland is Asomaliu Fou Tagiilima, who was a finalist in the Oceania category of the Smokefree Fashion Awards in 1997 and 1998 and a category winner in Fashion Pasifika 98. Like Paula Chan Cheuk, Tagiilima's work incorporates natural materials from the Pacific islands in combination with commercial cloths and fabrics.

As winner of the Menswear category in Fashion Pasifika 98, Tagiilima created a three-piece costume derived from the formal modern costume of Samoan, Tongan and Fijian men. It consists of a brown silk lavalava, a red velvet jacket and a taovala-style waist garment. The lavalava and jacket are decorated with loops of applied 'afa and small amounts of shells and feathers. The waist garment is made from an upper band of Tongan ngatu (tapa), from which hangs a thick fringe of fau fibre overlaid by a rectangular lattice of linked plastic petals or leaves.

The work of Samoan designers such as Shigeyuki Kihara extends the possibilities of Samoan and Pacific inspired fashion. Through her work in fashion design and art Shigeyuki makes commentary on issues of contemporary urban life, things that affect young people today. 'My medium is fashion and art and I like to play around with a concept I call 'fashionised art' it's something that should be recognised as part of Pacific art and contemporary culture.'

Her *Graffiti Dress* 1995 combines many facets of her urban environment. The graffiti on the dress (which signify teenage rebelliousness and rage) reflects the graffiti on a former Police building in Wellington. The dress itself is based on the mu'umu'u design; as Kihara says, 'the mu'umu'u was introduced into the islands as a way of suppressing women's sexuality. Although the dress covers the entire body some of the material is transparent, in an attempt to show that women's sexuality cannot be suppressed. The overlocking on the outside of the dress represents modern technology and the urban influence of Polynesian young people. The colours represent the rastafarian influence in local culture and the word volume represents the music of young Polynesians who are becoming well known nationally because of their use of rhythm and lyrics.' This dress won first place in the Lifestyle category in the Du Pont Lycra Student Design Awards in 1995. A recent work by Shigeyuki that took fashion away from the catwalk and into the museum and art gallery, was a set of tee-shirts titled, *The Teunoa'i – Adorn to Excess Collection*. Branded with recognisable but manipulated advertising slogans, the tee-shirts cast a sarcastic and humorous commentary on everyday products and consumables, as well as some of the large corporations who employ Pacific islanders as low paid workers. The collection reappeared alongside work by artist Pip Culbert, in an exhibition called *More or Less: Art and Fashion* (Te Papa, 2001). It was an exhibition that showed how these two artists used fashion as a starting point for making works of art. In describing Shigeyuki's work, curator Ian Wedde suggests that it is the word 'collection' that draws attention to Shigeyuki's strategy – using language of both fashion and the museum to present an artful undressing of the Pacific as exotic accessory.

In terms of Samoan fashion the conventional skills and garments are still there and form a foundation. But it is among the higher fashion garments, shows and pageants that we are seeing the most dramatic expressions of creativity. What is most encouraging is the sheer diversity of the work, the combinations of materials and the many statements that are being made. The past's expression in the present is an important element in the significance and value of a new portfolio of garments. It is a portfolio that incorporates the many cultures and ideas that make up the contemporary Samoan world.

Fig. 15.10 *Graffiti Dress*, Shigeyuki Kihara, 1995. (Museum of New Zealand, Te Papa Tongarewa, Ref. No: FE010561. Courtesy of artist)

FASHION DESIGNER: PAULA CHAN CHEUK

I was born in Western Samoa in a village called Sale'imoa, but I grew up mainly in Apia. My father is Chinese from Canton, China. My mum is half Samoan, half Chinese and comes from the village of Faleu, Manono. My parents are both tailors: dad specialises in men's tailoring and mum in ladies and childrenswear.

At a very young age I was interested in the art of sewing. I was so fascinated with dad because he used to take people's measurements and cut clothes out freehand without patterns. Mum was a good seamstress too but not as advanced as dad, he was more into the complicated things like suits, mum was more just a basic seamstress.

I came to New Zealand in the early seventies … 1974. I joined my sisters who were already in the sewing trade. In the evening I did a design course with the New Zealand College of Fashion Design. I took the course to further my knowledge in advanced designs and pattern drafting. My practical knowledge of sewing and garment construction helped me tremendously in completing the course in half of the expected time of three years.

In 1991 I was approached by Lucy Reedy to design outfits for Julia Toevai, who was entering the Miss Samoa New Zealand Pageant. She won and went on to compete in the Miss South Pacific, which she won as well. That's when people started noticing my work because it was so totally different from everybody else's.

I always think of my background as a Chinese-Samoan, so I sometimes incorporate my parents' cultures into my designs. I often combine the knowledge of siapo printing in Samoa, with the Oriental dress and the Mandarin collar.

With my traditional garments I look back through historical research and talk to my mum and friends. I create traditional costumes using organic materials and incorporate the influence of the two-piece puletasi with a more Western look. For me personally, I like simple, uncluttered designs, quality and good fitting. Classical … simple lines … that's me.

Fig. 15.11 Wedding dress made from tapa, shells, coconut fibre by Paula Chan Cheuk for Jakkie Leota-Ete, 1997. (Norman Heke)

CHAPTER 15

1. Te Rangi Hiroa (Peter Buck), 'Samoan Material Culture', *Bernice P. Bishop Museum*, Bulletin 75 (Hawai'i, Honolulu: 1930), p. 260
2. Te Rangi Hiroa, 'Samoan Material Culture', p. 273
3. Te Rangi Hiroa, 'Samoan Material Culture', pp. 273-274
4. J. Williams, in Moyle, R.M. (ed) *The Samoan Journals of John Williams 1830 and 1832* (Canberra: Australian National University Press, 1984), p. 147
5. G. Turner, *Nineteen years in Polynesia: missionary life, travels, and researches in the islands of the Pacific* (London: John Snow, 1861), p. 208
6. Grassi Museum fur Volkerkunde Zu Leipzig, Germany (PO544) and Museum of New Zealand Te Papa Tongarewa FE(011002)
7. Turner, *Nineteen years in Polynesia*, p. 208
8. W. Churchward, *My Consulate in Samoa: A record of four years sojourn in the Navigators Islands, with personal experiences of King Malietoa Laupepa, his country, and his men* (London: Richard Bentley & Son, 1887), p. 369
9. L. Jones, 'The Pareu: persistence and revival in a French Polynesian folk art', in Dark, Philip J.C. and Rose, R.G. (eds) *Artistic Heritage in a Changing Pacific* (Honolulu: University of Hawai'i Press, 1993), p. 85
10. F.J.H. Gratton, *An Introduction to Samoan Custom* (Papakura: McMillan, 1985, first published 1948), p. 160
11. J. Leota-Ete, 'Te Papa buys unique wedding dress' in *New Zealand Weddings: A Complete Guide* (1998)
12. Paula Chan Cheuk, interview with author (1999)
13. Paula Chan Cheuk, interview with author (1999)

CHAPTER 16

TOURIST ART

Souvenirs and handicrafts made for the tourist industry are not usually covered in books about the arts. But in the case of Samoan art they deserve discussion. After all, they are the most visible and accessible of Samoa's arts and probably the most widely dispersed representations of fa'asamoa. Moreover, some of these products are purchased by Samoans, both locals and visitors from overseas.

In Samoa the tourist arts and tourist industry create income opportunities for local people and in some cases keep the material and visual arts alive. On a large scale, projects like the building of the Sinalei Reef Resort – a major work for tufuga faifale Talamaivao Niko – provide income and learning opportunities. On a smaller scale, the tourist industry is an outlet and nursery for the skills and products of weavers, siapo-makers and carvers.

The tourist industry has brought with it great change and innovation, but the commercialisation of some Samoan arts is not always a nurturing and sustaining process. Tourist items say as much about those who produce them as those who purchase them. What is made provides a glimpse of what artists and sellers might perceive as representing 'classic' values, articles, and ideas of Samoan culture. What sells tells us a great deal about the tastes and expectations of the tourist. It is a case of demand influencing supply. The need to make a profit and maximise use of labour and time has led to deterioration of some arts and the development of others. Favoured timbers, feathers, shells and other natural products that were once abundant have become scarce or been replaced with new, imported and often synthetic substitutes. Likewise, processing and manufacturing methods have in some cases been shortened or streamlined to meet increased demand and save time. The impact of these developments depends on the attitude artists and sellers have toward making a quick profit and maintaining their own sense of artistic and/or cultural integrity.

While trade in artefacts had been common since the first contacts with Europeans, the visits of the first cruise ships heralded a new era of change, a further opening up of the Pacific. The growth of trade and relationships beyond Samoa's shores

Fig. 16.1 Cover illustration: Union Steam Ship Company of New Zealand Limited: tours to the South Sea Islands: Tonga, Samoa, Fiji. Three wonderful nations [Dunedin, N.Z.]: U.S.S. Co. of N.Z.,1907.

brought new ideas, incentives and motivations that would affect all aspects of life in the islands of the Pacific. A cruise brochure from 1895 paints a picture of a typical cruise, previewing what tourists looking for souvenirs could expect to pick up in the Samoan Islands:

Canoe after canoe sets out from various places on the shore: all converging on one point – the ship. Most of them are manned by women, and some by children little better than babies ... The occupants of the various canoes are on barter bent; each carries with her some piece of merchandise to be disposed of on board – a piece of tappa, a basket of limes, breadfruit, or bananas, a piece of woodcarving, a war club, a model canoe, a kavabowl, or some such trifle.[1]

The development of a tourist art industry undoubtedly had its beginnings in the visits of these late nineteenth century travellers. Since then, and probably for a few decades earlier, items have been especially made, modified and invented to meet the demand of the overseas visitor.

It was not until the 1920s, however, under the direction of the New Zealand administration, that any official encouragement was given to the handicraft industry in Samoa.[2] Initially the output was small and restricted to women who worked on the government plantations. But by this stage merchants were already making trips to Savai'i and out to Manu'a in search of quality work to export. One such merchant was Mary Pritchard, who had a business in Tutuila shipping siapo, floormats, tablemats and hula skirts to dealers in Honolulu.[3] She made a great physical effort to get Samoan products out to the world. Of one of her trips to Savai'i in 1929 she wrote:

Fig. 16.2 A man in a dugout paopao with produce and handicraft, 1938. (Alexander Turnbull Library, National Library of New Zealand, Te Puna Matauranga o Aotearoa. Ref. No: F20705 1/2)

When I had finished my buying at Sala'ilua, I had bought over 2,000 pieces of siapo on Savai'i. Small pieces of siapo, called vala, sold at that time for two shillings, or about fifty cents. During the two week trip I had also worn out two pairs of new tennis shoes.[4]

Into the late 1940s more and more villages worked to meet the demand from Apia merchants such as O.F. Nelson and Company and later Aggie Grey, both of whom had found an overseas market for handicrafts in the United States.[5]

In the last 40 to 50 years an increase in air travel and tourism has seen the market for tourist art continue to grow. A major study in the 1960s showed that handicrafts were an important earner for some Samoan villages. There were more village-based entrepreneurs and traders than ever before and in the case of the village of Malie handicrafts made up almost 9 percent of their yearly earnings.[6] Women's groups were involved in making mats and baskets, and with new tools and techniques, new products emerged: ornaments made from shell, brooches and pins made from toothbrush handles and rims of sunglasses, and even items of silverwork. In a survey of handicrafts sold over a two month period in 1964 by vendors in Apia, baskets, shell necklaces and bracelets proved the most popular.[7]

Another survey of Pacific island handicrafts during the same period listed items including tikis or ancestral figures, slippers, wastepaper baskets, lampshades and serving trays as being for sale. Siapo was supplied in any desired dimension, but interestingly, the usual size was described as being 9 ft x 6 ft long, large by today's

Fig. 16.3 Model tanoa fai ava (kava bowl) with 18 cylindrical legs. 230 mm (dia) x 55 mm (h). Collected by Mr J. Cook, Wellington Hospital Board. Presented by Mrs J. Cook mid 1900s. (Museum of New Zealand, Te Papa Tongarewa, Ref. No: FE003112)

standards, and the price was according to finish and quality. Turtle shell products, not banned at this time, were also available.[8]

By 1980 the industry was even more organised, and the main commercial outlet for Samoan tourist art was the Western Samoan Handicrafts Association established in 1965.[9] Items available for purchase included a wide range of baskets, plaited table-mats, fans, hats, sandals, shell jewellery, coconut shell ukeleles, model canoes, wooden bowls, small wooden figurines and models of fale.[10]

This growth continued into the 1990s, with more retailers involved in the tourist arts than ever before. This is probably due to an increase in air travel with more Samoans from overseas visiting or returning to the islands. The Savalalo markets in Apia as well as a large number of specialist shops provided a range of handicrafts and souvenirs for the tourist, including items from beyond Samoa's shores. Mother of pearl and turtle shell brooches from Fiji and carved items in wood from the Philippines were some of the exotic items imported and sold locally.[11] Without further research, it is difficult to say how these imports have affected local village tourist art production. Based on observations during the 1990s, Samoan articles seemed to retain a place on the retailer's shelf, albeit a shelf more diverse and multicultural in appearance.

Compared to an island group such as Hawai'i the tourist art industry in Samoa today is relatively small. Samoa does not have the same population levels as Hawai'i or the same levels of tourist traffic. As a tourist destination Samoa is still developing, as is the infrastructure, services and village-based industries that support it. For example, in Waikiki it is not difficult to walk into a store and pick up one of a dozen variations of a plastic Hawai'ian god, mass-produced in Hong Kong, often with a key ring attached. In Samoa there is little evidence of large-scale mass manufacturing. The production of most Samoan tourist art items remains largely the preserve of village groups such as the aualuma (women's committee) or individual artists. This is despite a growing number of items being imported including baskets from Vanuatu and tapa from Tonga.

Since the 1990s the number of outlets for tourist arts in Apia has remained relatively stable. Very few producers make items on a regular basis unless their village is visited as part of a tour route. Some are attached to particular stores or retailers who occasionally get large commissions or orders. However, some regions or villages maintain a long-established reputation for specific crafts or products. Artists from Fagaloa Bay, Uafato and Falealupo are known for the quality of their woodwork, and artists from Siutu and Palauli for their siapo. Art for tourists is still very much a secondary source of income. The usual situation is that artists generally come into market to sell if they require quick cash for upcoming family commitments or social occasions, or if primary sources of income such as crops are not stable.

There is a cross-section of local and overseas customers who keep the trade going. According to one retailer, the most popular items for non-Samoans – who are mainly tourists – tend to be model va'a or fale and small portable items such as jewellery. Samoan customers from overseas tend to buy things that 'look good and are well made'.[12] There is not too much concern as to whether an object is 'authentic' in the cultural sense; kava bowls or wooden platters with inset electric clocks sell as well as or better than those without. Items such as octopus lures and fishhooks, things that would more typically be attractive to the specialist collector than the regular tourist, tend not to sell so well. One group of customers who are more concerned with authenticity is Samoan government departments, who on occasion will buy to'oto'o, tanoa or fue for special gifts or presentations to visiting guests and dignitaries.

One item that Samoans both locally and from abroad tend not to buy is weapons. There is a great selection of clubs and bludgeons available, all heavily decorated, but they seem to have very little appeal. While they are interesting to other tourists their popularity as souvenirs is a far cry from last century when travellers and museums collected them in the hundreds.

For some of the stores it is not unusual to get large orders for a range of things or have specific items especially commissioned. For example, in 1999 a customer from Hawai'i commissioned ten model va'a as well as several large examples of siapo from one retailer.

One family from the village of Falefa on the north coast of Upolu receive their sole cash income making model va'a for a handicraft store. Mulivai and Shirley make examples of the full range of va'a, including va'aalo, amatasi and taumualua, and less frequently they make tanoa.[13] The retailer they supply researched the va'a and provided the couple with detailed historical drawings and images of what was required. Mulivai uses hand tools and fashions the models from timber, while Shirley prepares the woven sails from pandanus. Sailing rigs are tied with 'afa and miniature appendages are made with great attention to detail. It is a full-time occupation that results in fine, meticulous work and has provided much-needed income since 1994.

As described in Chapter 14, Adornments, there is a wide range of jewellery made in Samoa, much of it for the tourist industry. Strings of necklaces hang in the markets by the dozen. Most are made from local shells, fibres and seeds, although some stores

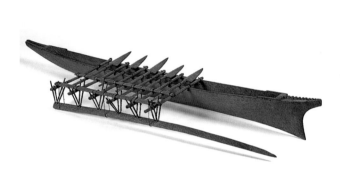

Fig. 16.4 Model va'a (dugout canoe) with six 'iato (booms) supporting outrigger float and platform. Made circa 1900. Label written in pencil on inside of hull reads: *First potato race on board S.S. Sonoma, April 24, 1907.* Collected and presented to the museum by Mr W. Evans. (Museum of New Zealand, Te Papa Tongarewa, Ref. No: FE003047)

stock strings of very small yellow shells imported from Niue and the Cook Islands.

Jewellery made from synthetic materials is also very common and is purchased more often by locals. Necklaces such as the 'ula lei, usually made from whale tooth, are now sometimes made from white plastic, and tauvae, usually made from seeds, from bottle tops. Also popular is jewellery manufactured from coconut shell. There seems to be no limit to the things that can be made with this ubiquitous material - decorative combs, belt buckles, bracelets, rings, necklaces and earrings.

There is a variety of wooden tanoa. The tanoa fai'ava or kava bowl is the most popular. They can be purchased with any number of wooden legs – from four up to 30. In contrast to the days before the tourist boom, they now come in a range of sizes, many of them small and portable enough to be carried in luggage. Another innovation with the tourist in mind is the appearance of engraved carvings and geometric designs on the outer surface of the tanoa. From at least the 1930s these have taken the form of straight parallel lines of different lengths and thickness arranged in patterns reminiscent of tatau or siapo motifs. Once made for ceremonial use in a local or village context, in the tourist's home tanoa fai'ava become important as items for display.

Weapons and slit-drums have undergone a similar transformation. Once used in war and sparsely decorated with geometric shapes and patterns, the wooden clubs and spears of the 1990s are smaller in size and decorated more extensively and elaborately, again to appeal to tourists' tastes. Similarly, slit-drums, formerly always plain, are now often decorated. Other wood-carved items include platters, model fale and small figurines, the latter usually depicting important community figures such as the tulafale and the taupou.[14] Carved 'upeti (wooden design tablets) used in siapo making are also sold, and to tourists at least are seen as art objects in their own right, their engraved patterns very much worthy of display.

Siapo is common in both the stores and the markets in the form of swatches or small samples that are easily portable. However, orders for larger pieces are becoming more common as tourists become more informed about the role of siapo in Samoan culture. As described earlier, recent illustrated publications on Pacific tapa have started a move by some siapo makers to revive old styles and designs in siapo decoration, the cleaner lines and details having a greater appeal than the more quickly produced pieces made for tourists. However, lengths of Tongan ngatu or tapa still remain common and in some cases are sold to unsuspecting tourists as Samoan siapo.

In the area of woven products, baskets have always been more popular than mats. There is a great range, characterised by structural detail and the incorporation of coloured cloths and plastics in the design. Samoan baskets are sold in almost every store, but often with colourful and finely-made examples from Vanuatu. Woven mats and 'ie toga are also available, though more readily from stalls at markets than established retailers. Buyers of these items are more often locals or Samoans visiting from overseas than the regular tourist.

Overall there is a great selection of collectibles for sale. So what do they say about those who make, sell and buy them? By and large they represent an internal view; one that reflects idealised Samoan values, history and culture. In many cases this is modified by and in tension with an external view representing market demand, values and taste.

Fig. 16.5 Model fale (house) presented to Gerard Eugene Mallon at Falealupo, Savai'i, 1968. Private collection.

As anthropologist Harry Silver has pointed out, the tourist market can often alter the patronage, production and distribution of indigenous art and material culture. Most artists, in preparing work for this market, consider very carefully the tastes of the consumers.[15] This market demand and taste may not always equate with local artistic conventions and practices and may change over time.

Whether the tourist art industry is beneficial or detrimental to Samoan culture depends a great deal on the attitudes and understanding of those producing and selling the products. For a country like Samoa, the manner in which this growing industry is managed is very important. As souvenirs for travellers from the outside world and symbols of pride in Samoa itself, the arts encouraged by the tourist market have the potential to promote pride and respect within a culture as well as destroy them.[16]

CHAPTER 16

1. Union Steamship Company, *A Cruise in the Islands: Tonga; Samoa; Fiji* (Dunedin: J. Wilkie & Co. Printers and Publishers, 1895), pp. 21-22
2. D. Pitt, *Tradition and Economic Progress in Samoa* (Oxford: Clarendon Press, 1970), p. 240
3. M.J. Pritchard, *Siapo: Barkcloth Art of Samoa* (Honolulu: University of Hawai'i Press in association with American Samoa Council on Culture Arts and Humanities, 1984), p. 9
4. Pritchard, *Siapo: Barkcloth Art*, p. 11
5. Pitt, *Tradition and Economic Progress in Samoa*, p. 147
6. Pitt, *Tradition and Economic Progress in Samoa*, p. 147
7. Pitt, *Tradition and Economic Progress in Samoa*, p. 240
8. A. McBean, *Handicrafts of the South Seas* (Sydney: Bridge Printery Pty. Ltd., in association with South Pacific Commission, Noumea, New Caledonia, 1964), pp. 85-86
9. P.J.C. Dark, 'Tomorrow's heritage is today's art and yesteryear's identity', in Hanson and Hanson (eds), *Art and Identity in Oceania* (Australia: Crawford House Press, 1990), p. 260
10. R. Neich, 'Material Culture of Western Samoa', *National Museum of New Zealand* Bulletin 23 (1985), p. 60
11. Dark, 'Tomorrow's Heritage', p. 251
12. Heidi Paul, personal comment (1999)
13. June 1999
14. C. Wilpert, *Western Samoan Handcrafts* (Reinbek, Western Germany: Hamburgisches Museum fur Volkerkunde, 1983)
15. H.R. Silver, 'Ethnoart', *Annual Review of Anthropology*, vol. 8 (1979), pp. 267-307
16. K. Clark, *Handcraft trade in the South Pacific: a case study - Trade Aid (NZ) Inc.* Pacific Handcraft Research Project Report no. 2 (New Zealand Coalition for Trade and Development, 1984), p. 52

CHAPTER 17

MUSIC AND DANCE

Samoan music and dance are the most communal of the Samoan arts. They reach and involve people of all ages and are a major part of fa'asamoa activities and entertainment both in Samoa and in Samoan communities overseas. Practitioners have always drawn on a wide range of influences, making music and dance diverse and changing art forms. Christian missionaries were to have the most profound effect, introducing different melodies and singing styles, and in one or two instances even insisting on the abandonment of certain dance forms.[1] But the value and function of music and dance in Samoa has persisted along with a spirit of creativity, reinterpretation and competition. From customary songs and dances that reflect local life, histories and achievements, Samoan music today also reflects Samoan experiences of places beyond the village. The present Samoan music and dance repertoire extends to brass bands, opera, rock and roll, and hip hop.

This chapter briefly surveys some of the instruments, musical genres and dance forms of Samoa, with a focus on contemporary artists and recent developments. Richard Moyle's *Traditional Samoan Music* (1988) provides a more comprehensive survey of Samoan music, drawing on historical accounts and his own extensive fieldwork.

Fig. 17.1 Logo (slit drum) at Sinalei Reef Resort, Upolu, 2000. (Sean Mallon)

MUSICAL INSTRUMENTS

Over the last 200 years a number of different instruments have been documented as being used in Samoa. Musical instruments were an accompaniment, secondary to the words and poetry of song, but providing the rhythm and pulse that words, voice and movement could build upon. Today many of the old instruments have disappeared from use and have been replaced by the guitar, organ, keyboard and drum machine.

One of the most familiar types of instrument in the Pacific is the slit-gong, a percussion instrument usually made from a short log or section of tree hollowed out with a long slit cut into one side. In Samoa four different types of slit-gong have been identified since at least the 18th century.

The nafa was a slit-gong also called fa'aali'i meaning in the 'manner of or pertaining to a chief'.[2] Made up to one metre in length, it provided an accompaniment to dancing by matai or dancers and singers of high social standing.[3] The nafa seems to have disappeared from use in the mid-19th century. Te Rangi Hiroa's investigations in 1926 failed to find one or get one made, although an old man in the village of Taputimu in Tutuila did provide a demonstration of how the nafa was played.

Two sticks were used and various tunes and rhythms were produced by the expert who showed off his skill by beating the sticks together and tossing them in the air in time to the tune he was playing. Evidently a greater range of play was associated with the nafa than with the lali.[4]

The lali, a larger form of slit-gong is said to have originated in Fiji and come to Samoa from there after it was introduced to Tonga. Appearing in Samoa in the mid-18th century, the lali was used as an entertainment and signalling device on 'alia (large double-hulled sailing canoes). These sailed between the three archipelagos and undoubtedly had a role in the introduction of the lali to Samoa. In the village the lali is still sometimes used to signal the commencement of events, meetings and church services. Usually beaten in pairs, the larger lali is called tatasi and the smaller talua. If a third lali is used it is called tatu'u. Each was typically up to a metre in length, but a small difference in size could produce a big difference in sound.[5] In the 1960s Moyle noted that the task of beating the lali was allocated to specific individuals. Father and son combinations were common. The father would beat out the varied rhythm on the talua with the boy beating out the less complicated rhythms on the tatasi.[6]

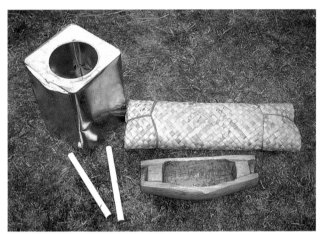

Fig. 17.2 Tin, pate (slit drum) and fala drum as used at Polyfest, 2000, Manukau, Auckland, New Zealand. (Sean Mallon)

The logo and lali are often confused, but the logo differs from the lali in that it has 'a longer and less curved body (from two to three metres in length), a larger more cavernous slit, and a different beating method'.[7] The logo is the largest of the slit-gongs and at one time could be heard every Sunday calling people to church services. Today the logo is gradually being replaced by tall metal gas cylinders which serve the same function and are more easily procurable.

The pate is another much smaller slit-gong used primarily as a signalling device when meetings or gatherings are announced. Made with handles that make them easy to carry, they are hit with one stick when used for signalling, and two sticks when used to accompany dances or songs. The pate was first introduced to Samoa in the 1830s by Rarotongan missionaries arriving with John Williams. It is usually constructed from solid wood that has been hollowed out with a long slit, but thick bamboo tubes are an alternative that enable the instrument to be made more quickly.

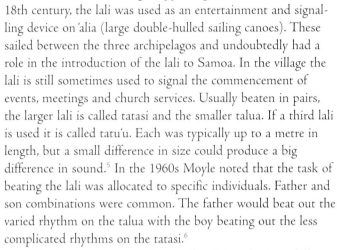

Fig. 17.3 Pate, Savai'i, 2000. (Sean Mallon)

Another type of percussion instrument is the fala or pandanus floor mat. When rolled into a tight cylinder the fala is played to maintain timing and provide accompaniment for group performances. To improve on the sound and increase the volume, lengths of bamboo or bottles are sometimes inserted inside the rolled fala. When this is done the instrument is called tu'itu'i.[8]

A lesser known and extremely rare instrument is the pulotu, a small sounding board which is played with two sticks. The only surviving example of this instrument is held by the Museum of Mankind in London. The Reverend J.B. Stair gives us a rare description of the pulotu:

… was formed by fitting loosely a thin slip of board into a bed of close grained wood. It was beaten with two small sticks, and although the sound produced could not have been very pleasing,

it was used exclusively by the higher chiefs, some of whom were considered to excel both in this instrument and in that of the Nafa.[9]

Other percussion accompaniments included bamboo stamping tubes, handclapping and body slapping, and the use of ipu (coconut shell halves that were clapped together).

Aerophones used in Samoa included the faʻaili (panpipe)[10], fagufagu (nose-flute)[11] and pu (conch trumpet)[12]. Both the faʻaili and fagufagu seem to have disappeared from use by the late 19th century. Faʻaili were like panpipes and made of several small bamboo pipes of different lengths held together with bindings tied to a stick frame. Only two examples are believed to exist today and there are very few references in the historical literature to its use. In the 1920s one of Te Rangi Hiroa's informants re-ported hearing the faʻaili played in Falealupo, saying that ʻAn old man played a plaintive tune upon them, while an old woman sang in a nasal tone a song in time to the tune.'[13]

Fagufagu were nose-flutes made from a single thick section of bamboo and played by blowing through a small hole with the nostril. They could measure up to 45 cm in length and examples in museums indicate that they may have had between one and four holes.[14] However, not all of these holes would be played by the fingers. The sound of the nose-flute has been described as ʻa faint and feeble note, too small of volume to accompany the voice, and with too little flexibility to reproduce the tunes of the common songs'.[15]

Pu are conch shell trumpets made from the *cassis cornuta* and *triton tritonis* species of shell. They are played by blowing through a small hole pierced through the sharp end or side of the shell. In pre-Christian times pu were believed to represent and house the voice of local war gods. Common throughout Polynesia, it is used today mainly as a signalling device to announce special occasions, arrivals and the commence-ment of events.

Modern instruments such as ukuleles and guitars have long been popular in Samoa. They are an accessible and convenient accompaniment for impromptu singalongs and widely used at many social occasions. Keyboards and electric pianos are also becoming increasingly common. Some models feature built-in drum machines and horn and string sections, and are much sought after by Samoan churches. As they become cheaper they are likely to replace the long-serving harmoniums and pianos.

SONG

Song has always been important in Samoa and group singing was well-established long before the advent of missionary choirs. Conveying the poetry of the song's lyric is the most important function of Samoan song. Some songs are performed by groups and others by individuals. There are over 30 types of song reflecting on many facets of Samoan life and culture. These include ʻlullabies, juggling chants, marriage songs, laments, paddling songs, dance songs, historical songs and songs of praise.'[16]

The most important song type in Samoa is generally considered to be viʻi (praise songs). These are typically composed to honour the village and its various achieve-ments in sporting and social endeavours. Village lands are praised and in some cases viʻi are composed to honour the memory of deceased matai.[17]

Group singing in Samoa usually involves a choir seated in a semicircle of rows around a standing fuataimi (conductor). This animated figure urges, prompts and encourages the choir using various expressions, gestures and hand signals. The fuataimi will also often be the original fatupese (composer) of the song being performed. In Samoa fatupese are engaged on an irregular basis to compose songs on behalf of the village for special occasions or events as they arise.

Paid with either cash or 'ie toga, the loyalty of the fatupese is first to his own village or district, although for at least 40 years talented fatupese have been sought far and wide. In the 1960s, for example, Tu'i Samuelu from Samata village was requested several times by villages other than his own to compose a song for a particular occasion.[18] Likewise in March 2000, in preparation for the American Samoa flag day celebration marking the 100th year of the relationship between American Samoa and the United States government, composers from Western Samoa were sought by two American Samoa villages to assist with their song writing efforts.[19] Such is the importance and prestige a village can acquire through the words and performance of a song.

Fatupese also make a strong contribution in contemporary popular music. As ethnomusicologist Ad Linkels notes: 'Part of the repertoire consists of old Samoan songs which are given contemporary arrangements. New songs are sometimes written, although it is also very popular to attach new Samoan lyrics to well-known Western pop melodies.'[20] Auckland-based groups such as Jamoa Jam and Lole are two of many contemporary groups continuing the practice of rearranging old Samoan favourites and making them accessible to the listening tastes of the current generation, as well as developing their own original compositions.

A fatupese who has enjoyed some popular success is Galumalemana Afeleti Tuiletufuga Hunkin. He now resides in New Zealand and is Head of Samoan Studies at Victoria University, Wellington. Galumalemana comes from a family with a long involvement in Samoan music, and composition in particular. Both his father, Papali'i Tuiletufuga Hunkin, and grandmother, Pu'aea Fai'ivai Hunkin, were fatupese. Galumalemana has added his own achievements to that legacy.

GALUMALEMANA AFELETI TUILETUFUGA HUNKIN

I started picking up the ukelele as a young, young boy, but the musical side of myself I didn't really know about until years later when I became very interested in music and I started to look at my own ability in composing songs.

In the late 1960s I had been to Teachers College in New Zealand and it was there that we had to take practical teaching subjects and one of them was music. When I got to Samoa, I found that I had picked up a particular style of guitar playing in fa'asamoa, but with a folk style influence. So my musical ear and my ability to play the guitar combined with encouragement from my father really got me thinking one day when I was teaching in Samoa, Heck I could probably sit down and compose some simple songs... Samoan songs to teach the children. It so happened that there was an American Peace Corp worker at that time [1970] that was running a children's programme on the local radio station, 2AP. And after she heard me take the whole school singing one time she approached me and said, 'I'd like you to come and help me sing a couple of your Samoan songs on radio.'

Her name was Karen Weiss. She had a wonderful voice. So the following Saturday we appeared on the radio... she read a children's story in English and I read the version in Samoan, and then we sang a couple of Samoan songs – some children's songs. One of them was 'Pusi Nofo' – 'Pusi nofo, nofo i luga o le fala, e po atu e ia imoa, Pusi nofo, Nofo i luga o le fala, Pusi, mata, tio peti, nofo i luga o le fala'. But what interested people was the way our two voices combined with the guitar, this new style of picking or playing. And it made such an impact that the following day I got rung up by the radio station: 'Say! We've had people ring up and say "Could

Fig. 17.4 Galumalemana Afeleti Tuiletufuga Hunkin. (Sean Mallon)

we play those two songs by the Peace Corp's group?" They didn't know I was not a Peace Corp worker. So they played it again and then the following week the radio station said, 'Could you record some other songs, some other simple Samoan songs, children's songs?'

So we sang two more songs plus the others. The following week the radio station combined the whole four songs and put them on tape and then played them and then about two weeks later the head of the music department of the entertainment department of the radio station rang me up and said, 'Why don't you compose some Samoan songs?' And I said, 'But I've never composed Samoan songs before.' He said, 'Do it!' and that was the catalyst that got me going. My very first composition was based on the tune of 'Good-bye Joe, we gotta go me-o-my-o,' and the song, which is called 'Sau sau ia,' goes 'Sau sau ia, Ta fiafia, i lenei taimi manaia, fa'agalo uma ou fa'alavelave 'ae pesepese maia, Mata 'ata'ata pe vae la'ala'a e miliona uma lava, Fuga sau ia ta fa'atofa 'ua lava lea.' The first verse happened to be a protest really against some of the local shop keepers who were always glum. But it was the chorus and the tune and that verse which made the song popular, so popular that about a month or two later it played on the radio station, under the name 'Samoa Fiafia Trio' consisting of Karen Weiss, my sister 'Otilia and myself. Then I wrote another song, which was on our first album, based on another favourite country western tune - Ua 'ou fiafia ua 'ou fa'alogo 'ua 'e taunu'o - Crying Time. The song was a love song, the story of a young man who had gone to New Zealand and left behind his sweetheart, his Samoan sweetheart. When the sweetheart, who all this time had been wondering... 'Where on earth is my darling?', hears that he is returning from New Zealand, she comes to the airport to see if he remembers her, and as it turns out in the last verse he does remember her. He does see her there and he goes up to her and she says, 'Oh my dreams, my prayers have been answered, I thought that you were going to turn your back on me, but now we are going to live forever'... and so this song became another hit. So that very first album consisted of 'Sau sau ia' and this other love song 'Alofa Fa'amaoni' plus two other new songs which I had composed. I just couldn't stop once I started and I have been composing ever since. But I don't record any longer. What has happened now is that I still compose songs for Learning Media, for use by school children in New Zealand, and I continue to enjoy all kinds of music. I have also encouraged my own children to compose their own songs.

As well as the old Samoan songs I enjoy the modern groups like Jamoa Jam that have come and taken some of those older songs and reshaped them. When I heard my children singing 'Vauta o le meamatu'a lelei' I said to myself I could never have sat them down and said 'Come on, we'll learn this song!' because they would have said 'Boring dad'. But it is the way that the old songs have been re-presented and re-fashioned by Jamoa Jam that really fascinates me. I took Western-styled songs and turned them into Samoan music by using Samoan words and putting in the Samoan with my style of playing. That was a moment, that was a birth in itself of Samoan music of a different type. Jamoa Jam have come in and taken old Samoan songs and reinterpreted them in their own genre and their own style, with their own wonderful renditions. That's what really makes music dynamic and so wonderful to work with, because it keeps on reproducing itself at different levels and through different generations.

CHURCH-BASED CHOIRS

Secular group singing has a long history in Samoa, although with the introduction of European hymns and songs these pre-Christian forms were greatly transformed. Church-based choirs were first established in Samoa with the arrival of the missionaries in the early 19th century. Samoan pastors trained at the seminaries of Malua and Piula played an important role in the formation of the first church-based choirs by taking hymns to the villages and teaching congregations how to sing them.

Based around the standard four part model of soprano, alto, tenor and bass, most Christian religious songs in Samoa were and continue to be translations from English and American hymn books.[21] In more recent times, however, choirs have become more innovative in their approach to music and more open to the influences of other musical styles and genres such as rhythm and blues and hip hop.

In New Zealand, Samoan choral activity also centres on the church. Outside of the close-knit Samoan village context, the church provides a regular meeting place for families living across large areas and suburbs. They are a focal point for worship and social events, a venue for homework centres and bible classes, and they provide valuable cultural, spiritual and welfare support. It is not surprising then that aspects of community spirit and identity are built around the church and its activities.

Choral competitions are thus another forum for a sense of community identity to be nurtured. The competitive context creates a medium for new ideas, compositions, arrangements and songs. The competitions in Auckland's Samoan community are usually organised on the basis of religious denomination. Some are for all of Auckland and others are divided into individual pulega (unit of the church) and dioceses. This is by necessity as organisers have found it difficult to find and manage a single venue for as many as 35 choirs in one day. As well as points for musicianship, awards are presented for best uniforms and presentation. There is a high level of competition with one choir in recent times hiring an orchestral accompaniment for their performance.

Fig. 17.5 Fuataimi and choir, Apia, 1999. (Craig Potton)

It is the Samoan choirs in New Zealand that tend to be most innovative in their approach to church-based music. These developments are partially spurred on by the high level of competition, but also because singers, choir directors and composers are more regularly exposed to a wider range of musical influences and a higher level of musical training. Leaders and innovators in Samoan choral singing in New Zealand include Peter Sua, Ron Lauese, Igelese Ete and Richard Moyle. Their work not only maintains long-established ideas in Samoan choral singing but also adds a great deal through new interpretations and arrangements. It combines musical styles drawing on popular as well as classical genres and increasingly includes aspects of American gospel, rhythm and blues and hip hop.

Another area where voice performance is finding a new interpretation is in classical singing and opera. Samoan singers have found success on opera house stages worldwide playing characters and singing songs from a range of cultural traditions and historical backgrounds. Iosefa Enari and Fa'afetai Jonathan Lemalu have pioneered the territory for Samoan singers' involvement in opera.

Enari (1954-2000) was an admired New Zealand baritone and a pioneer for Pacific people's involvement in opera singing. From the moment he won the New Zealand Herald Aria Competition in 1987 he gained recognition both locally and internationally. His many roles included Baron Scarpia (*Tosca*), Porgy (*Porgy and Bess*) and Figaro (*Le Nozze Di Figaro*). His work also extended to musical theatre where he played Old Deuteronomy in the Auckland and Adelaide productions of *Cats*. He took leading acting roles in dramatic theatre, starring in the successful plays *A Frigate Bird Sings* (1996), *Sons* (1997)[22] and *Dawn Raids* (1998).[23]

Jonathan Lemalu is one of a number of other talented Samoan opera singers to gain international recognition. Described as 'a young bass of great distinction' he has won all the major scholarships in Australasia including the Mobil Song Quest and the Sister Mary Leo Scholarship. He currently studies at the Royal College of Music in London where he was the winner of the inaugural Llangollen International Singer Competition 2000.

With talent such as Enari and Lemalu and a host of other emerging singers moving along in their training, the timing was right to showcase the talent that Pacific opera singers and classical musicians had to offer. Gathering a company of performers and a creative team comprising of Igelese Ete and Teokota'i Paitai, Enari conceived and produced *Classical Polynesia*, a fusion of classic Samoan songs, contemporary dance and classical opera.

First performed in 1998 as part of the New Zealand International Festival of the Arts, with a later tour in 2000, *Classical Polynesia* recreated life in a Samoan village over the course of one day. Through the use of 12 popular historic songs and modern choreography, the moods and activities of the village were brought to life in a way never seen before. From dawn till dusk, people's lives, loves, work and emotions were revealed in song and movement as they went about their daily tasks. It was a groundbreaking production in many ways, but particularly because it bridged a cultural gap, presenting Samoan song and culture to a wider, non-Samoan audience, in a context and form that they were familiar with. It was a performance that brought together two classic musical traditions while also honouring the past and present composers of Samoan music.

Other artists from the Samoan and New Zealand art community involved in *Classical Polynesia* include choreographer Teokotai Patai, classical violinist Sam Konise and pianist Robert Wiremu. The voices and characters were provided by bass Jonathan Lemalu, tenor Ben Makisi and soprano Daphne Collins, with Mabel Faletolu and the Lota Nu'u Choir in chorus. The new arrangements of the well-known songs were made by choral and vocal director Igelese Ete.

An established choir director, Ete had experienced success with other large-scale choir and musical productions such as *Malaga* (1997) (2001) (2002).[24] In the early 1990s he dabbled with the commercial pop charts with the single 'Groovalation' (1995), but his strongest interest had always been in choirs. His groundbreaking work is an example of the current creativity and innovation in Samoan choral performance. His key focus for many years has been to introduce classical style and training to Samoan singers and more recently to combine these with the different genres such as hip hop and gospel, mixing old and new together to create new hybrid styles. Having studied at the Conservatorium of Music and Victoria University Wellington and holding a Bachelor of Music degree in performance singing, he has a strong musical foundation on which to base this work. Currently he is Vocal Director at Vision Leadership College in Hamilton, New Zealand.

IGELESE ETE

My father is Risatisone Ete and he is from Fusi on Savai'i and my mother, Fereni Ete, she is from Falealupo on Savai'i.

When you are a pastor's son music is pretty much an automatic thing that you find yourself doing. You always help out in the worship, playing the piano and taking the choirs. But I guess my interest in music really began when I was 12 and won a talent quest for writing a song, an original composition. From then on I decided I wanted to be a musician and chose to pursue the career and take music during intermediate, college and then at university.

Fig. 17.6 (top) Poster for Classical Polynesia concert, 1998. (Courtesy of Igelese Ete)

Fig. 17.7 (bottom) Poster for Malaga concert, 2001, Auckland, New Zealand. (Courtesy of Jacob Luamanuvae)

Fig. 17.8 Igelese Ete.

Going through college I auditioned for the New Zealand Secondary Schools Choir then the National Youth Choir. Getting into both was like an encouragement for me. I had a lot of passion for taking choirs, I was taking choirs within the church and I thought I might extend that and pursue the career of choral conductor/composer/performer/singer. So I went to university and did a degree in music and opera singing. I didn't really like opera initially, but once I got into it I found it was an amazing art form. I thought I could use the best of that and sort of fuse it into my own culture. Learning the actual technique of singing and the different languages such as French and German, I thought surely you could do these things with Samoan music. Hence projects such as Classical Polynesia.

In my approach to choral work a director must have good listening skills: you must be able to relate to the people you are working with. I have been working with children's choirs, adult choirs over 60 and teenage choirs. Each has their own unique requirements/wants; the old people like the classical style with the hymns, the young love hip hop, rap and gospel. In major productions such as Malaga *I like to bring all those sounds together; the nasal heritage singing of our parents and grandparents, juxtaposing this against classical opera, or the chants and prayers of old with rap. I love to challenge people, our own included... keep them guessing as to what musical style will follow.*

In 2000 we went to Samoa for the Millennium Celebrations. The reaction there to my work was positive, they loved it; I don't know why they loved it, but they loved it. A lot of people were talking about it and saying what an amazing sound. I think that stemmed back to the fact that it was just a different sound production. It was more rounded vowels, more towards the classical style of singing rather than the contemporary or traditional style of Samoan singing.

This is an important difference. With the influences we have here you have Samoan singers and musicians who are classically trained. Back in Samoa its more a traditional style that incorporates the nasality in the actual sounding of the voice. Here they are more aware of the classical and gospel as well as the traditional. Whatever the style, the music is always firmly planted in Pacific pride, and most importantly with an innate spirituality; our god, our atua. These are my roots, to which I try to remain true.

DANCE

Samoan dance is usually performed by groups for an audience. On some occasions individuals will represent or dance on behalf of a group, but will be supported in their efforts by the group's singing or the accompaniment of a beat played on a fala or a drum. As well as the identity of the group, the dance is a process that mediates the identity of the individual.

Samoan dance is yet another aspect of music that has always allowed scope for creativity and invention – especially through the process of competition and the composing of new works. Today Samoan dance draws upon many styles and cultural influences, but new works remain rooted in a strong conceptual base built upon fa'asamoa and reinforcing elements of the Samoan social order. Through negotiating the space of the dance floor, the performers are respecting relationships within Samoan society and giving dignity to the occasion.

According to Moyle, transformations in Samoan dance over the last 200 years appear to have come from within Samoa 'as a function of changes or shifts of emphasis within social institutions'.[25] The missionaries did, however, play a part in the suppression and subsequent demise of some dance forms. Their most determined opposition was to the poula (night dance). Held in the main fale of the village under torchlight, the naked dances called sa'e which came towards the end of the evening were consid-

Fig. 17.9 Group in Samoan dancing attire circa 1920. (Photograph Alfred John Tattersall. Alexander Turnbull Library, National Library of New Zealand, Te Puna Matauranga o Aotearoa. Ref. No: PA1-0-445-57)

ered obscene. But despite the poula being abolished in some areas, in other places it persisted, often with the intercession of Samoan Christian ministers, until the end of the 19th century.[26]

Likewise, through a degree of Samoan agency, missionary hymns also found a place in the events of the poula.[27] In the 1830s missionary John Williams wrote:

I enquired of the teachers why they had not taught them to sing. They informed me they had commenced but the females immediately took what they obtained to the dancing houses & sang it to their dances. They were therefore afraid to teach them any more at present.[28]

The void left by the banning of the poula saw the creation of another dance, the ma'ulu'ulu, by at least the 1870s. The ma'ulu'ulu is comprised of three parts: the laulau siva, an introductory song; the sasa, a wordless dance performed seated with clapping and slapping sychronised with the beating of a rhythm on fala or drum; and the ma'ulu'ulu itself. The dance remains part of the Samoan dance repertoire both in Samoa and overseas, and has continued to change in small ways and incorporate new words and movements.

In terms of movement, the hands, legs and head are an important part of a Samoan dancer's performance. They have key communicative and expressive roles. The complex movements made by the hands and arms are known as taga, and, according to Samoan music scholar Tialuga Sunia Seloti, have multiple functions:

They allude to sung words, comment on implied concepts, and decorate and connect musical phrases. Taga use flexible wrists. Movements and positions of fingers and palms occur in a limited number of arm positions. Men's and women's hand-and-arm movements may be soft, but men's may use stiffer wrists or clenched fists, and may be faster and freer.[29]

The hands are also used in the men's fa'ataupati dance, where body slapping plays a prominent role. In this dance all the movements are performed at a furious pace, as the dancers slap their thighs, chests and feet in a synchronised group effort.

Tialuga Sunia Seloti goes on to say that the head and face should mask emotion, noting that the taupou (ceremonial village maiden), when performing the taualuga (last dance) 'fixes her facial muscles into a weak smile, maintaining an aloofness that onlookers interpret as dignity'.[30] In a dance such as the taualuga other male and female dancers will clown around the taupou, with wild gestures and expressions that further enhance the dignity of her performance.

This scenario of a taupou surrounded by clowning dancers highlights an aspect of Samoan dance that points to the way in which dance reveals the nature of relationships in Samoan society. The organisation of the dance floor reinforces the social order through the distinction of siva (dancing proper) and 'aiuli (clowning).[31] In the 1970s anthropologist Bradd Shore spoke to Samoans about the symbolic associations of Samoan dance. He describes the dance floor as a kind of microcosm of the larger village arena where a distinction between the a'ai or malae (village centre) and the periphery (bush or 'back' of the village) is made:

On the dance floor, the periphery is associated with the orator or those representing the orator, the males, the untitled, and those showing respect. The centre is left for the ali'i, the taupou, or, more generally, for anyone commanding respect and deference.[32]

Samoans who talked with Shore shared with him the following two insights:

The ali'i dances inside [i totonu] and he dances well [e siva lelei]. He dances gracefully [onomea]. But the 'aiuli, the clown he doesn't dance gracefully like that. The 'aiuli is pretending to dance from the sidelines ['autafa]. We say in Samoan that they plead to the main dancers inside to dance nicely.

The 'aiuli is the dance of the tulafale, and the taulele'a - the sons of the tulafale. And if the taupou is dancing, the daughters of the tulafale should 'aiuli to her. Similarly, the wives of the 'aiuli should dance 'aiuli to those of the ali'i.[33]

Apart from ceremonies and formal occasions the most common stage for Samoan dance is found at festivals. These events provide a focal point for the performing arts, keeping alive a spirit of creativity as well as competition. The most significant occasions for dance are Flag Raising Day in American Samoa and the annual Independence Day celebrations. The annual Teuila Festival provides a competitive forum where the art of Samoan dance can be shared with tourists and visitors to Samoa.

Another common environment in which dance takes place in Samoa is at floorshows or fiafia nights hosted by local hotels and resorts. At these venues the visitor can see a packaged performance under lights from their dinner tables. While the dances are Samoan, they also incorporate elaborations and exaggerations to make them an appealing and entertaining spectacle for the tourist.

Figs. 17.10 (top) and 17.11 (bottom) Samoa National Dance Troupe, Apia, 2001. (Sean Mallon)

The stronghold for Samoan dance in New Zealand is found with the groups and tutors in high schools and community groups. Apart from community-based functions, events like the annual Auckland Secondary Schools Maori and Pacific Islands

Cultural Festival, also known as Polyfest, provide the main stage for new work in dance and performance. Similar smaller-scale competitions are held throughout the New Zealand and the competition is intense. A great deal of time both in and out of school is invested over several weeks in rehearsal.

Judges are appointed from the Samoan community, with the judging criteria reflecting important cultural forms and values but also allowing some scope for innovation and creativity. The marking schedules for Samoan performances at Polyfest 2000 included scores for synchronised actions, enthusiasm, and stance and posture. Taupou and manaia were judged on their costume and ornamentation, as well as the use of appropriate actions in their dance. Groups were also judged on originality and creativity. In the Auckland Boys' Grammar School performance this aspect of competition took the form of hip hop/breakdancing. To the side of the main body of performers backspins and breakdancing poses added a further contemporary element to an already innovative performance.

Samoan dance is further extended through the work of two professional contemporary dance companies based in New Zealand. Black Grace and MAU draw upon many diverse dance forms to produce a unique union of style and performance. In both these dance companies there is an emphasis on finding new ways and means of expression and movement, extending the idea of what Samoan dance can incorporate and what dance in general can be.

Black Grace is an all-male dance company led by Samoan choreographer Neil Ieremia. Their work has made a strong impression on the local dance and theatre scene. Black Grace often looks beyond the motif and familiar styles of Pacific dance, creating their own movements and responses within a broad range of narratives. Drawing on song, dance, music and the Pacific and Maori cultures of its cast, Black Grace makes a temporary but memorable commentary and record on the circumstances of life in the present. With works such as *Black Grace, Fia Ola – Let Me Live* and *Relentless* they have explored themes of journeying, transition, displacement and identity. These are significant issues for recent generations of Samoans as they travel and migrate to different parts of the world.

One of these travellers is Samoan dancer and director of MAU Dance Theatre, Lemi Ponifasio. Drawing on his extensive travels and experiences in New Zealand, Japan, Scandinavia and Russia, Ponifasio encourages his dancers to 'cast off the burdensome armour of convention' and remove the intention to consciously perform. Like other aspects of Samoan dance, Ponifasio's work is about negotiating relationships and space, and in this role he has been described as a modern taulaitu or shaman, one who mediates between the living and the dead.[34] It's an engagement that has seen him look to the ancient concepts of Samoa for inspiration and an anchoring:

The concept of Samoan existence is called va and I base my dance on that. It means space and it means we are always negotiating the truth at that moment. Nothing is absolute. A Samoan house is a good example of this concept. It's open, there's no privacy, you have to negotiate how you exist in that. A Western house has closed doors so it's easy.[35]

In finding his place in theatre and dance Ponifasio has been an agent of change, inviting the audience to change in the process.

Fig. 17.12 Performers from Otahuhu College, Auckland, Polyfest 2000. (Jeff Evans)

LEMI PONIFASIO – MAU DANCE THEATRE

I was born on the island of Savi'i in the village of Lano. My parents were faife'au (pastors, ministers). My father's first name is Ponifasio. I use this as my last name because that's the Samoan way. My father is from the aiga sa Tuala and sa Sala of Leauvaia. My mother's name is Gafa o Malietoa and she is from the aiga sa Faiamausili of Malie.

I was never interested in dance until I came to New Zealand. In Samoa dance was not something people got interested in, it was just something you do, like you are not interested in fishing, you have to fish. When I arrived in New Zealand in 1978 it was the height of the disco era. I was a very good disco dancer and that's how I started to somehow make people think I was a dancer. From then on I started to think of myself as a dancer.

I studied ballet because someone said it would make me a better disco dancer. My first ballet class was in a studio in Karangahape Road. It was a rude culture shock and utter humiliation. I remember trying to figure out the ballet exercises and vocabulary as they were in French, let alone trying to understand English, the classical music and grown men in black tights. I was wondering how this was going to make me a better disco dancer. At one point the class had to dance a section from Swan Lake. I wasn't sure what a swan was, but I imagined it was a kind of a duck. So I tried to impress the class with my own duck dance. There are no swans in Samoa. I found out that ballet originated in Europe and it transformed into different styles in different countries and made its way all the way down to K Road where this confused Samoan boy was being humiliated. It was also the first time I saw a piano. There were no Samoans studying ballet or contemporary dance at the time. This initial dance experience and embarrassment, however, made me wonder what my own dance was.

Fig. 17.13 MAU Dance Theatre. (Courtesy of Joseph Brown)

As a professional dancer I lived most of my adult life in Japan, Europe and what was then the Soviet Union, where I was exposed to many ideas and forms of performance theatre. However, I still wasn't able to renew the Western dance forms to dance the stories I wanted to tell. So from 1988 to 1990 I stopped performing altogether. I began to seriously try to answer the question of what my dance was.

The experience in the theatre in New Zealand is fundamentally European and the so called Pacific island theatre here doesn't represent me. I didn't have a Porirua or a South Auckland experience. I also consider Samoan dances such as the sasa or ma'ulu'ulu as those of my ancestors and I love them all. But what do I have to contribute to that legacy?

I call my dance MAU. Mau is the Samoan word for my point of view or vision. My dance is of the experience of my life and body. I see the body as a memorial vessel. So when I am performing, I am also aware that I am dancing the dance of my mother, father, family and country. This is the foundation of my work.

Fig. 17.14 Lemi Ponifasio. (Jeff Evans)

BRASS BANDS

Brass bands were introduced to Samoa during the colonial period when they provided entertainment for the European settlers, particularly during the German administration. Brass bands contribute to a sense of community spirit and competition; the music is very popular and played regularly on local radio. Representing churches, villages and in one case a school, brass bands, like choirs, have become a symbol of community identity and pride, as well as a focus of inter-village competition. It is probably this competitive and community aspect of being involved in a brass band that has made it such a long-lasting institution in Samoa. For similar reasons, brass bands enjoy huge popularity in places such as Great Britain and the United States.

In Savai'i there are about four well-established village brass bands, in Upolu about seven. There is also one school band that belongs to the school of the Church of Jesus Christ of Latter Day Saints in Apia. Most brass bands in Samoa play at weddings, birthdays and church dedications. Bands are usually mixed in age and experience. The music they play is varied, as well as popular Samoan song and dance tunes, German marches and popular English and American music also features.

There are two main competitions for brass bands in Samoa, the Independence Day competition and the Teuila Festival. At these events the bands compete for cash prizes. In 2000 the Teuila Festival attracted a band from Avondale in Auckland, New Zealand. The contest was won by a brass band from Sala'ilua on Savai'i, with Avondale coming second.

The most prominent brass band is the Police Band of Samoa based in Apia. They play each morning at the ceremonial raising of the flag on Beach Road, and are also in attendance at important government functions and occasions. The band leader and director is Superintendent Sefuiva Sani Epati.

Fig. 17.15 The Police Band of Samoa, 2001. (Sean Mallon)

SUPERINTENDENT SEFUIVA SANI EPATI: POLICE BAND OF SAMOA

Fig. 17.16 Superintendent Sefuiva Sani Epati. (Sean Mallon)

I started to learn music when I was nine years old. My parents are originally from Sale'imoa next to Malua Theological College. My father, he was a very smart man, he bought books about music and spent a great deal of time teaching himself how to play. He bought books about different instruments and later on he taught me how to play the euphonium and saxophone.

The Police Band of Samoa was established in 1978 by a local musician Levao Avau, then carried on by Karl Tuilupe who was an ex-navy trumpeter. More than ten police officers started off in this band using instruments that were a gift from Germany to Samoa's Head of State. I became involved with this band in 1983 after working with the Development Bank.

In the band there are 43 members. They are all very good. About 34 of them are former keyboard players and about 23 of them have had training in Australia and New Zealand, doing one year courses playing various instruments. We have two bands, a mixed brass and a combo band. We also have the Samoa Police Male Voice Choir, consisting of 130 voices. The brass band practises on Mondays and Thursdays, twice a week for the whole day. The combo practises only on Wednesdays. The band plays every morning with the flag raising parade and is also responsible for government ceremonies and functions. We have also gone to Tonga to play for the King's birthday twice.

We are more influenced by English tunes that we get from Australia and New Zealand, but we also have about 20 German marches that we play. Most of them we memorise. In Samoa we do not really have concert bands that sit. We do not have concert band competitions. The bands in Samoa are different from other bands in the world. We play and sing and play and dance. This year when Manu Samoa played Italy in a rugby game which we won, we split the Police band in two, each with different uniforms. The drum major came onto the field with no band stick... no mace, he came in with the ball along with the referee. The ball was passed from player to player and we had a game of rugby while we played the instruments.

CONTEMPORARY STYLES

Other types of bands inspired by popular modern musical styles have led to further arrangements and new interpretations of Samoan music. Pop, rock and hip hop are contemporary genres where Samoan composers and musicians are creating their own sound. Through radio and recordings people in Samoa have become more familiar with foreign styles of music. Some have become celebrated artists in introduced genres. The late Mavis Rivers (1929-1992) was one Samoan singer who found international success as a jazz singer. 'Frank Sinatra is said to have described her as the "purest voice" in jazz, comparing her to Ella Fitzgerald'.[36] As well as experimenting with contemporary arrangements and writing original songs, writing new Samoan lyrics to well-known Western pop melodies has also been popular.[37]

In New Zealand there are many bands that provide favourite Samoan tunes for weddings and other social occasions. Some have become established and gone on to record their music for sale. Well-known Samoan bands over the last 20 years have included The Mount Vaea Band, The Golden Ali'is, the R.S.A. band Tatiana and singers such as Jerome Grey and Felise Mikaele.

Fig. 17.17 The Five Stars. (Courtesy of Kiwi Pacific Records International Ltd)

One of the most successful has been The Five Stars. Taking their name from the five stars that fly on the Samoan flag, the band was founded by Afoa Alapati Tu'uga in the early 1970s. This family band initially started playing in Auckland, New Zealand, and was one of many family bands playing at weddings and other social functions among the expatriate Samoan community. Signing and releasing an album with Kiwi Pacific Records, The Five Stars popularity soon extended across the Pacific. With harmonised lyrics sung over the gentle melodies of the electric guitar, The Five Stars music comprised new arrangements of popular Samoan songs and a selection of original compositions. It was a combination that saw them produce 16 albums, including three compilations, over a 20 year period.[38]

The strong following The Five Stars enjoyed took them on three tours to Samoan communities in Los Angeles. They also visited Papua New Guinea, Hawai'i, Samoa and American Samoa. One of the U.S. trips was with another well-known Samoan singing group The Yandall Sisters. But their fans were also found in great numbers on the other side of the Pacific, demonstrating the power of music to bring people together and the way that Samoan music has given something to the music of the Pacific. As Afoa still recalls with amazement:

We were invited to the Solomon Islands and Papua New Guinea, and I tell you all those people in those places can sing our songs, the songs we love. It was amazing, in the Solomon Islands and Papua New Guinea the audience would call out the songs they wanted us to sing. They would call out 'Samoa Matalasi!' and 'O La'u pele 'ea!' and when the boys started to sing, they all started singing. You know what? We ended up touring to Papua New Guinea three times![39]

But of all the contemporary styles of music it is hip hop that has most captured the imagination of the present generation of Samoans. Hip hop combines the skills of the DJ (disc jockey), the MC (master of ceremonies), the graffiti artist and the breakdancer. These forms of expression are a potent medium for communicating and documenting the lives and experiences of hip hop's practitioners and protagonists in different communities across the world.

Although its origins are said to lie in Jamaica, hip hop emerged most strongly in the communities of inner city New York during the 1970s and early 1980s. Its beats, rhythms and attitude soon caught on elsewhere and its popularity quickly spread beyond the environs of the city. Today hip hop enjoys a strong following across the United States, Europe, Asia and the Pacific.

Samoan hip hop has been most recently documented by Pacific historian April Karene Henderson. Her 1999 study 'Gifted Flows: Netting the Imagery of Hip Hop across the Samoan Diaspora'[40] reveals the Samoan involvement and contribution to the genre to be as varied as the places and circumstances young Samoan musicians find themselves in.

Fig. 17.18 *Savage Thoughts*, King Kapisi, 2000. (Courtesy of artist and Festival/Mushroom Records, Auckland)

It is probably no surprise that the pioneers of Samoan hip hop, Boo-Yaa T.R.I.B.E., come from the United States. They first appeared in the early Los Angeles hip hop scene as a group of dancers known as Blue City Crew, before going on to make their own music, blending several musical styles, including rap, funk and metal. Today they are the most successful of the Samoan hip hop acts in the United States.

The sons of Reverend and Mrs Taulima Devoux, Boo-Yaa T.R.I.B.E.'s initial training and interest in music started with their involvement in the musical activities of the church. It was a quiet beginning for a group of brothers whose own music would spread a different message, one that described who they were, where they lived and the circumstances of life in the ganglands of suburban Los Angeles. As Henderson comments:

Boo-Yaa T.R.I.B.E.'s music represents an ironic synthesis; talents nurtured in church are directed at addressing the secular realities of the street, specifically ganglife. On the T.R.I.B.E.'s 1997 release, Angry Samoans, *recurrent lyrical themes include homicide, carjacking (strongarmed autotheft), and marijuana use, all set to a driving drum beat and rock guitar riffs. Boo-Yaa T.R.I.B.E. claim to represent what they know in their music. They translate the grittiness and violence of Los Angeles ganglife into growling lyrics and shrieking guitars...* [41]

Henderson goes on to note that although fiercely proud of their Samoan ancestry and the influence of fa'asamoa values, Boo-Yaa T.R.I.B.E. are intent on remaining true to their urban California upbringing. Similar sentiments are held an ocean away in the urban South Pacific.

In New Zealand, Auckland-based Samoan hip hop artists rhyme about an urban environment far removed from the tropical homelands of their parents and the mean streets of Los Angeles. While deeply rooted in the values and culture of their Samoan parents and sharing something of the imagery and style of their American counterparts, their music incorporates an uniquely local perspective. The beats and rhymes are as fresh and as geographically and culturally specific as they are derivative or global. In some instances Samoan language tints the lyrical content and there are tracks where you will hear the ukelele, pate or slit gong drop into the mix. These elements give

Samoan hip hop down under an almost distinctive sound and expression.

Artists such as Ermehn and collectives such as Footsouljahs and Dawnraid have cast a Samoan gaze over the history of Samoan people in New Zealand. But the most recent and commercially successful exponent of Samoan hip hop in New Zealand is King Kapisi (aka Bill Urale). In interviews Kapisi has repeatedly distanced himself from the American experience and the gangster style of hip hop.

The main thing is that I'm trying to uplift hip hop in the South Pacific. I basically make Samoan hip hop and aim to get kids aware of conscious shit, not just I'll-shoot-you-with-my-gun sort of raps. I'd rather hear 'What's up bro' instead of 'Whats up nigga'. If someone called me nigga, I'd want to slap them. [42]

In 2000 Kapisi released *Savage Thoughts*, an album concerned with Samoan migration, histories and experiences in New Zealand. In the track 'Fix Amnesia' Kapisi reflects on the importance of remembering the lessons of the past and encourages young Samoans and Polynesians not to forget their roots and their histories.

That's why I make my music - so they are proud of being a Tuakana or Uso. To get pride in the Pacific... informing the youth about the injustices done to our peoples... There needs to be more people that acknowledge our past. Just be aware that all things have not been hunky dory in the South Pacific. [43]

Kapisi's sentiments and insight into the Samoan migrant experience are found throughout the lyrics of this landmark album. The following extract, from '2nd Migration', records a negative aspect of the New Zealand-Samoan migrant experience, but goes beyond that to become a staunch, non-aggressive celebration of Samoan history and identity, including an environmental message for the future. It's another important contribution to Samoa's rich musical heritage, giving voice to the experiences of young migrant Samoans who are now travellers, citizens and musicians of a wider world beyond the village.

My laidback islander feel is world wide
Pacific 2 atlantic overstayer on the mic
(Birds of steel) migration from apia to welli
2 my sister in kansas, 2 my peoples in cali
Samoan hip hop is on the rise (you better recognise)
With king kapisi and tha feelstyle it's all nice
But with that constant unnecessary misuse of government
Power
Crack down on my peoples in the early hours
The classic dawnraids, in other words return you back 2 sender
Even in exile my people wont surrender
Traditions older than the books in your archives, we survive
Nuclear free pacific is the only way of life...[44]

CHAPTER 17

1. R.M. Moyle, *Traditional Samoan Music* (Auckland; Auckland University Press, 1988), p. 201

2. Moyle, *Traditional Samoan Music*, p. 27

3. Moyle, *Traditional Samoan Music*, p. 27

4. Te Rangi Hiroa (Peter Buck), 'Samoan Material Culture', *Bernice P. Bishop Museum* Bulletin 75 (Honolulu: 1930), p. 578

5. Moyle, *Traditional Samoan Music*, p. 32

6. Moyle, *Traditional Samoan Music*, p. 34

7. Moyle, *Traditional Samoan Music*, p. 36

8. Moyle, *Traditional Samoan Music*, p. 43

9. J.B. Stair, *Old Samoa; or flotsam and jetsam from the Pacific Ocean* (Papakura: Southern Reprints, 1983, [First published, 1897]), p. 136

10. Moyle, *Traditional Samoan Music*, p. 52; also notes the use of the term fa'aili ofe and cites Stairs' use of the term fa'aali.

11. According to Moyle, *Traditional Samoan Music*, pp. 48-49, also referred to as fa aili.

12. Te Rangi Hiroa, 'Samoan Material Culture', p. 578, also known as foafoa (*cornuta*) or faofao (*tritonis*)

13. Te Rangi Hiroa, 'Samoan Material Culture', p. 580

14. Moyle, *Traditional Samoan Music*, pp. 49-50

15. L.P. Churchill, 'Samoa Uma: where life is different', quoted in Moyle, *Traditional Samoan Music*, p. 49

16. Ad Linkels, *Fa'a-samoa, The Samoan Way Between Conch Shell and Disco* (Tilburg: Muno Etnico Foundation, 1995), p. 49

17. Moyle, *Traditional Samoan Music*, p. 189

18. Moyle, *Traditional Samoan Music*, p. 15

19. F. Sagapolutele, 'Samoan Song/Dance Talent in High Demand', *Samoan Observer* (March 3, 2000)

20. Linkels, *Fa'asamoa*, p. 50

21. Tialuga Sunia Seloti, 'Samoa', in Kaeppler, A.L. and Love, J.W. (eds), *The Garland Encyclopaedia of World Music Volume 9, Australia and the Pacific Islands* (New York and London: Garland Publishing Inc., 1998), p. 807

22. Victor Roger, *Sons* (Auckland Season, 1995)

23. Oscar Kightly, *Dawn Raids* (Christchurch Season, 1997)

24. Commissioned for the opening of the Museum of New Zealand Te Papa Tongarewa, Wellington, February 1997.

25. Moyle, *Traditional Samoan Music*, p. 199

26. Moyle, *Traditional Samoan Music*, p. 206; Colvin, 1925, cites a letter written by R.L. Stevenson

27. J. Garrett, *To Live Among the Stars: Christian Origins in Oceania*, World Council of Churches in association with the Institute of Pacific Studies (Geneva and Suva: University of the South Pacific, 1982), p. 122

28. R.M. Moyle quoting J. Williams in, *The Samoan Journals of John Williams 1830 and 1832* (Canberra: Australian National University Press, 1984), p. 117

29. Tialuga Sunia Seloti, 'Samoa', p. 798

30. Tialuga Sunia Seloti, 'Samoa', pp. 798-799

31. Bradd Shore, *Sala'ilua: A Samoan Mystery* (New York: Columbia University Press, 1982), p. 259

32. Shore, *Sala'ilua: A Samoan Mystery*, p. 260

33. Shore, *Sala'ilua: A Samoan Mystery*, p. 259

34. A. Refiti and A. Wendt, 'Boneflute Ivi Ivi', *essays in dance programme*, MAU Dance Theatre, 2000

35. M. Amery, 'A Dancer Alone', *Sunday Star Times* (July 16, 2000)

36. Rivers, Shane, 'Rivers, Mavis Chloe 1929-1992', *Dictionary of New Zealand Biography*, updated 18 March 2002, [online] available URL: http://www.dnzb.govt.nz/

37. Linkels, *Fa'asamoa*, p. 50

38. Kiwi Pacific Records International Limited

39. Afoa Alapati Tu'uga, interview with author, 2001

40. A.K. Henderson, 'Gifted Flows: netting the imagery of Hip Hop across the Samoan diaspora' (University of Hawai'i: Unpublished M.A. Thesis, 1999)

41. Henderson, 'Gifted Flows', p. 35

42. *Rip it Up*, (October 2000), pp. 44-45

43. King Kapisi, 'Savage', *New Zealand Musician* (October/November 2000), p. 55

44. King Kapisi, '2nd Migration', Savage Thoughts, Festival Records (2000)

BIBLIOGRAPHY

Aiono, Fanaafi Le Tagaloa. *Confessions of a Bat* (Savali: July 1984)

American Samoa Historic Preservation Office. 'Culture History of American Samoa' (1997) [online]. Available URL: http://ashpo.org/Samoan_Cultural_History.html

Amery, M. 'Flower Power', *Pavement* 30 (Auckland: 1998)

Anonymous, 'Interview with The Brownies', *Pacific People Magazine* No. 6 (Auckland: April 1999)

Arbeit, Wendy. *Baskets in Polynesia* (Honolulu: University of Hawai'i Press, 1990)

Best, S., Sheppard, P., Green, R. and Parker, R. 'Necromancing the Stone: Archaeologists and Adzes in American Samoa', *Journal of the Polynesian Society* 101 (1992), pp. 45-85

Churchill, William. 'Club Types of Nuclear Polynesia', *The Carnegie Institution*, Publication No. 255 (Washington: 1917)

Churchward, William. *My Consulate in Samoa: A record of four years sojourn in the Navigators Islands, with personal experiences of King Malietoa Laupepa, his country, and his men* (London: Richard Bentley and Son, 1887)

Clark, J.T. 'Samoan prehistory in review', in Davidson, J.M., Irwin, G., Leach, B.F., Pawley, A. and Brown, D. (eds) 'Oceanic Culture History: Essays in Honour of Roger Green 1996': *New Zealand Journal of Archaeology Special Publication* (1996), pp. 445-460

Clark, Kevin. 'Handcraft trade in the South Pacific; a case study - Trade Aid (NZ) Inc.', *Pacific Handcraft Research Project Report*, No. 2 (New Zealand Coalition for Trade and Development, 1984)

Clunie, Fergus. 'Fijian Weapons and Warfare', *Bulletin of The Fiji Museum* No. 2 (Suva: 1977)

Clunie, Fergus. *Yalo i Viti*, A Fiji Museum Catalogue (Suva: Fiji Museum, 1986)

Crawford, R.J. 'The Lotu and the Fa'asamoa: Church and Society in Samoa 1830-1880', Unpublished Ph.D. thesis (New Zealand: University of Otago, 1977)

Dark, Philip J.C. 'Tomorrow's Heritage is Today's Art and Yesteryear's Identity', in Hanson and Hanson (eds) *Art and Identity in Oceania* (Australia: Crawford House Press, 1990)

Davidson, Janet M., Irwin, G., Leach, B.F., Pawley, A. and Brown, D. (eds) 'Oceanic Culture History: Essays in Honour of Roger Green', *New Zealand Journal of Archaeology Special Publication* (1996), pp. 445-460

Davidson, Janet M. 'Samoa and Tonga', in Jennings, J.D. (ed) *The Prehistory of Polynesia* (Cambridge, Massachusetts: Harvard University Press, 1979), pp. 82-109

Davidson, Janet M. 'Settlement Patterns in Samoa before 1840', *Journal of the Polynesian Society* 78 (1969), pp. 44-82

Davidson, Janet M. 'The Wooden Image From Samoa in the British Museum: A Note on Its Context', *Journal of the Polynesian Society* 84 (1975), pp. 352-5

Davidson, J.W. 'Lauaki Namulau'ulu Mamoe, a traditionalist in Samoan Politics', in Davidson, J.W. and Scarr, D.A. (ed) *Pacific Island Portraits* (Canberra: Australian National University Press, 1970), pp. 267-299

Dominion (March 29, 1999)

Dominion (April 7, 1999)

Duncan, Betty K. 'A hierarchy of symbols: Samoan religious symbolism in New Zealand', Unpublished Ph.D. thesis (Dunedin, New Zealand: University of Otago, 1994)

Dunmore, J. (ed) *The Journal of Jean-Francois de Galaup de la Perouse 1785-1788* (London: Hakluyt Society, 1995)

Duranti, A. 'Doing Things with Words: Conflict, Understanding and Change in a Samoan Fono', in *Disentangling: Conflict Discourse in Pacific Societies* by Watson-Gegeo, K. and White, G. (eds) (Stanford: Stanford University Press, 1990), pp. 459-89

Duranti, A. *From Grammar to Politics: Linguistic Anthropology in a Western Samoan Village* (Berkeley and Los Angeles: University of California Press, 1994)

Duranti, A. 'Heteroglossia in Samoan Oratory', in *Pacific Studies Special Issue: The Arts and Politics* Vol. 15 No. 4 (Hawai'i: Institute of Pacific Studies, Brigham Young University, 1992), pp. 155-175

Duranti, A. 'Language and Bodies in Social Space: Samoan Ceremonial Greetings', in *American Anthropologist* Vol 94, (1992), pp. 657-91

Duranti, A. 'The Samoan Fono: A Sociolinguistic Study', in *Pacific Linguistics Monographs*, Series B. Vol. 80 (Canberra: Australian National University, Department of Linguistics, Research School of Pacific Studies, 1981a)

Duranti, A. 'Samoan Speechmaking Across Social Events: One Genre in and out of a Fono' in *Language in Society* Vol. 12 (1990), pp. 1-22

Duranti, A. 'Speechmaking and the Organisation of Discourse in a Samoan Fono', in *The Journal of the Polynesian Society* 90(3) (1981b), pp. 357-400

Duranti, A. 'Universal and Culture-Specific Properties of

Greetings', in *Journal of Linguistic Anthropology* 7(1), pp. 63-97

Egri, Lajos. *The Art of Creative Writing* (New York: Carol Publishing Group, 1995 [first published 1965])

Ella, S. 'The Samoan "Taumualua"', *Journal of the Polynesian Society* 7:247 (1898)

Enright, John. 'The Westernisation of Time and Samoan Folk Arts', in Dark, P.J.C. and Rose, R.G. (eds) *Artistic Heritage in a Changing Pacific* (Honolulu: University of Hawai'i Press, 1993)

Enright, John and Herdich, D.J. *Star mounds* (1998), [online]. Available URL: http://ashpo.org/Enright_articles.html

Erskine, J.E. *Journal of a cruise among the islands of the Western Pacific including the Feejees and others inhabited by the Polynesian Negro races in Her Majesty's ship Havannah* (London: John Murray, 1853)

Eustis, N. *Aggie Grey of Samoa* (Adelaide, Australia: Hobby Investments Pty Ltd., 1980)

Evening Post (December 2, 1976)

Fairbairn-Dunlop, Peggy. 'Samoan Writing: Searching for the Written Fagogo' in Sharrad, Paul (ed) *Readings In Pacific Literature* (Wollongong, New South Wales: New Literatures Research Centre, University of Wollongong, 1993), pp. 136-160

Feu'u, Fatu. 'Samoan Artists in Samoa and New Zealand', *Art and Asia Pacific* Vol. 2:4 (1995)

Fletcher, G. *The Painted Life of Teuane Tibbo*, Manuscript held at Hector Library (Museum of New Zealand, 1996)

Freeman, Derek. *Margaret Mead and Samoa: The Making and Unmaking of an Anthropological Myth* (Canberra: Australian National University Press, 1983)

Garrett, J. *To Live Among The Stars: Christian Origins in Oceania*, World Council of Churches in association with the Institute of Pacific Studies (Geneva and Suva: University of the South Pacific, 1982)

Gell, Alfred. *Wrapping in Images: Tattooing in Polynesia* (Oxford: Clarendon Press, 1993)

Geurnsey, Allen A.E. 'The Ritual of Architecture: The Creation of Samoan Guest Fale', *Pacific Arts* Nos. 9 and 10 (1994)

Gilson, Richard P. *Samoa 1830-1900: The politics of a Multi-Cultural Community* (Melbourne: Oxford University Press, 1970)

Goldman, I. *Ancient Polynesian Society* (Chicago and London: University of Chicago Press, 1994)

Gratton, F.J.H. *An Introduction to Samoan Custom* (Papakura: McMillan, 1985. First published, 1948)

Green, Roger C. 'A review of the portable artifacts from Western Samoa', in Green, R.C. and Davidson, J.M. (eds) *Archaeology in Western Samoa Volume II*, Bulletin of the Auckland Institute and Museum 7 (1974), pp. 245-275

Green, Roger C. 'Early Lapita art from Polynesia and Island Melanesia: Continuities in Ceramic, Barkcloth and Tattoo decorations', in Mead, S. (ed) *Exploring the Visual Art of Oceania* (Honolulu: University of Hawai'i Press, 1979)

Grimwade, J. 'Tattoo Tricks catch on again among Samoans', *Pacific Islands Monthly* (September, 1993)

Haddon, J.C. and Hornell, J. 'Canoes of Oceania', *Bernice. P. Bishop Museum Special Publications*, 27, 28, and 29 (Honolulu, Hawai'i: Bishop Museum Press, 1991. First published, 1936)

Handy, E.S.C. and W.C. 'Samoan Housebuilding, Cooking, and Tattooing', *Bernice P. Bishop Museum* Bulletin 15 (Honolulu, Hawai'i: Bishop Museum Press, 1924)

Hart, J.W. *Samoan Culture* (Apia: Ati's Samoan Print Shop, 1996. First published, 1966)

Harvey, N. 'Craft Revival', *City Voice* (Wellington, 15 February 1996)

Henderson, April K. 'Gifted Flows: Netting the Imagery of Hip Hop across the Samoan Diaspora', Unpublished M.A. Thesis (Hawai'i: University of Hawai'i, 1999)

Herdich, D.J. 'Towards an Understanding of Samoan Star Mounds', *Journal of the Polynesian Society* 100 (1991), pp. 381-435

Hereniko, Vilsoni. 'Clowning as Political Commentary: Polynesia Then and Now', in *The Contemporary Pacific, A Journal of Pacific Island Affairs* Vol. 6, No. 1 (Hawai'i: University of Hawai'i Press, Spring 1994), pp. 1-29

Hereniko, Vilsoni. 'Comic Theatre of Samoa: an interview with John A. Kneubuhl', *Manoa: a Pacific Journal of International Writing* Vol. 5, No. 1, pp. 99-105

Herman, Brother. *Tala O Le Vavau: The Myths, Legends and Customs of Old Samoa*. Translations adapted from the collections of Steubel and Brother Herman (Auckland: Polynesian Press, 1987)

Hjarno, J. 'Social Reproduction: towards an understanding of aboriginal Samoa', *Folk* Vol. 21-22 (1979), pp. 73-123

Hood, T.H. *Notes of a Cruise in H.M.S. Fawn in the Western Pacific in the year 1862* (Edinburgh: Edmonston and Douglas, 1863)

Howe, K.R. 'The Fate of the 'Savage' in Pacific Historiography', *Journal of New Zealand History* Vol. 11, No. 2 (1977), pp. 137-154

Howe, K.R. *Where the Waves Fall* (Sydney: George Allen & Unwin, 1979)

Hunkin, A.L. *Gagana Samoa: A Samoan Language Course Book* (Auckland: Polynesian Press, 1998)

Huntsman, Judith. (ed) *Tonga and Samoa Images of Gender and Polity* (Christchurch, New Zealand: University of Canterbury, Macmillan Brown Centre for Pacific Studies, 1995)

Ioane, Sefulu. 'Western Influences on Samoan Poetry', *SPAN South Pacific Arts Newsletter* (1984)

Jennings, J.D. 'The Ferry Berth Site, Mulifanua District Upolu' in Green, R.C. and Davidson, J.M. (eds) *Archaeology in Western Samoa* Volume II. Bulletin of the Auckland Institute and Museum 7 (1974), pp. 176-178

Jones, L. 'The Pareu: Persistence and Revival in a French Polynesian Folk Art' in Dark, P.J.C. and Rose, R.G. (eds) *Artistic Heritage in a Changing Pacific* (Honolulu: University of Hawai'i Press, 1993)

Jowitt, G. and Shaw, P. *Pacific Island Style* (Auckland: David Bateman Ltd., 1999)

Kaeppler, Adrienne. 'Exchange Patterns in Goods and Spouses: Fiji, Tonga and Samoa', *Mankind* 11 (1978), pp. 246-52

Kaeppler, Adrienne. 'Art and Aesthetics' in Howard, A. and Borofsky, R. (eds), *Developments in Polynesian Ethnology* (Honolulu: University of Hawai'i Press, 1989)

Kaeppler, Adrienne. *Poetry in motion: studies of Tongan dance* (Nuku'alofa, Tonga: Vava'u Press, 1993)

Kaeppler, Adrienne. 'Kie Hingoa: Mats of Power; Rank; Prestige and History', *Journal of the Polynesian Society* 108:2 (1999), pp. 168-232

Kane, H.K. *Voyage, The Discovery of Hawai'i*, Knowlton, William (ed) (Hawai'i: Island Heritage Ltd., 1976)

Keesing, F.M. *Modern Samoa: its government and changing life* (London: George Allen & Unwin Ltd., 1934)

Kightly, Oscar. *Dawn Raids* (1997)

Kikuchi, W.K. 'Petroglyphs in American Samoa', *Journal of the Polynesian Society* 73:1 (1964), pp. 163-166

Kikuchi, W.K. 'Additional Petroglyphs from American Samoa', *Journal of the Polynesian Society* 76:3 (1967), pp. 372-373

Kneubuhl, Victoria, 'Traditional Performance in Samoan Culture: two forms', *Asian Theatre Journal* Vol. 4 (1987), pp. 166-176

Kramer, Augustin. *The Samoan Islands Vol. I and II* (Auckland: Polynesian Press, 1994 and 1995)

Larsson, K.E. 'Fijian Studies', *Etnologiska Studier* 25 (Etnografiska Museet Goteborg, 1960)

Leota-Ete, Jackie. 'Te Papa Buys Unique Wedding Dress', in *New Zealand Weddings: A Complete Guide* (1998)

Linkels, Ad. *Fa'a-samoa: The Samoan way between conch shell and disco* (Tilburg: Muno Etnico Foundation, 1995)

Luschan, F. von *Beitrag zur Kenntniss der Tattowirung in Samoa* (Berlin: Verlag von A. Asher & Co., 1897)

Macpherson, Cluny. 'On the future of Samoan Ethnicity in New Zealand', in Spoonley, P., Macpherson, C., Pearson, D., and Sedgewick, C. (eds) *Tauiwi: Racism and Ethnicity in New Zealand* (Palmerston North: Dunmore Press, 1986), pp. 107-126

Mallon, S. and Pereira, F.P. *Speaking in Colour: Conversations with Artists of Pacific Island Heritage* (Wellington: Te Papa Press, 1997)

Marquardt, C. *Die tatowirung beider Geschlechter in Samoa / The tattooing of both sexes in Samoa*. English Translation by Sibyl Ferner (Papakura, New Zealand: R. McMillan, 1984)

Marsack, C.C. *Samoan Medley* (London: Robert Hale Ltd., 1961)

Martin, J. (Mariner, William) *An Account of the Natives of the Tongan Islands* (London: John Murray, 1818)

McBean, Angus. *Handicrafts of the South Seas*. South Pacific Commission, Noumea, New Caledonia (Sydney: Bridge Printery Pty. Ltd., 1964)

McKenzie, A. *Samoan Customs* (Samoa, Apia: [no date])

McLeod. R. 'The Innocent Eye: Folk Art at the Dowse Art Museum' *Art New Zealand* 48 (Spring, 1988), pp. 75-79

McNaughton, Howard. 'Drama' in Terry Sturm (ed.) *The Oxford History of New Zealand Literature in English* 2nd edition (Auckland: Auckland University Press, 1998)

Ma'ia'i, F. *Stories of Old Samoa* (Wellington: Whitcombe & Tombs Ltd., 1960)

Mead, M. 'Social Organisation of Manu'a', *Bernice P. Bishop Museum Bulletin* 76 (Hawai'i, Honolulu: 1969)

Meleisea, M. *Lagaga: A Short History of Samoa* (Suva: University of the South Pacific, 1987[a])

Meleisea, M. *The Making of Modern Samoa* (Suva: Institute for Pacific Studies of the University of the South Pacific, 1987[b])

Meleisea, M. '"To whom gods and men crowded": chieftainship and hierarchy in ancient Samoa', in Huntsman, Judith (ed) *Tonga and Samoa Images of Gender and Polity* (Christchurch, New Zealand: Macmillan Brown Centre for Pacific Studies, University of Canterbury, 1995)

Milner, G.B. 'Samoan Tattoos and Structural Analysis', *Man* 10 (1973), pp. 307-308

Moore, Albert. C. *Arts in the Religions of the Pacific: Symbols of Life* (London: Pinter, 1995)

Moyle, Richard M. *Fagogo: Fables from Samoa in Samoan and English* (Auckland: Auckland University Press, 1981)

Moyle, Richard M. (ed) *The Samoan Journals of John Williams 1830 and 1832* (Canberra: Australian National University Press, 1984)

Moyle, Richard M. *Traditional Samoan Music* (Auckland: Auckland University Press, 1988)

Neich, Roger. 'Samoan Figurative Carvings and Samoan Canoes', *Journal of the Polynesian Society* 93 (1984), pp. 191-197

Neich, Roger. 'Processes of Change in Samoan Arts and Crafts', in Dark, P.J.C. (ed) *Development of the Arts in the Pacific*. Pacific Arts Association, Occasional Papers No 1. (New Zealand: Government Printer, 1984)

Neich, Roger. 'Material Culture of Western Samoa', *National Museum of New Zealand* Bulletin 23 (1985)

Neich, Roger. 'Samoan Figurative Carvings and Taumualua Canoes - A Further Note', *Journal of the Polynesian Society* 100 (1991), pp. 317-328

Neich, Roger and Neich, L.L. 'Some Modern Samoan Beliefs Concerning Pregnancy, Birth and Infancy', *The Journal of The Polynesian Society* Vol. 83, No. 4, 1974

Neich, Roger and Pendergrast, Mick. *Pacific Tapa* (Auckland: David Bateman Ltd., 1997)

Nordstrom, Alison Devine. 'Popular Photography of Samoa: Production, Dissemination and Use', in Blanton, Casey (ed) *Picturing Paradise: Colonial Photography of Samoa 1875 to 1925* (Southeast Museum of Photography: Daytona Beach Community College, 1995)

O'Meara, T. *Samoan Planters: Tradition and Economic Development in Polynesia* (Fort Worth, Texas: Rinehart and Winston, 1990)

Pacific Islands Monthly (May, 1974)

Pacific Islands Monthly (June, 1971)

Parnham, B.E.V. 'Plants of Samoa', *New Zealand Department of Scientific and Industrial Research Information Series* no. 85

Partsch, Olivia. 'Malu: Samoan Women's Tattoo', Unpublished Research Paper, Diploma of Social Work (Wellington: Victoria University, 1993)

Pitt, D. *Tradition and Economic Progress in Samoa* (Oxford: Clarendon Press, 1970)

Pritchard, Mary J. *Siapo: Barkcloth Art of Samoa* (Honolulu: University of Hawai'i Press in association with American Samoa Council on Culture Arts and Humanities, 1984)

Rampell, E. *Velvet Venuses*, Director Sima Urale (1999), [online]. Available URL: http://www.geocities.com/Wellesley/3321/win16c.htm

Reid, A.C. 'The Fruit of the Rewa Oral Traditions and the Growth of the Pre-Christian Lakeba State', *Journal of Pacific History* Vol. 12 part 1 (1977), pp. 3-24

Richards, R. *Samoa's forgotten Whaling Heritage. American Whaling in Samoan Waters 1824-1878* (Wellington: The Western Samoa Historical and Cultural Trust. Lithographic Services Ltd, 1992)

Rodgers, Victor. *Sons* (1995)

Rowe, N.A. *Samoa under the Sailing Gods* (London and New York: Putnam, 1930)

Sagapolutele, F. 'Samoan Song/Dance Talent in High Demand', *Samoan Observer* (March 3, 2000)

Sahlins, Marshall. 'On the Anthropology of Modernity, or, some triumphs of culture over despondency theory', in Hooper, Antony (ed) *Culture and Sustainable Development in the Pacific* (Canberra: Asia Pacific Press, 2000)

Schoeffel, Penelope. 'Samoan Exchange and Fine Mats', *Journal of the Polynesian Society* 108:2 (1999), pp. 117-148

Schultz, E. *Samoan Proverbial Expressions Alaga 'upu Fa'a – Samoa* (Auckland: Polynesian Press, 1994)

Scott, S.D. 'A Human Image from Samoa – Some Observations', *Journal of the Polynesian Society* 91 (1982), pp. 589-92

Sharp, Andrew. (ed) *The Journal of Jacob Roggeveen* (Oxford: Clarendon Press, 1970)

Shore, Bradd. *Sala'ilua: A Samoan Mystery* (New York: Columbia University Press, 1982)

Siers, James. *Samoa in Colour* (Wellington: A.H. & A.W. Reed Ltd., 1970)

Silver, H.R. 'Ethnoart', *Annual Review of Anthropology* 8 (1979) pp. 267-307

Sinavaiana, Caroline. 'Comic Theater in Samoa as Indigenous Media', *Pacific Studies* Vol. 15, No. 4 (December, 1992)

Sinavaiana, Caroline. 'Where the spirits laugh last: comic theatre in Samoa', in *Clowning as critical practice: performance humour in the South Pacific*. William E. Mitchell (ed) (Pittsburgh: University of Pittsburgh Press, 1992)

Sinavaiana, Caroline. 'Music and Theater: Samoa', in Kaeppler, A.L. and Love, J.W. (eds) *Garland Encyclopaedia of World Music Vol. 9 Australia and the Pacific Islands* (New York: Garland Publishing, Inc., 1998)

St Cartmail, Keith. *The Art of Tonga* (Nelson: Craig Potton Publishing, 1997)

Spirits in Samoa internet discussion, [online], available URL: http://www.samoa.co.uk/qanda/5513.html

Stair, J.B. *Old Samoa; or flotsam and jetsam from the Pacific Ocean* (Papakura: Southern Reprints, 1983. First published, 1897)

Stephen, Ann. Introduction in *Pirating the Pacific: Images of Travel, Trade and Tourism* (Australia: Powerhouse Publishing, 1993)

Stevenson, Karen. 'Culture and Identity: Contemporary Pacific Artists in New Zealand', *Bulletin of New Zealand Art History*, Vol. 17 (1996), pp. 59-68

Summerhayes, G.R. 'The face of Lapita' *Archaeol. Oceania* vol. 33 (1988)

Sutter, Frederick K. *Amerika Samoa: An Anthropological Photo Essay* (Honolulu: University of Hawai'i Press, 1996)

Sutter, Frederick K. *Samoa: A Photographic Essay* (Honolulu: University of Hawai'i Press, 1982)

Sutter, Frederick K. *The Samoans: A Global Family* (Honolulu: University of Hawai'i Press, 1989)

Tapu, T. 'Tattoo Ritual in Samoa' in Deverell, Bruce and Deverell, Gweneth (eds) *Pacific Rituals: Living or Dying* (Suva: University of the South Pacific, 1987)

Teaiwa, T. and Figiel, S., *Terenesia: amplified poetry and songs by Teresia Teaiwa and Sia Figiel* (Honolulu: 'Elepaio Press and Hawai'i Dub Machine, 2000)

Te Rangi Hiroa, (Buck, Peter) 'Samoan Material Culture', *Bernice P. Bishop Museum* Bulletin 75 (Hawai'i, Honolulu: 1930)

Te Rangi Hiroa, (Buck, Peter) 'Material Representatives of Tongan and Samoan Gods', in Fraser, D. (ed) *The Many Faces of Primitive Art, A Critical Anthology* (New Jersey, Englewood Cliffs: Prentice Hall Inc., 1966)

Teilhet, Jehanne. (ed) *Dimensions of Polynesia* (San Diego: Fine Arts Gallery of San Diego, 1973)

Thomas, Allan. 'Dance Costume in the Central Pacific Islands', *Studia Choreologica* Vol. 1. (Instytut Choreologii w Poznaniu: 1999), pp. 39-56

Thomas, Nicholas. 'Pacific Dualities: Bottled Ocean in Wellington and Auckland', *Art New Zealand* 74 (1995), pp 46-50

Thomas, Nicholas. *Oceanic Art* (London: Thames & Hudson Ltd, 1995)

Thomas, Nicholas. 'The Case of the Misplaced Ponchos: Speculations Concerning the History of Cloth in Polynesia', in *Journal of Material Culture* Vol. 4 (1) (1999), pp. 5-20

Tu'i, T.F.M. *Launga: Samoan Oratory*. Western Samoa Extension Centre, National University of Western Samoa (Suva: Apia Institute of Pacific Studies, University of the South Pacific, 1987)

Tuimaleali'ifano, Morgan A. *Samoans in Fiji: migration, identity and communication* (Suva: University of the South Pacific, 1990)

Tunumafono, Apelu. 'Reviving an old art for $35,000', *Pacific Islands Monthly* (January, 1982)

Turner, George. *Nineteen years in Polynesia: missionary life, travels, and researches in the islands of the Pacific* (London: John Snow, 1861)

Turner, George. *Samoa A Hundred years ago and long before* (London: 1884)

Union Steamship Company. *A Cruise in the Islands: Tonga, Samoa, Fiji* (Dunedin: J. Wilkie & Co. Printers and Publishers, 1895)

Urale, Makerita. 'Telling it how it is: Pacific Island Theatre in Aotearoa New Zealand', *Artlink* Vol. 16, No. 4 (1997)

Va'ai, Sina. *Literary Representations in Western Polynesia: Colonialism and Indigeneity* (Apia: National University of Samoa, 1999)

Vercoe, Caroline. 'A Pacific Presence Tautai at the Sixth Australian Art Fair', *Art New Zealand* No. 90 (1999), pp. 40-41, 87

Vercoe, Caroline. *John Ioane Fale Sa* (Auckland: Auckland Art Gallery, Toi O Tamaki, 1999)

Vercoe, Caroline. 'Fantasy Islands: Hollywood's Samoa', in Smith, A. and Leonard, R. (eds) *Bright Paradise: Exotic History and Sublime Artifice* (Auckland: Auckland Art Gallery Toi O Tamaki, 2001)

Vivieaere, Jim. 'The Island Race in Aotearoa', *Artlink* Vol. 16:4 (1997)

Wakefield, E.J. *Adventure in New Zealand from 1839 to 1844 with some account of the beginning of the British Colonisation of the Islands* (Whitcombe & Tombs Ltd, 1908)

Wedde, Ian. (ed) *Fomison: What Shall We Tell Them?* (Wellington: City Gallery, 1994)

Wendt, Albert. (ed) *Nuanua: Pacific Writing in English Since 1980* (Auckland: Auckland University Press, 1995)

Weiner, A.B. *Inalienable Possessions: The Paradox of Keeping While Giving* (Berkeley: University of California Press, 1992)

Wilkes, Charles. *Narrative of The United States Exploring Expedition during the years 1838, 1839, 1840, 1841, 1842* (Strand: Ingram, Cooke & Co. 227, 1852)

Wilpert, C. *Western Samoan Handcrafts* (Reinbek, Western Germany: Hamburgisches Museum fur Volkerkunde, Ferd. Baruth, 1983)

Yarwood, V. 'The Backyard in History', *New Zealand Geographic* No. 33 (January-March, 1997), pp. 124-127

Internet sites:

Samoa Sensation, URL: http://www.samoa.co.uk/whatsnew.html

Creative NZ website, URL: http://www.creativenz.govt.nz/

INDEX